FAIREY FIREFLY

THE OPERATIONAL RECORD

FAIREY FIREFLY

THE OPERATIONAL RECORD

William Harrison

Airlife
England

Copyright © 1992 by William Harrison

First published in the UK in 1992
by Airlife Publishing Ltd

British Library Cataloguing in Publication Data
A catalogue record for this book
is available from the British Library

ISBN 1 85310 196 6

Printed by Livesey Ltd, Shrewsbury

Airlife Publishing Ltd
101 Longden Road, Shrewsbury SY3 9EB

Contents

Acknowledgements

The original research for this book started in 1962 and became a thirty-year labour of love with an aeroplane I had never even flown in. Even when I had put the bones of the book together no publisher would handle it as it was considered a 'high risk' project with an unknown market value. I persevered and continued to add to the material I had collected until Airlife agreed to take it on. Over the years I have had the opportunity to meet with many people asssociated with the Firefly and this is really their story – and I envy them. It is also a story of political and ministerial interference reflecting the policies and world situation at the time, a condition not restricted to the Firefly unfortunately. There may well be information in this book that the pundits will say is untrue. To them I say only that I have not used any previously published works on the Firefly, finding as I did that many contained untrue information that seems to have been perpetrated down the years without anyone bothering to check the authenticity.

My sources came from the original Fairey Aviation Co. documentation made available to me, supported by ministerial and Admiralty files contained in the Public Record Office at Kew. To those were added many interviews with the people who designed, built, worked on and flew the Firefly. I hope I have done some justice to the time they so generously gave to help this project reach fruition. Unfortunately, some of those people are no longer with us but that makes their contribution all the more valuable. Throughout the thirty-year period it was my wife Mary, son Karl and daughter Wendy, who supported and helped me to beaver away and not give up.

It is not possible to list every single person who helped over the years but if they seek their name and it is not here, please accept my apologies, it is not intentional. I would therefore like to thank my friend Jan Algera in Holland, A. N. Angus, John and Angela Adams, Captain D. W. Ashby OBE RN, Len Batchelor, P. H. Bliss DSC RNR, Ken Brown, Captain E. M. Brown CBE DSC AFC RN (Retd), Lt/Cdr M. S. Boissier RN (Retd), Harry Bennett for his invaluable assistance with British foreign policy in the post war period, V. M. G. Bennett for copies of his excellent water colours of 1770 ops, Alan Braithwaite, David Birch and Mike H. Evans of Rolls-Royce Heritage Trust, Michael J. F. Bowyer, Robert J. Carter, Lt/Cdr D. Carter, Lt/Cdr R. H. Chalker DSC VRD RNR, Major V. B. G. Cheesman DSO MBE DSC, Lt/Cdr J. G. Corbett MBE RN (Retd), C. E. Chaplin (Designer of the Firefly), J. C. F. Coles, J. Davis, F. de Friatas, Lt/Cdr S. Dixon-Child RNVR, Lt/Cdr J. D. Eagles AFC RN (Retd), Neville Franklin, Lt/Cdr E. M. Fraser RN (Retd), Richard Griffiths, R. S. Griffith, J. M. G. Gradidge, G. P. Gill, J. C. Harrison MBE RNVR, Lt/Cdr K. Holme RN (Retd), Lt/Cdr J. F. K. McGrail RN (Retd), G. R. MacDonald, Lt/Cdr J. R. Hone RN (Retd), Ian Huntley of Aerocam, Lt/Cdr M. B. W. Howell RN (Retd), Mike Hooks, Lt/Cdr W. J. Hanks RN (Retd), Leif Hellstrom of Sweden, Peter Illiffe, Rear Admiral J. A. Ievers CB OBE RN (Retd), George Jenks, Lt/Cdr J. H. Kneale RNVR, E. A. Key, Benny Karlsson of Sweden, Hans Kofoed and Jens L. Hvid of Denmark, P. Law, Lt/Cdr B. C. Lyons RN (Retd), Lt/Cdr R. B. Lunberg RN (Retd), Jergen Larsen of Denmark, Lt/Cdr J. E. Maddocks RN (Retd), Alec Mathews, Mrs Wendy Mills, Brian Morecroft, Duncan Menzies, Sam Moseley, Lt/Cdr P. Millett DSC RN (Retd), David Masters, Ole G. Nordbo, John S. L. Oswald BSc C Eng, J. M. Palmer, V. M. Piper, Cdr D. R. O. Price DFC RN (Retd), John D. R. Rawlings, Cdr S. H. Suthers DSC DFC RN (Retd), W. Sleigh, Ray Sturtivant, P. Stonehouse, G. P. La T. Shea-Simonds, R. K. Simmonds, Group Captain Gordon Slade, Cdr J. H. Stenning RN (Retd), Lt/Cdr Peter Twiss DSC RNVR, P. Warner, Norman Wiltshire, Eric Watts and Alan J. Wright. To these must be added the staff members of the Imperial War Museum, Public Records Office (Kew), RAF Museum, many friends in Air-Britain (Historians) Ltd., Svensk Flygjanst of Sweden, *Flight International,* information offices of the Royal Danish Air Force, Royal Australian Navy, Royal Thai Air Force, Indian Navy, Royal Netherlands Navy and the Canadian Department of Defence. Any Crown copyright material in the Public Record Office is reproduced by permission of the Controller of Her Majesty's Stationery Office.

Chapter 1
N5/40

IN MARCH 1939 the Air Ministry proposed circulating requirements to a number of firms for a single-engined two-seater fixed gun fighter for use in the Fleet Air Arm. There was some discussion with the Admiralty about the draft specification and requirements. These requirements were passed to the firms on a list who were invited to submit tenders when the specification was issued. The firms were:

> Blackburn Aircraft Co. Ltd.
> Boulton Paul Ltd.
> Fairey Aviation Co. Ltd.
> Gloster Aircraft Co. Ltd.
> Hawker Aircraft Co. Ltd.
> Vickers Armstrong Ltd.
> Westland Aircraft Ltd.

Specification N8/39 was approved on 21 June 1939, along with N9/39 which called for a similar aircraft but fitted with a gun turret, the major differences after this being confined to armament and equipment. Tenders were invited from the above companies on 10 August with designs to be submitted by 19 September. Westland asked for more time but was refused, and then the Admiralty upset everyone by asking for the folded wing width to be reduced even further. This was passed to the tenders on 17 August, and Gloster, at least complained that the new requirement would

make it extremely difficult to revise their submission in time.

Tender designs were submitted by Blackburn, Gloster, Hawker, Fairey and Vickers Armstrong to both specifications on 19 October, the revised date. The Director of Technical Development at that time, Rear Admiral M. S. Slattery, said that he proposed to treat the two designs together as both could probably be derived from one basic airframe.

Fairey tendered designs to both requirements. The two-seater front-gun fighter to Specification N8/39 was a low-to-mid wing design with a 48 ft wingspan and 39 ft 3 in fuselage. Alternative powerplants were offered and these comprised the Rolls-Royce Griffon and Boreas, Fairey Queen and Bristol Taurus. Comparative performance was estimated in the table below.

There did not seem much doubt as to the best choice, the Griffon gave the best performance and retained its power well at altitude, the only concession being the higher AUW and slightly higher stalling speed. The first three tenders utilised a three-blade propeller but the Fairey Queen was offered as a contra-rotating engine with two three-blade propellers rotating in opposite directions. The Queen was the result of many years research into aircraft power plants by Fairey culminating in the contra-rotating P24 engine which, when fully developed was giving over 2000 hp – and that was before World War II.

	TAURUS	BOREAS	GRIFFON	QUEEN
Total all up weight (lb)	9355	9570	10,775	9975
Max speed at SL (knots)	221	212	236	209
Speed at 15,000 ft (knots)	257	236	277	254
Time to 15,000 ft (min)	9.1	10.4	6.45	11.0
Service ceiling (ft)	29,750	28,000	31,600	28,000
Stalling speed (knots)	56	56.5	59	57
Engine power at T/O (BHP)	1200	1150	1600	1320
Engine power at 15,000 ft	1170	950	1445	1170

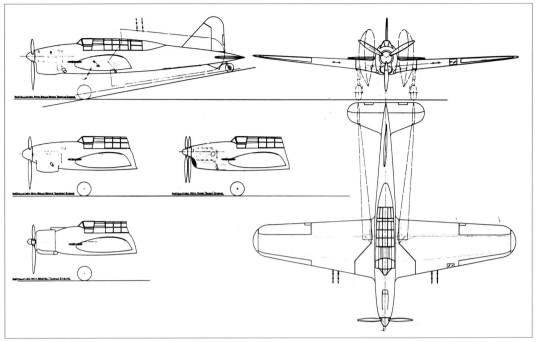

The original design by Marcel Lobelle for a two-seat, front-gun fighter to Specification N8/39.

The chief designer at Fairey at that time was a British domiciled Belgian named Marcel Lobelle. His designs were not unlike the Fairey aircraft then in or entering production, i.e. Battle and Fulmar. His design, as can be seen in the accompanying drawings, were similar except for the two-seat turret fighter, which instead of a faired-in observer's cockpit housed a gun turret. The performance of the two aircraft was similar but the drag from the turret pulled the top speed down by nearly twenty knots.

Although there was pressure to get the new naval fighters into production as quickly as possible, they still had to go through the system. The Tender Design Conference (already delayed twice by the Admiralty) was set for 5 January 1940. By early December 1939 word had leaked out that the Admiralty were in favour of dropping the N9/39 turret fighter and going for (a) N8/39 as a two-seat naval fighter, and (b) a single-seat fixed-gun naval fighter – both to be derived from the same basic design. These new requirements were circulated to those firms that tendered to the N9/39 specification. This led to some confusion, but when it was realised that the aim was to gain two aeroplanes from one design, firms tendered for both, increasing the confusion. At any rate, the Admiralty stated in late December 1939 that after giving further consideration to the tendered designs to N8/39 they

were not satisfactory. As a result, the requirements were modified and proposals for the two revised designs circulated. This cleared the confusion but meant everyone going back to the drawing board. The performance requirements for the single-seat fighter specified a maximum speed at 15,000 ft of not less than 330 knots (385 mph) with the figure for the two-seater being 300 knots (350 mph).

Fairey's new designs showed a marked improvement over the earlier ones. This was due to Fairey appointing a new chief designer – H. E. Chaplin. Marcel Lobelle had left the company and eventually set up on his own as ML Aviation Ltd, which is still in business, but with different fields of interest. Herbert Eugene Chaplin (known to all as 'Charlie') had served his apprenticeship with Adlam & Sons at Bristol, and in 1917 joined the design staff at Geo. Parnall & Sons. His first job was on the Parnall Panther and he stayed with that company until 1929. He joined the design staff at Fairey in 1930, working on the original designs of the Swordfish, Albacore and Battle. In 1938 he prepared the complete project design of the FC-1 airliner which was halted by the war. He took over as head of the Firefly design team in 1940, halfway through the specification proceedings. In an interview with the author he said, 'I reviewed the specifications and the design work done previous to

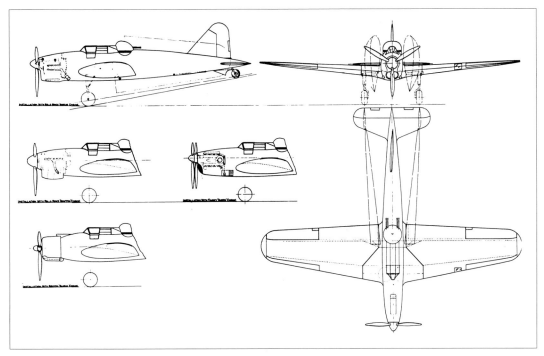

The original design by Marcel Lobelle for a two-seat turret fighter to Specification N9/39.

my appointment, put them all on one side and set out afresh to design the best aircraft I could within the limitations of the specification'. During the interview he recalled that he had not originally wanted to work in the aviation industry but wanted to be a marine engineer – indeed his bungalow at Tatlow had very little on Fairey or aviation, his bookshelves being lined with marine technical books. He later went on to lead the Fairey project design office and was responsible for the 'droop snoot' used on the Fairey FD2, later incorporated into the Concorde design.

Chaplin's designs were submitted on 18 December 1939 and were for two aircraft, a single-seat front-gun fighter and a two-seat front-gun fighter, both to N9/39. It was the latter design that was to become the Firefly. Extracted Fairey comments to this revised specification are important and interesting – 'The new specification (the revised N9/39) for a single-seat front-gun fighter in parallel with the revised specification is of very great interest, indicating as it does a performance requirement considerably in excess to that hitherto called for in Fleet Air Arm fighters. To obtain the necessary performance, the greatest attention to clean design is made with the absence of any excrecences. It will be seen that the speed laid down

is higher than that obtained by any single-engined fighter at present in service and operating from land aerodromes, and to that must be added the fact that this new aircraft must be capable of having folding wings, catapulting and accelerated take-offs, deck arresting and take-off and land under restricted conditions. There are furthermore, limitations which do not appear in the specification but with which we have been brought into close touch and have had to overcome during a long period of building aircraft to Fleet Air Arm requirements. The limitations are associated with robustness of structure to withstand rough usage, freedom from corrosion in a salt laden atmosphere, view and controllability when making the approach to the deck in bumpy and disturbed conditions, handling in confined spaces and necessary holding down provisions. A further and very important point which we have carefully kept in mind is the possibility that this aeroplane will be introduced into production within two years and if this procedure were carried out, there would be no chance of going through extensive prototype trials and development which might warrant unorthodox design or construction. The existence of these factors, i.e., past experience and production virtually off the production board, have the effect of introducing a conservative note into our design and

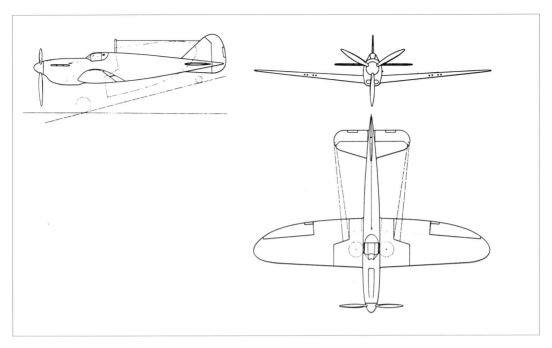

The new designs of H. E. Chaplin for the two requirements from one airframe to the revised Specification N9/39.

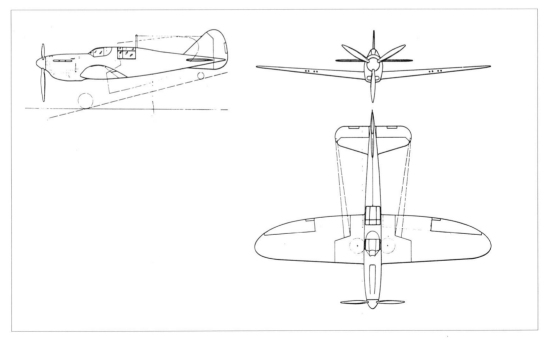

have avoided going to wing loadings which we consider too high for practical aircraft carrier operation, adopting 35lb/sq ft as our best com-promise. We have submitted two designs, the primary one being that using the Rolls-Royce Griffon engine, and a second design using the

Napier Sabre. The layout of both is similar but the Sabre-engined version is slightly larger and heavier. The obvious advantage on production of having one basic aeroplane which could be used either as a single or two-seater, are too great to need stressing here. The two-seat version may have a space problem for the observer's cockpit but we could raise the hooding, which would not interfere with the main production. Unfortunately with the limited time at our disposal we have not been able to make a mock-up of this part of the fuselage. Only a full scale investigation could decide whether we need to increase the height of the hooding or not. We have taken every step possible to come up with the cleanest design possible and we feel that if this design adhered to, and the temptation resisted to add external fitments, the result should prove to be an aeroplane of extremely high performance and one which will be highly satisfactory in service and operation.'

The comparative performance figures were:

	GRIFFON	SABRE
All up weight (lb)	9300	10,800
Wing loading (lb/sq ft)	35	35
Speed at SL (kts)	285	310
Speed at 15,000 ft (kts)	332	357
Time to 15,000 ft (min)	4.45	3.40
Service ceiling (ft)	34,000	40,000
Engine power at t/o	1600 at 2750 rpm	2500 at 4200 rpm

Fairey added: 'The performance figures indicated a superiority of the Sabre engine over the Griffon as regards speed, climb and take-off run. It should be borne in mind that the exceptionally high take-off power loading combined with the small diameter airscrew may well lead to difficulty in directional control during take-off – particularly important in the case of deck operated aircraft having a restricted take-off run.' The Firefly that eventually went into production with the Griffon engine was prone to this problem, i.e., torque stall, which is what happened when the throttle was slammed open to catch a difficult situation and the aircraft went outside its performance envelope, usually rolling heavily to the right. What the above statement implies is that with the Sabre this problem would be more severe. The conversion of the single-seater to a two-seater would have involved the following changes:

1 Weight increased by at least 470 lb
2 Frontal area slightly increased
3 Top speed reduced by 2 knots
4 Time to 15,000 ft increased by 22 seconds
5 Take-off run increased by 25 ft
6 Duration reduced by 24 minutes
7 C of G range increase in the aft position.

The Tender Design Conference of 5 January 1940 was attended by many representatives from the Air Ministry and Admiralty. The design submissions were discussed in detail and the original specification abandoned in favour of the single and two-seat aircraft plans. A question was raised as to why the new requirements had not been thought of in the first place! The Director of Air Material at the Admiralty outlined the considerations which had given rise to the changes, saying that the original requirements had actually been laid down before the war. The tenders had been submitted after two months of war, and even in the light of that short experience it had become evident that performance was paramount and fighters with low speeds could not be considered. This statement marked a change in Admiralty policy with regard to fleet fighters. It was at last recognised that to obtain the desired performance the equipment normally carried would have to be drastically reduced. The linking of the designs initiated in the two original specifications was discarded as having adverse effect on the design. The single-seat designs, brought in at a late date, had been invited primarily for comparative purposes between tenders. It was felt that, if at the end of the Conference two designs could be selected for production, the efforts of the investigation would have been worth it. It was also recognised that whatever the designs were, the chief technical obstacles to carrier-based fighters still remained, i.e., folding wings, small dimensions, limited take-off run and low stalling speed. Production would be desired in eighteen months' time!

Some alternative ideas came up at the Conference: one was to modify a Hawker Tornado to gain time in production, but this would have involved having new wings and a modified fuselage and tail unit. Modifying existing single-seat fighters was not ruled out and the Spitfire had been tendered with a Griffon engine. There was some disappointment that it had not been possible to select a design powered by the Napier Sabre engine, but the Air Ministry said that the increase in weight precluded the use of this engine, and indeed Fairey had shown in their submission that it would have produced undesirable characteristics for deck landing. Exhaustive discussion indicated that the overriding factor controlling the designs was the stalling speed. During the conference all other tender designs were examined but discussion had definitely established that the Fairey design (for the two-seater) was the most acceptable. The revised speed of 330 knots was regarded as optimistic but it was thought that the design showed better appreciation of the Admiralty's requirements than the others. It was decided that (a) the modified Fairey design with the Griffon engine was the most suitable and could be adopted as the basis for production orders; (b) the Blackburn design with Hercules HE6M engine had valuable features which should be tried and an order for twenty-five aircraft be placed. (This became the Blackburn Firebrand.)

On 27 February 1940 in an official letter from the Admiralty to the Air Council it was stated: 'While appreciating that the Fulmar should prove a valuable weapon for the Fleet Air Arm we are anxious that a fighter of higher performance should be brought into service as early as practicable. To this end we propose that production of the two-seat front-gun fighter to revised specification N8/39 should be undertaken without going through the full prototype procedure. We gather that no difficulty is anticipated in arranging production at the Fairey works at Stockport (later changed to Hayes) to follow on and replace the Fulmar. An initial order of 200 aircraft is suggested with a view to reaching a peak output of some 27/30 aircraft a month.' However, it was felt that as Firefly production would run concurrently with the Barracuda at Stockport that twenty a month of each type was more realistic. Just prior to this a request had been raised for permission to replace the revised N8/39 specification, i.e., the Fairey N9/39 new design, with N5/40F to avoid confusion! This was agreed and copies of the new draft specification were sent to the Resident Technical Officer at Fairey, Mr H. G. Harrison.

The Advisory Design Conference on Fairey's naval fixed-gun fighter took place on 11 March 1940. This was to clear up any points in design problems and how to meet them. It was of the utmost importance that any such requirements should be decided at this conference. The consequences of changes in the design of Fleet Air Arm aircraft, which were subject to stringent limitations in weight, were far reaching and would, if called for later in the programme, inevitably involve sacrifice of some of the qualities of the aircraft. The conference therefore marked a definite stage beyond which requirements could be regarded as definite and settled. A mock-up of the aircraft was to be made available for inspection within two months of receiving the order. Rolls-Royce had already provided the necessary information on the Griffon engine and visited the Admiralty in March 1940 to discuss the forthcoming programme.

On 23 April 1940 the Admiralty put in a requisition for the purchase of 200 Fairey fleet fighters to the new specification N5/40F. They indicated that the engine would possibly be the Rolls-Royce Griffon, and this was confirmed at the Mock-Up Conference at Fairey's Hayes factory during 6/7 May 1940. Two prototypes were ordered on 13 May followed by eleven development machines and 187 production aircraft on 12 June. With things now under way it was to be December before the name – Firefly – was chosen. During the following year there were numerous conferences and visits by the Air Ministry and Admiralty culminating in the final Firefly examination and conference during 7/8 May 1942. The first true production Firefly was delivered the following month – but the way had not been easy.

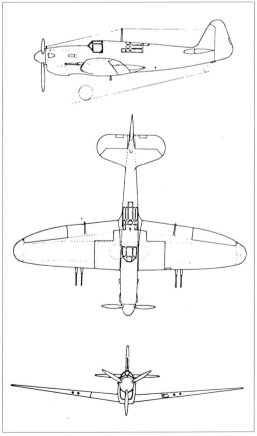

Chaplin's revised drawing to the new Specification N5/40F.

Chapter 2
Early Production Problems

WITH THE ink barely dry on the contract for 200 Fireflies, Fairey launched into 1941 with a vengeance. They were offering a proposal to the RAF to use the Firefly as a two-seat night fighter to Specification F18/40. Not content with that, they also tended a single-seat version to F19/40. The original version of Specification F18/40 called for a two-seat night fighter with 20 mm cannon mounted in each wing. An amended version of this specification was issued later calling for an alternative removable turret, together with radar and an operator. Although totally impracticable in the light of Defiant experience, Fairey pointed out that they were building a two-seat naval fighter to Specification N5/40F, and, disregarding the turret problem, said that the similarity between the two specifications could be met by the new design. They pointed out the advantages to both services by using the same type

of aircraft, with commonality of spares and centralised servicing in some theatres of the war. In a comparison between the F18/40 original specification and the Firefly, they said both aircraft were almost identical except for the removal of naval requirements such as folding wings, catapult and arresting gear etc. which could be accommodated on the production line. Fairey said that in order to reach the top speed of 330 knots at 20,000 ft with a suitably rated Griffon, it was necessary to design a wing with a loading of 43 lb/sq in – which was roughly seventy per cent greater than fighter types then in service. To meet the required speed range, especially at the lower end, Fairey said their Youngman flap, being used on the N5/40 design, would improve control and stability at the stall, thus giving a better turning performance. Summing up, they said that since the drawings were already at an advanced stage, its

A general arrangement drawing of the final Firefly design.

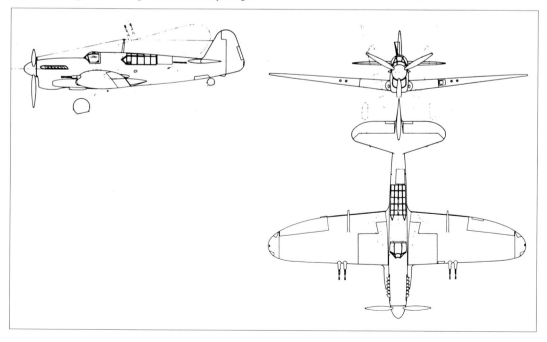

adaption would give simplification of production, with a rapid and economical introduction of a new type. And this before the Firefly had flown! The other specification, F19/40, called for a long-range single-seat fighter and Fairey offered a single-seat version of the Firefly. At an AUW of 12,370 lb it would have had a maximum speed of around 320 knots of 20,000 ft with a range of over 1500 miles at a cruising speed of 200 knots. Neither tender was taken up of course.

On 5 March 1941 the Ministry of Aircraft Production (MAP) informed Fairey of planned Firefly production – one by December that year, one in January 1942, two in February, five in March, ten in April, seventeen in May and twenty-five in June. In reply, Fairey thought this a trifle optimistic and put forward for one in June 1942, three in July, six in August, eight in September, ten in October, fourteen in November, sixteen in December and twenty per month from January 1943. Fairey also suggested an order for a further 500 Fireflies, plus 200 for General Aircraft, the sub-contractor. Production figures and schedules were to be changed continually between then and the final Mk 7 batch. To go through these would be pointless as they are nothing more than lists of Firefly types required month by month. The details of changes are included where necessary for continuity of the story. The first works drawings were released on 31 March 1941 but these were still secret and for Ministry use only. The MAP told

Fairey to go ahead and order material for another 100 Fireflies on 21 April 1941, these being additional to the 200 already on order. Serial ranges were given as DT926–DT961, DT974–DT998 and DV112–DV150.

It was during 1941 that the first three aircraft, Z1826–Z1828, were hand-built in the Experimental Shop at Hayes to act as prototypes while the fourth machine, Z1829 was to be a Royal Aircraft Establishment (RAE) structural test airframe.

Although the Firefly resembled its predecessor, the Fulmar, it was much more robust, had heavier armament and looked more aggressive. The fuselage was actually built in two halves which came together along a vertical centreline, featuring no longitudinal stringers. Strength was derived from twenty-one 'U' frames contained within the flush-riveted light alloy monocoque structure. The centre section was a light alloy structure comprising front and rear spars, diagonal bracing diaphragms, oil tank bearers and eight ribs on each side of the centreline. Fitted to the fuselage were four catapult spools, the front ones being retractable and the rear ones, when not in use, were stowed in the fuselage. When the aircraft was launched by catapult however, the spools were locked down and could not be retracted. The deck arrester gear comprised a transverse torque shaft from which two tubes converged to their attachment with the the hook, which was held in a snap gear mounted at the bottom of frame 19. The hook was released from

Hawker Henley L3414, seen here at the Rolls-Royce Flight Test Establishment at Hucknall, was used as a Firefly Griffon IIB engine installation test bed. *(Rolls-Royce PLC)*

The Firefly prototype Z1826, as rolled out after final assembly at the Great West Aerodrome in December 1941. It is still in natural metal, with fabric covered control surfaces. *(Westland Aircraft Ltd)*

the snap gear by means of a hook-shaped lever in the pilot's cockpit. The pilot's hooding consisted of three transparent panels in light tubular and plate-like structure which slid back as a unit on rails. The observer's hood had a panel on the port side, hinged to the fuselage decking, through which normal entrance and exit was made. The tail unit comprised a tailplane and fin fixed to the fuselage, and a rudder and elevators fitted with trimming tabs. The tailplane and fin were covered with a flush-riveted metal skin and faired into the fuselage with fillets.

The rudder and elevators were of the horn-balanced type with mass balance weights bolted to the leading edges of the horn. The undercarriage was fully retractable and consisted of two shock-absorber struts carrying wheels. Each strut was braced against lateral and rearward movement by link struts. The shock-absorber struts carried fairings which formed the underside of the centre section when the struts were retracted. The tail wheel was housed in a fork at the bottom of the shock-absorber strut, itself anchored to the rear

Another view of the prototype Z1826, at the RAE at Farnborough in March 1942. Note the wooden mock-up cannon and the missing pilot's cockpit hood. *(Crown Copyright)*

wedge structure at its mid-position. A friction device was fitted to the strut to dampen wheel shimmy when taxying over rough ground. The outer wings were flush-riveted in light alloy and consisted of front and rear spars, main and nose ribs, a detachable wingtip, ailerons and flaps. Hinges at the root ends of the rear spar allowed each outer wing to be folded back alongside the fuselage and secured at the outboard end by a reception sleeve which engaged a locking stay mounted on the rear fuselage. When the wings were spread for flight they were locked by manually operated latchpins.

Two 20 mm cannon were fitted in each wing and operated electro-pneumatically from a firing button on the control column. The Youngman flaps were quite an innovation. They were fully retracted when in high speed flight but when trailed in the cruising position gave an early form of variable geometry and greatly reduced the turning radius – very important in combat. The excellent manoeuvrability that was one of the outstanding characteristics of the Firefly was due to these flaps. The Fairey design team exercised their ingenuity in managing to combine the flap linkage system with a wing folding arrangement, eventually accomplished by means of a new wing fold joint which provided a lock of great strength. The Firefly was one of the first British aircraft to use a power-egg, the rapidly detachable engine system straight off the firewall.

In the middle of December 1941 the first prototype, Z1826, was taken to the Great West Aerodrome at Heathrow, now fully absorbed by London Heathrow Airport. It was assembled in a semi-painted condition with only the serial number on the rear fuselage. On 20 December F/Lt Chris Staniland spent seventy minutes carrying out taxying trials and getting the general feel of the new aeroplane. Chris Staniland was Fairey's chief test pilot and the very epitome of the pre-war schoolboy's dream; ex-RAF fighter pilot, wizard on the track (whether car or motorcycle) and chief test pilot of one of Britain's premier aircraft companies. Staniland took Z1826 on her first flight on 22 December 1941, being airborne for thirty-five minutes and going up to 8000 ft. Two more trips were made the following day with one trip to 27,000 ft. Staniland started 1942 on New Year's Day with a flight in Z1826 at an AUW of 10,338 lb. Thereafter he continued to fly the new prototype almost on a daily basis, making twenty-five flights by the end of January. At last the flight test programme was under way. F/Lt Dixon, one of the Fairey production test pilots flew Z1826 on

2 January at a reduced weight of 9971 lb. During February Staniland flew the prototype twenty times, and Dixon three – but both were doing other test flying as well. With March came some of the improvements suggested by Staniland and these resulted in sixteen flights by him and five by Dixon. More changes were made from the end of March but it wasn't until 15 April that flying recommenced. A de Havilland propeller was tried on 23 April but was discarded the next day. The prototype made three more flights over the next two days with Staniland delivering it to Boscombe Down on 28 April – arriving minus the pilot's cockpit hood which was lost on the way! And there was no spare! However, Boscombe, knowing how important it was to get this aircraft into production, said they would accept it anyway as it was required at Fairey's for more work on 2 May.

The purpose of the short stay was for brief handling trials in order to assess any adverse features in its flying characteristics or design. At this early stage in the programme there were still items not fitted to the aircraft. Four wooden 20 mm mock-up cannon were fitted but no real armament; aerial masts and locations were fitted, but no aerials. The general impression of the aircraft layout was good, any adverse comments being restricted to recommended minor changes. There was quite a bit of interest in the flap arrangement and the report said: 'The flaps were controlled by a large crank handle on the left of the cockpit and fitted with a press button release. The Youngman flaps could be selected to move to either of four positions – up, cruising, take-off and landing. The word "cruising" is rather a misnomer as it applied to the condition when the flap is first lowered, its chord remaining approximately parallel to its position when shut, and this position was used to obtain added manoeuvrability. For take-off the flap moved through a small positive angle from cruising so that lift increased without too much increase in drag. For landing, the flap moved through a large angle so that its leading edge moved up and practically met the trailing edge of the wing, so producing high lift and drag. Extending the flap from shut to cruising took about seven seconds, but the other movements were less than that.'

Because of the short time available it was decided to fly the aircraft at almost both extremes of its flight envelope. The two conditions were:

AUW	C OF G POSITION
10,240 lb	33.3 in forward of datum
11,230 lb	29.8 in forward of datum

The C of G limits for the Firefly design were from 33.67 in to 29.5 in forward of datum at an AUW of 11,400 lb. From the two conditions it is fairly obvious that Z1826 was only 170 lb below its maximum weight and the aft C of G position was only 0.3 in forward of the design aft limit. The majority of the flying was done under these conditions.

The report continues . . . 'The aileron control was light throughout the speed range, but appeared to be over-balanced for large movements at low speeds. Large movements at high speeds tended to produce a "snatch". The effectiveness at high speed was good and although it fell off with decreasing speed it remained adequate. The fall off in effectiveness however, combined with the over-balance, produced a complete lack of "feel" in the ailerons at low speeds. The rudder control was light and effective and considered quite satisfactory. The elevators were of the horn-balanced type, and the elevator control suffered from the snatchiness often associated with this type of elevator. The "snatch" occurred with small elevator movements, while for large movements the control was heavy. In bumpy conditions there was a continual fore and aft movement of the control column with a resulting movement of the aircraft, and this produced a feeling of instability.'

Boscombe said that they found the stick-free stability to be satisfactory, but the elevators were too heavy and possessed some undesirable characteristics. Readers might like to note that the Firefly suffered from this longitudinal instability right from the start and was to be plagued by it throughout its life. Staniland informed them that he had flown Z1826 without a horn-balanced elevator and round a big decrease in stick-free stability. Boscombe stressed that the horn should be deleted, but in order to retain stick-free stability the C of G would have to be moved forward. After some discussion with Fairey it was decided to dispense with only part of the horn balance, with the elevator hinge moved further aft in order to produce a lighter control. Stalling characteristics, aerobatics, approach and landing were all satisfactory, except for this lack of 'feel' on the ailerons at low speeds. Stalling occurred at 81 knots clean, 70 knots with everything out. The design limit diving speed was just over 390 knots, but because of the missing hood, dives were limited to 315 knots with no problems. In summarising, Boscombe stated that the items needing attention were the over-balanced ailerons and horn-balanced elevators. 'If these controls can be satisfactorily modified, the aircraft should make a satisfactory

naval fighter . . . despite its weight the aircraft possesses the characteristics and manoeuvrability of a smaller and lighter aircraft. There should be no difficulty in operating it from the deck of an aircraft carrier.'

Staniland flew Z1826 back to Heathrow on 2 May with this knowledge. Five days later both he and Dixon were flying Z1826 fitted with a new rudder. Acting on the information coming back from Boscombe, Fairey attempted to improve the handling qualities throughout May. In the meantime Fairey had received another order, this time for 300 Fireflies on 9 May with serial ranges, MB378–419, 433–479, 492–536, 549–593, 613–649, 662–703, 707–758. Production, said the MAP, should run at fifty aircraft per month until the end of 1944.

Staniland took Z1826 back to Boscombe on 22 May for further handling trials. The condition of the aeroplane was basically as for the previous tests except, annoyingly, the pilot's cockpit hood was still missing and there had not been time to manufacture a new one. In fact, it wasn't until 16 June that a new hood was fitted. Boscombe found that the following alterations had been made:

(a) The square cut horns on the elevator were replaced by triangular horns.
(b) The elevator hinge line was moved about two inches further aft.
(c) The nose balance of the elevator was increased by one inch.
(d) The upward movement of the elevators was reduced from 30 degrees to 23 degrees.
(e) The nose shape of the ailerons was modified.

Flight tests started on 25 May and continued until 1 June when Staniland collected the aircraft again. The tests this time were to see what Fairey had done against the criticisms from the first trials, and whether the changes would cause adverse effects on stability and general flying characteristics. It was found that the controls were very considerably improved, in particular, the elevator 'snatch' had all but disappeared, but it was still too heavy for large control movements at low speeds although the effectiveness was adequate. Ailerons were still light but the over-balance had been taken out. The lack of 'feel' and effectiveness at low speeds still persisted, and more so when the flaps were down. It was also found that when flying with the engine on and flaps down, the ailerons refused to stay central and moved from side to side. The only other unsatisfactory point was that when trimmed for level flight the force required to hold the aircraft in a dive was excessive. At least the results were encouraging and it wasn't anticipated that these problems would persist. From 16 June until early October Z1826 went back into the factory for further modifications and fitting up of equipment not previously carried.

The flight test programme was, however, carrying on. The second machine Z1827 was test flown by both Staniland and Dixon on 4 June and flying got under way. At 11.35 a.m. on 26 June 1942 Z1827 crashed killing Staniland. This was a tragic blow to Fairey; they lost their popular chief test pilot and suffered a setback in the Firefly programme at a crucial time. Staniland was buried at Keddington Church, Louth, Lincolnshire, on 2 July 1942. The programme stopped until investigations were complete. The cause, it was said at the time, was due to fabric failure on the elevators which gave an imbalance. Rumours of difficulties in opening the hood also abounded as did one of panels coming adrift, either being blamed for Staniland's death. When investigations were made the question of fabric covered control surfaces was debated, although not to a satisfactory conclusion. While there was a lull it seemed an opportune time to review another problem, the lack of performance. For a fighter the Firefly lacked speed. It was felt that with a more powerful engine it would put it in the single-seat class. Fairey's Technical Office offered their own P24 engine with an initial take-off rating of 2150 bhp at 3000 rpm.

This would have taken the maximum speed at 19,000 ft up around 330 knots. A more powerful rating of 2500 bhp would be available later in the programme. The P24 was always a non-starter, the Ministry had already turned down numerous applications for it on the basis that there were already more than enough aero engine companies in business and they would not support another. Undeterred, Fairey proposed the Firefly as a torpedo carrier powered by a higher rated Griffon of 1830 bhp. AUW would have been 14,850 lb and take-off run into a twenty-five knot wind would have been 437 ft. This project, like numerous other Firefly ones, fell by the wayside. In conjunction with this proposal was a series of tests to see what speeds the Firefly could get up to in terminal velocity dives with different flap settings. One of the Fireflies demonstrated that in a seventy degree dive with full flap, or bellows brake flap, an indicated airspeed of around 260 knots was achieved. With less flap these increased, until, in a clean configuration, the pilot was going down at 435 knots, or nearly 500 mph. When this was corrected for atmospheric and compressibility factors the corrected true airspeed was 500 knots. This was well outside the design limiting speed of 390 knots and says much for the structural design. Naval pilots were to verify this speed later . . .

The third machine, Z1828, joined the flight test programme on 26 August. After acceptance tests it

The wreckage of the second prototype Firefly Z1827 after the crash that killed Fairey Chief Test Pilot F/Lt Chris Staniland. He was thirty-six at the time of the accident, which was attributable to collapse of the tailplane in up-load when fabric-covered elevators failed. *(Westland Aircraft Ltd)*

flew to Boscombe on 22 September for handling and performance trials with checks on flame damping. Z1828 went on to do trials of all descriptions in support of the Firefly programme, spinning trials, navigation equipment, radio and radar, handling after mods etc. until March 1945 when it was finally handed over to the FAA at Stretton. The fourth machine, Z1829, destined to go to the RAE as the structural test specimen, was used in the development programme to replace Z1827. Despite rumours to the contrary it was Z1828 that did the deck landing trials aboard HMS *Illustrious* with its bedmate of N8/39 days – the Blackburn Firebrand.

Z1826 rejoined the programme on 12 October 1942 and the flying progressed, being done mainly by Dixon. He was joined later by a new test pilot, F/Lt J. Colin Evans, who had been taken on to help out after the loss of Staniland. Z1826 was flown with 16 ft and 17 ft span tailplanes covered in wool tufts to show how the airflow was behaving. By the end of the year Dixon had completed over thirty test flights in support of the Firefly programme. The Firefly was by now well behind its planned programme with the MAP and Admiralty justifiably concerned – all the problems had not been with the aeroplane!

Sir Ernest J. H. Lemon was asked to look into the production problems of the Firefly. Sir Ernest Lemon at that time was Special Advisor to the Ministry of Aircraft Production, and had previously been Director General of Aircraft Production at the Air Ministry, and was therefore ideally suited to sort out the production problems at Faireys. A meeting was set up between Fairey and the MAP on 19 December to discuss the situation. In summary afterwards Sir Ernest Lemon said: 'Failure to achieve the original programme, or even the revised programme, can be ascribed to unjustifiable optimism on the part of the management, to delay in the supply of certain drawings for tools and to delays by sub-contractors. The aircraft is not yet acceptable for operational use and development work has not yet been completed.' After the enquiry he put into operation a Group Co-ordinating Office at Hayes to handle all phases of the problems as they arose. The office, manned by representatives from Fairey, General Aircraft and Aero Engines, came under MAP control and was managed by Wing Commander S. T. Freeman. The original programme had asked for sixty-six Fireflies by the end of 1942, but when the programme started to lag behind this was changed to twenty. At the time of the enquiry only six Fireflies had been produced. The Air Supply Board also looked into the

production problems and in a memo to the Minister on 22 December 1942 stated . . . 'It has been found, however, that owing to inadequate planning by Fairey in the first instance, the quantity of machine tools included in grants was insufficient. The result of this is now being felt in the shortage of machined wing root-end fittings which in turn is one of the major reasons for the slow build up of the Firefly. An additional 150 workforce will be required.'

With the problems identified and the co-ordination office functioning it was felt 1943 would be a better year. In fact 1943 was the turning point for the Firefly, not only was there an extremely busy year of development flying, but it was introduced into FAA service both as a day and night fighter. These three 'prongs' in the story are all different ones in their own right and I have treated them as such. Not to have done so would have made an extremely complicated chapter trying to include three different stories in one. This chapter continues the story of Firefly development and production, while the day fighter story is told in Chapter 3, and the night fighter one in Chapter 4. There will, of necessity, be some slight overlap for continuity of the story. Under the revised production arrangements following the enquiry, it was planned to deliver five Fireflies in January 1943 increasing gradually to forty-five per month by the end of the year and through 1944. The first night fighter, Firefly NFII Z1831 came off the line in February and went to Boscombe on 10 March for night fighter trials. Z1830 had arrived at Boscombe just before this to carry out gunnery trials, and, except for a few days back at Fairey for slight changes, was there until September. It was during February that the Admiralty, now firmly following the night fighter plan recounted elsewhere, came up with their requirement for 100 Firefly night fighters. This obviously changed requirements on the production line and a MAP memo of 28 April stated that under the revised programme, production would now be 300 Mk I, 100 NFII and 200 Mk III.

In March 1943 Z1826 went back to Boscombe to flight test elevator characteristics at high speeds. As a result of the accident that killed Staniland Fairey had modified the elevator. Eight additional riblets were introduced aft of the tailplane spar, and an improved method of attaching the fabric to the elevator was tried. Trials continued through March and April but Boscombe were still not happy with the elevator. They recommended a small increase of tailplane incidence, combined with some stiffening of the tailplane and elevator structure. It was hoped that this would help correct the undesirable elevator control characteristics and so eliminate any chance of over-stressing the tailplane and elevator structure. After a short stay back at Fairey for modifications Z1826 returned again, this time for aileron assessment. The original report about the lightness of aileron control prompted Fairey to try out a number of improvements. Although Z1826 started the trials it was recalled for some urgent work and Z1828, at Boscombe for spinning trials, carried them on. Unfortunately the ailerons on Z1828 were different from those of Z1826, being of the earlier type. It was hoped that the modified ones on Z1826 would prove to be all right as they were expected to be the production shape. Just to confuse things further, a new stiffened type of aileron was being tested on Z1832. Various trials were conducted with Z1828 including removing the wingtips to see if that affected aileron control, which it didn't. The outcome of all these tests was that the earlier type of aileron was unsuitable for a fighter aircraft and more so for a carrier fighter where control at slow speeds was essential.

To keep the programme moving Fairey proposed that the first seventy Fireflies be built with the revised ailerons as per Z1826. This entailed fitting an upturned metal strip along the trailing edge of each aileron. Subsequently they would produce a production aileron similar in profile to those on Z1826, but with the leading edge strengthened by a heavier gauge of metal. These would then be fitted to the earlier Fireflies in service retrospectively. Fairey also announced they were designing a new aileron incorporating spring tabs and these, it was hoped, would provide a cure for the faults. In the meantime Z1832 was conducting trials with the strengthened aileron and a tailplane incorporating a two-degree increase in incidence. The problem with the ailerons was that the Fairey design office was coming up with ideas to cure the undesirable characteristics faster than they could be flight tested. Performance with Z1832 proved to be acceptable but it was noted that there was evidence of either twisting or surface distortion of the tailplane, although not severe, and elevator control characteristics could still further be improved by stiffening the structure or surface involved.

In June 1942 Z1842 was accepted for trials as being representative of early production aircraft (listed as the first seventy machines) and Boscombe were to check whether it was suitable for release to the Service, and if not, what improvements would be required to clear it. After the flight trials Boscombe declared the Firefly unfit to be released for fighting operations, although it could be released for training purposes until approved. This was something of a blow as it was felt with the

modifications to the control surfaces they were almost there. The items condemning it were:

(a) Excessive elevator loads required to hold a change of speed.
(b) Excessive heaviness of the ailerons at high speed.
(c) Directional oscillation at all speeds, i.e. 'porpoising'.
(d) Insufficient left rudder for deck landing requirements.

It was pointed out that items (a) and (b) were the most serious and rendered the aircraft inacceptable as a fighter. It was noted that something was being done about those items and the seventy aircraft already produced would be modified. Defect (c) was apparently curable by fitting cords to the trailing edge of the rudder, and (d) needed some rectification. In all fairness it should be said that although Z1842 was selected as a typical production machine, research has proved it to be a hybrid, in that some of the control modifications had been done and some not. Naval pilots who flew Z1842 confirmed that there was insufficient left rudder available to keep straight on take-off, or for correction when landing or over-shooting. The ailerons were only just acceptable and no further deterioration could be allowed. Not a suitable machine one could say for the trials it was supposed to represent.

While this was going on two other Fireflies, Z1834 and Z1837 arrived to carry out intensive 100-hour flying and maintenance trials. Both aircraft were fully equipped Firefly Mk Is and representative of production machines, except however for the ailerons, elevator and tailplane settings which were of the pre-70 standard. Both aircraft had flown less than five hours when delivered and the 100 hours was increased to 150 at a later date. The flying was done mainly by naval pilots with ground maintenance carried out by naval ratings, with advice from Fairey's representatives and Boscombe's permanent intensive flying staff. Z1834 was flown between 14 May and 11 July 1943 for a total of 102 flights in 148 hours 5 minutes. It made 173 landings, of which 49 were on hard runways and the rest on grass. The stern frame and rudder were damaged by failure of the tail oleo leg after 125 landings, both being repaired on site. Z1837 was flown between 23 May and 3 July for a total of 104 flights in 146 hours 35 minutes. Some 131 landings were made of which only three were on hard runways. No landings were made using deck arrester gear. Both aircraft were subjected to dives of between 300/350 knots although a few were made at 380 knots. They took part in a number of dog-fights with other types of aircraft. Four engine failures occurred – three of these being the seizure of the super-charger change speed in FS gear. Considerable tailwheel shimmy was experienced on both aircraft, this resulting in the breakage of the oleo on Z1834. A new one was fitted with a new type of spring loaded damper and this eventually cured the problem. Fairey had already assisted the RAE by measuring the vibratory stresses in the Firefly due to tailwheel shimmy. There was some concern that this might lead to fatigue problems so during the winter of 1944/45, at the RAE's request, Fairey again measured tailplane vibrations which were being caused by resonance at three times propeller speed. From these results RAE concluded that no strengthening of the tail unit was necessary to avoid any fatigue failure that might have been caused by such vibrations. No problems were found with the maintenance, only minor problems expected with the introduction of a new type into service.

The naval crews expressed dissatisfaction with rudder power on two counts. Firstly, at take-off there was a considerable tendency to swing to starboard and not enough travel to correct it; secondly, when approaching to land at low speeds with full power a large degree of port rudder was required but there was not enough reserve to make a left turn out in the event of a baulked landing on a carrier deck. In the general assessment, as flown, the two Fireflies were considered unfit for serious operational duties owing to their control and stability characteristics. It was suggested that if the modifications on the way improved the problems, the Firefly would be a considerable improvement on similar types in service. Performance was considered reasonable for a low altitude fighter and things were not good with the control inputs and it was hoped by all that the problems would disappear when the full range of modifications in the pipeline were incorporated.

In June 1943 a review of the Firefly situation was made:

Z1826	At RAE Farnborough
Z1827	Written off
Z1828	Spinning trials at Boscombe – then to RAE
Z1829	Test airframe at RAE
Z1830	At Boscombe for armament trials
Z1831	Night fighter – at Boscombe
Z1832	At Boscombe for elevator trials
Z1833	Night fighter – at TRE Defford
Z1834	Intensive flying trials at Boscombe
Z1835	Mk III prototype – at Rolls-Royce, Hucknall
Z1836	Night fighter – at TRE Defford
Z1837	About to join Z1834 for intensive flying trials
Z1838	Fairey test aircraft
Z1839	At RNAS Crail – due to return
Z1840	Night fighter trials with Z1841
Z1842	At Boscombe
Z1843	Fairey – elevator development machine
Z1844	At Rolls-Royce, Hucknall, for flame damping trials
Z1845	Night fighter with Z1846
Z1866	At Rotol with runaway propeller problem
Z1873	At RAF Sealand for packing trials
Z1970/G	Set aside for ASH nacelle trials

Some of the early production machines started to be delivered to the MU at Wroughton from July 1943.

On 7 July 1943 the Firefly FMk I was released to the Service for use and on 17 July the MAP ordered an additional 200 Fireflies with serials PP391–437, 456–497, 523–567, 580–623 and 639–660. The same source informed Fairey on 10 August that the production programme was now to be 500 Mk I, 200 NFII and 100 Mk III. Production of the Firefly was now being rushed through all departments at Fairey to such an extent that some loyal company employees that year worked through their summer holidays!

Between 20 July and 25 August Z1832 and Z1867 were at Boscombe testing metal covered elevators. The design was the same but with the fabric replaced by a metal skin. On Z1867 the leading edge of the elevator was extended forward slightly but both machines had the two-degree tailplane incidence change. The trials included handling and quantitative measurements of stick forces and accelerations under various conditions of dive and recovery, and, in the case of Z1832, measurement was made of elevator and trimmer angles in relation to the trimmed out machine. The tests showed that the metal elevators were a considerable improvement over the fabric covered ones, but that now the C of G needed to be kept within 33.1 to 28.6 forward of datum. This could be achieved by removing 200 lb of ballast from the engine bearers. Interestingly, it was noted that by using two similar aircraft together any slight differences due to manufacturing inaccuracies showed up. It was felt that if these could be more standardised in the factory then the flying

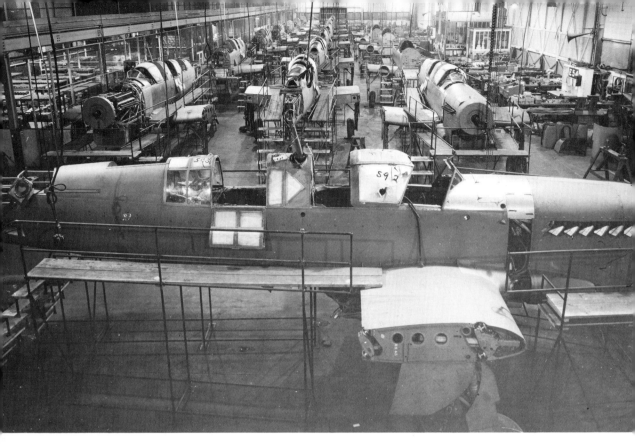

Fireflies on the assembly line at Fairey's Hayes factory in 1944; the three down the right-hand lane are NFIIs. There appear to be about twenty aircraft in the picture. *(Ian Huntley Collection)*

characteristics in all areas would be more acceptable for operational flying. This was confirmed later in the year when Z1888 went to Boscombe for flight trials of the metal covered elevators proposed for production aircraft, along with production type ailerons. The report stated that the Firefly with elevators and ailerons such as fitted to Z1888 was acceptable for operational use. It was pointed out that the problems were by no means over, and maybe only spring tabs fitted to control surfaces would alleviate the problem. At least the aircraft was now clear to be used for its proper role. Another change in the programme came on 13 October when MAP said the plan now was for 350 Mk I, 350 NFII and 100 Mk III.

While Fairey had been sorting out its production and stability problems their Design Office had been looking at ways of improving performance and came up with some interesting projects. The reason behind this was that the Design Office thought that the Firefly was a sound design with excellent stability and control characteristics, of robust construction but lacking power to compete with enemy fighters. Two of the projects involved alternative power plants, the Bristol Centaurus XII and the Rolls-Royce X45 Pennine. More of these later, suffice to say at this stage that the profiles

with these engines were bulkier, more ugly and the drag from the enlarged frontal areas would have negated any possible performance increase. They also came up with the idea of fitting a jet unit in the fuselage just aft of the pilot's cockpit and exhausting out of the rear fuselage under the tail. The jet unit was located in place of the observer's position, making the aircraft a single seater. As

Diagrammatic layout of the Ryan FR1 Fireball, which shows the twin engine arrangement planned for the Firefly.

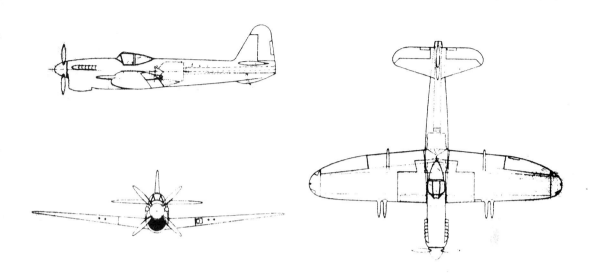

The Firefly project to fit a Whittle-type jet engine in the rear fuselage.

can be seen from the accompanying illustration the pilot's cockpit had a glazed section added and faired down to the lower decked fuselage. The fin and rudder were taller and of less chord with a finlet under the rear fuselage below the tailplane. Initially it was intended to use a test Firefly powered by a Griffon IIB engine but the design was based around the later Griffon 71 powered Firefly Mk III. The 'Whittle' type jet unit would provide around 1600 lb of thrust to start with but 2000 lb was expected after development. With both power units operating the Firefly would have achieved 372 knots at rated altitude. Rate of climb was to be 3000 ft/min. The modifications required to fit the jet unit were quite reasonable. One of the main problems was how to feed the jet unit with air in sufficient quantity. It was proposed that retractable air scoops be incorporated at shoulder level behind the pilot, then, when operating with the piston engine only, the scoops could be retracted out of the airstream. The fuselage aft of the pilot's cockpit was to have a break point to totally remove the rear fuselage to allow servicing and removal of the jet unit. All this was based on available information at the time (August 1943). The concept of dual powerplants was not new but in this arrangement was unique. Although Fairey's

project got no further, the concept was carried to a successful conclusion just after the war by the American company Ryan with their FR-1 Fireball. The illustration opposite is not unlike the Fairey proposal. One of the big disadvantages was the space requirement for two different types of fuel.

Another idea, and much more feasible, was the removal of the frontal radiator beneath the nose and putting it under the rear fuselage, not unlike the Mustang intake only smaller. Putting forward the project the Design Office stated: 'Investigations have been made into the possibility of improving the aerodynamic cleanliness of the Firefly, with a view to increasing the performance. Development work on these lines prompts us to put forward the following proposal: the Rolls-Royce Griffon IIB engine is installed, and a standard 15-inch bay, as now used on the night-fighter version, is incorporated. The radiators are taken from under the engine and are repositioned as follows:

(a) The redesigned oil cooler, a three-row Morris F type be housed in the centre section leading edge, on the port side, by deleting the 23-gallon leading edge fuel tank on that side. The duct entry is in the nose of the aerofoil with a controlled flap outlet immediately forward of and below the front spar.

(b) The cabin and gun heater is transversely housed in the centre section leading edge with an air intake further outboard than that for the oil cooler.

(c) The coolant radiator is positioned under the rear cockpit floor.'

The fore and aft dimensions of the duct were limited at the forward end by the flap link boxes when folding, and at the rear by the deck hook frame. A boundary layer inlet was to be positioned in the lower body in front of the main duct, and the outlet was in the wing fillet on each side of the aircraft. This resulted in a much more pleasing profile and looked quite promising. However, the Aerodynamics Laboratory at Hayes informed the Design Office that the project was not feasible on the existing Firefly structure. Drag, they said, for various reasons would be higher than the existing arrangement and the ideal layout was the leading edge radiator scheme with well shaped exits superior to both. Their observations were based on extensive test data on ducted radiators (largely from full scale work in the 24 ft wind tunnel at Farnborough) that showed the drag of ventral radiators placed in the aft positions was higher than when placed well forward. They summed up loftily by saying, 'It is possible therefore to estimate drag and cooling flow problems of such a proposed system with a considerable measure of confidence.' One cannot help feeling, with hindsight, that perseverance with the ducted radiator scheme might well have given the Firefly that performance edge it lacked.

Another project, prompted this time from the Ministry, was for a long-range reconnaissance version of the Firefly. Armament would be reduced to one gun per wing to make way for extra fuel. Blisters were to be added to the observer's hooding to improve the view. This was not proceeded with

even though a mock-up of the revised rear hooding was examined at length by Air Ministry officials.

In November 1943 Z1840 started its night-fighter trials, joined later by Z1831. As 1943 drew to a close it seemed the Firefly programme heralded a much better picture with things looking up. Fairey's Design Office got the new year of 1944 off to a start with more of their projects. These were revised plans for the set aside Centaurus/ Pennine projects. Engine manufacturers were promising great things (for 1946) from their existing designs and new engines. Alternative engine performance was expected to produce the figures from the Firefly airframe shown in Table 1.

Naturally nothing came of these projects.

On 9 February 1944 Fireflies Z1908 and Z1910 flown by Lt Underwood and Lt Gunn respectively flew aboard *Pretoria Castle* for deck landing trials. Over two days they did more than fifty deck landings with no problems.

Tragedy struck the Firefly programme on 1 March when Z1839 operating out of Boscombe crashed killing the pilot. Wing Commander Peter F. Webster DSO DFC and bar had taken off around 3 p.m. to carry out rate of roll tests at increasing speeds. An hour later he crashed at Bury Hill Camp, near Andover, about twelve miles from Boscombe. He had joined the RAF in 1936 and had accumulated 1450 hours on fifty-four types. He was in fact a graduate of No 1 Course, Empire Test Pilot's School. As stated, he was carrying out rate of roll tests at increasing speeds, and it is known that at the time of the accident he was diving at 365 knots and banking to port. The starboard wing failed in upload when subjected to high 'G', resulting in very violent rolling to starboard during which the tail collapsed. The only difference between this and earlier flights was that different ailerons had been fitted, but these were not considered a contributory cause, the wing being over-stressed.

Fairey's meantime were suffering from the

Table 1.

	PENNINE	CENTAURUS IMPROVED	CENTAURUS STANDARD	GRIFFON
AUW (lb)	13,800	14,000	12,500	12,130
Wing loading (lb/sq ft)	41.8	42.4	43.9	36.8
Max speed at SL (knots)	327	312	295	261
Max speed at 21,500 ft	370	370	350	281
Range (miles)	–	690	315	840
Endurance (hours)	–	3.45	1.75	4.20
Time to 20,000 ft (min)	–	7.0	8.0	12.45
Engine at t/o (bhp)	3480	3000	2320	1740

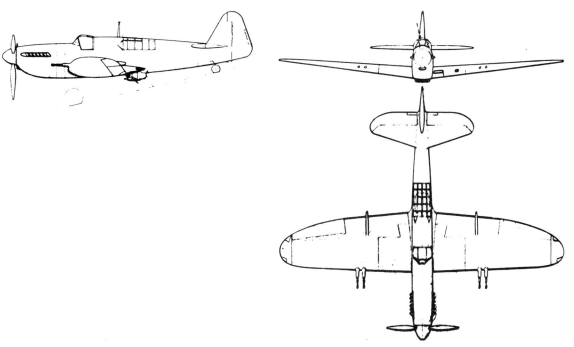

The under-body radiator scheme for the Firefly showing the location.

effects of losing Staniland. The Firefly test programme had got behind and then Dixon had to leave for an operation. There was a backlog of test flying to be done. Between 9 March and 8 May 1944 Lt G. P. La T. Shea-Simonds was 'loaned' to Fairey for test flying duties. Lt Shea-Simonds was also a graduate of No 1 Course of the Empire Test Pilot's School and a friend of W/Cdr Webster killed in Z1839. His duties included test flying repaired or overhauled Swordfish and Albacores at Eastleigh or Hamble, Barracudas at Ringway, Fulmar and Firefly at the Great West Aerodrome. Apart from clearing some twenty-six Fireflies from the backlog he also did some test flying when asked. One Firefly he flew was Z1984 on 25 March when he was carrying the AID inspector Mr Stally. Lt Shea-Simonds recalled that day: 'The aircraft was being flown for the purpose of checking the carbon

Close-up of the under-body radiator scheme.

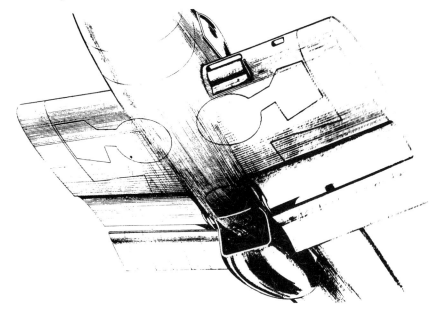

monoxide contamination in the rear cockpit, Mr Stally being the observer for this test, and also to check the weight and trim of the ailerons following adjustments carried out as a result of a previous flight, and to check the effect on a previously reported engine roughness resulting from a change of propeller. Following the completion of tests referred to above, I discovered that the main landing wheels would not lower, either by use of the normal or emergency methods. At approximately 6000 ft I started to lose height slowly by orbiting the aerodrome slowly in a power glide with the propeller GS control lever set to the maximum rpm position and a small throttle opening – giving approximately 2400 rpm at 170 knots ASI. I lowered the flaps to the cruise position after reducing speed to around 150 knots ASI. I selected undercarriage (we called it the chassis in those days) down, getting a green for the tailwheel but reds for the main wheels. I continued to select undercarriage up and down but to no avail. As the visibility was very poor at this time I did not wish to climb up again and risk the probability of losing sight of the aerodrome and finally having to land with the main wheels unlocked or retracted somewhere else. I therefore reduced speed during

my last circuit, lowering the flaps to the landing position at around 1000ft, and came in to touch down in a tail down attitude – switching off both ignition switches just before making contact with the ground. I had not been able to communicate with the observer during the time that I was endeavouring to lower the undercarriage, but neither he nor I was injured in any way.' Must have been a bit of a surprise for Mr Stally who was expecting a normal landing! Lt Shea-Simonds also flew Z1826, the original prototype, fitted with leading edge mock-up radiators in support of the Firefly Mk IV programme, and then returned to Boscombe Down.

Firefly Z1867 was at Boscombe at this time finishing live firing trials of a new weapon – the rocket projectile, or R/P as it was known. Z1867 had been fitted with what was called a standard Mk I Rocket Projector. This consisted of a framework attached to the blast plate beam lugs by which each R/P was suspended from hooks on the underside of the wing. The installation was jettisonable from a button in the cockpit. The trials included air firing, ground firing, harmonisation, accuracy and attitude measurements. Some 524 R/Ps were fired, 316 being 25 lb shot heads and

This shot of a later production Firefly DK418 not only shows off its pleasing lines, but also the raised windscreen and cockpit hood. *(Author's collection)*

the rest 60lb shell heads. One salvo of eight 60 lb shell type was fired in a dive at about 350 knots. There were no problems. Other trials being conducted towards the end of 1944 were Z1909 on gun firing, Z1835 performance and handling, MB395 investigating vibration problems, DT985 on drop tank tests, these including both the 45-gallon Hurricane and 90-gallon Thunderbolt types and Z1970 on radio trials. In October 1944 the Firefly started to suffer from severe vibration problems but only on aircraft produced after the 160th machine. MB395 was one such 'problem' aircraft but after trials at Boscombe the problem was not considered enough to make it unfit for service use. It did persist however and Commander Bassett at the Admiralty would not let service pilots fly 'problem' aircraft, stating that the ATA could deliver them! The source of the problem was difficult to isolate. Vibrations were felt through the control column seemingly emanating from the tail area. Damping was put into the control circuit and stick but it didn't really cure it. Naval pilots said the Firefly always seemed to suffer from vibrations anyway.

In October there was another memo from the MAP. The number of Fireflies on order was to be reduced by 126 aircraft, leaving 674 on order. The totals were thus revised to 587 Mk I, 37 NFII and 50 Mk III. This wasn't really surprising, the NFII was not suitable and the Mk III was turning into a disaster.

Before the year's end the Design Office released details of two new projects. One was a design study for a single-seat fighter using mainly Firefly components and powered by a 70 series Griffon, an alternative powerplant being the Pennine. The second design looked more promising and quite exciting. The design team had taken a basic Firefly airframe and modified it to take two Merlin 20s – mounted in tandem! Fairey were looking at providing the best view possible for a pilot by sitting him right up front and putting the engines behind him. The idea of using tandem engines was not new, Italy having used them in the Fiat 6 Schneider Trophy engine. The Merlins (or possibly Griffons in a later version) were to drive contra-rotating propellers through a common gearbox, both engines being able to operate independently when required. It was claimed that a pilot would have twin-engine reliability over the sea, without the dangers associated with asymmetry. The Design Office preferred this layout to the piston-plus-jet concept since it only used one type of fuel and thrust efficiency would be much higher resulting in better take-off and landing performance. At an

AUW of 15,750 lb the maximum speed at 18,500 ft would have been over 350 knots. Rate of climb was 20,000 ft in seven minutes and range at 15,000 ft some 880 miles on internal tanks. This had exciting potential and may well have been better in the long run than the Sea Hornet (speeds on developed versions approached 435 knots).

The Fairey Firefly was first demonstrated to the press on 1 November 1944, when Dixon put a production machine through its paces. *The Aeroplane* announced its existence in the 3 November issue using pictures of the early F Mk 1 with a low windscreen and unfaired cannon and also the later model with a blown hood and faired cannon. This one also showed the Youngman flap in the cruise position. More details were mentioned in the 10 November issue with pictures of the wing fold mechanism. The journalist said: 'One notable impression left after the inspection of the Firefly is the ingenuity devoted to the solution of detail problems.'

Flight in their 9 November issue said of the Firefly, 'The translation of the staff tactical ideas into flying form is the normal headache accepted by the design company and the technical personnel of the Navy installed in the Ministry of Aircraft Production under Commander Slattery RN. Contrary to the widely accepted belief, the chief worry is how to get off the deck rather than how to land. This major factor has debarred many good aircraft from consideration for naval flying, but in the new Firefly the Griffon engine has solved this difficulty . . . Control surfaces, with the exception of the rudder, are all metal (the rudder is fabric covered), and it is interesting to learn that the ailerons, which are pressed out in fairly heavy gauge sheet, are all made so accurately that there is virtually no detectable difference in aileron response between different aircraft. A most unusual thing!'

At the beginning of 1945 a review of the aircraft state was:

Z1826 FI	Company hack
Z1831 NFII	No working being done on this one
Z1835 Mk IV	Prototype in shops
Z1838 FI	Awaiting scrap
Z1843 FI	Torsion bar spring tab development
Z1875 NFII	Awaiting scrap
Z1895 NFII	Company hack
Z1909 FI	At Boscombe
Z1970 FI	Initial ASH installation – at Boscombe

Z2118 Mk IV	Flight trials Mk IV
DT985 FI	Drop tank trials – at Boscombe
DT986 FRI	In for modifications
MB404 FI	Trials
MB561 FRI	In for modifications
MB621 FRI	Trials aircraft for Mk IV

Firefly Z1970/G was at Boscombe during this time for ASH trials. The aircraft, a standard FI, had been modified in detail to represent the FR Mk I which consisted of a nacelle under the forward fuselage housing a radar scanner and equipment in the rear cockpit. Directional oscillation appeared worse than usual. Moving, or even removing the nacelle did not improve matters and the report recommended that the aircraft with ASH radar equipment be accepted for service use under the same conditions as the original acceptance. All other handling was acceptable including trimmed dives at 350 knots. The Firefly FR Mk I was released for service use on 16 February 1945. MB404 was first flown as an FI by Colin Evans on

13 October 1944 and subsequently went on to do trials with the company, first at the Great West Aerodrome, then Heston and finally White Waltham. It was used for numerous trials including all the varied types of loads a Firefly could carry – it was still flying in 1949. MB621 followed a similar path being used only for testing different wings and ailerons. After flying with its own wings it had those from Z1875, then from Z1831, then Z1875 again, then Z1831, then Z1835 and Z1831 and Z1843 . . .

In January 1945 the MAP informed Fairey that they were revising the programme again. Firefly Mk Is were to continue in production until the middle of 1946 averaging about 25/30 aircraft per month but tailing off once into 1946. Firefly Mk IV production would start in January 1946 and be divided up between the FR and NF versions at a ratio of 4 NF:3FR. Not only that but the following month they were reinstating the 126 Fireflies cancelled previously and these would consist of 123 Mk I and three Mk IV. The revised details came on 16 February – 710 Mk I, 37 NFII and 53 Mk IV

Cutaway of the Firefly FR1.

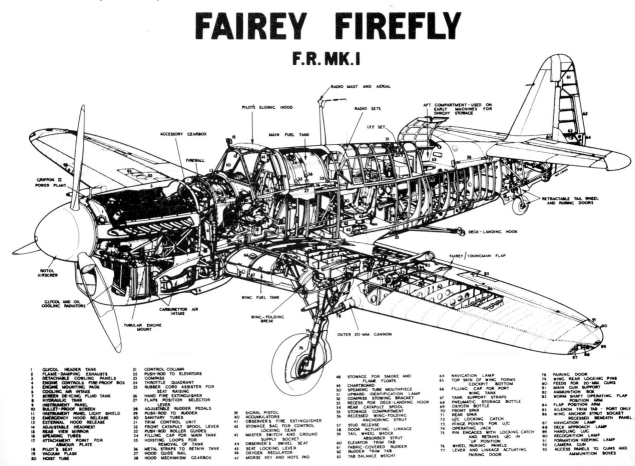

(the Mk III having been cancelled). However, the MAP were not done – on 4 April they reallocated the 800 Fireflies on order as: 297 FMk 1, 273 FRMk I, 140 NFMk I, 37 NFMk II, 30 FRMk IV and 23 NFMk IV. The demise of the Mk III and rise of the Mk IV are told in that chapter. The introduction of 140 NFMk I Fireflies reflected the serious thinking of the Admiralty at that time on this subject, the full story being in that chapter. Fairey wrote back to MAP informing them: 'Owing to the failure of General Aircraft Ltd to produce the programmed number of fuselages, for which they are our sub-contractor, the programme put forward in your letter will be unobtainable. We attach herewith a programme for 1945, subject to General Aircraft Ltd being able to secure sufficient labour to produce the planned fuselage programme for 1945.' Despite this the programme stuck for a while.

A meeting between the MAP, Air Ministry, Admiralty and Fairey took place on 11 September 1945 to review all aircraft development work at Fairey. The object, as it was with all the other aircraft companies at that time, was to review the aircraft work in hand, and, pending direction of policy for post-war aircraft types, to decide what work might be cancelled, or held in abeyance, and so make more design capacity available for new developments in the post-war era. Work which was required solely for the war against the Japanese could be stopped and possibly the number of roles for each type reduced. Among the Fairey discussions was an indication of possible Firefly developments – an anti-submarine version to replace the Barracuda III, and an advanced trainer. Both these were snapped up by Fairey and their story is told later.

The test programme suffered a double setback towards the end of the year when, on Saturday 13 October F/Lt J. G. Seth-Smith was killed test flying PP417 and Colin Evans went the same way on 27 November in PP463.

Throughout the mid-to-late '40s the development of the Firefly continued apace, so much so that hardly had one mark gone into service before another seemed to be joining or even replacing it. A lot of project work went on and one of the more noteworthy tests was that of utilising vertical wing folding. In January 1946 there were piles of ex-FAA Firefly 1s outside the Structural Test lab at Hayes and it was decided to convert one of these. The outer wings were hacked off about a foot outboard of the usual wing fold joint, and installed by hinges at the spar positions. By means of a mobile crane, and later a gantry, the hinged outer portion was spread and folded, with measurements and photographs being taken during the operation. The project was abandoned, possibly due to the time, cost and effort involved, especially the redesign of the Youngman flap system. The requirement was not there, the British small carriers would probably not have the headroom for vertical wing fold in the hangars, and the GR17/45 (Gannet) was already being talked about.

The Firefly FMk IA was released to the service on 19 March 1947 for training purposes and in the

Demonstration of Firefly wing-folding method. Each wing was hinged at the root ends of the rear spars, each outer plane being folded back against the fuselage and secured at the outboard end by a reception sleeve which engages with a locking stay mounted on the rear fuselage. *(Fox Photos Ltd)*

A Firefly in the USA. This one has the low windscreen of the early marks of Firefly and is almost certainly Z1908, which was used as a 'hack' by Lt Peter Twiss when he was a member of the British Air Commission. A Firefly was listed as available for evaluation by the Joint Fighter Conference in the USA where it was considered that 'Performance too low for modern warfare but stability controls and general handling qualities good for night fighting.' *(US Navy)*

reconnaissance role under similar terms to the FRMk I release. The FMk IA was an FMk 1 Firefly converted in service (based on drawings supplied by Fairey) to carry AN/APS-4 radar equipment. These conversions were formerly known as ASHCAT aircraft, but by the more familiar name of ASHCAN in the Service.

In the immediate post-war period Robert Carter was a Fairey apprentice and remembers some of those days: 'MB649 was the second prototype Mk IV and I recall the trial installation of the one-piece pilot's hood. MB757 was the flying mock-up for the Mk 7, and consisted of a Mk I airframe fitted some time previously with a very old pair of wings – I believe the number we found under the paint was Z1831, a fin from the other prototype Mk IV Z2118, which was in the structural test shop doing breaking trials, and rounded off with an ex-Barracuda Griffon engine installation. TW695 was the original contra-prop installation but unfortunately they had taken this off when it arrived at White Waltham and I only saw it with an

experimental ordinary prop on. TW735 was a fairly standard Mk IV which at one time was fitted with Mk I wingtips and flame dampers over the exhaust stubs. The one thousandth Firefly was shown at Farnborough in 1948. When the aircraft went into service sometime later everybody at the Hayes works was given a glass of beer – everybody that is, except the apprentices. I saw some of the target tugs, including the later version where the winch was carried under the fuselage. I saw the Dutch Firefly FII.6 fitted with one on one of its visits.

'I also watched the wing-breaking trials. With the manually folded wings a long pole was supplied to lift the wing 'up and over' when folding. It was discovered that Royal Navy groundcrews were in the habit of tying a rope to the wing tip and pulling down aft – a method which folded the wing all right, but had an inclination to break the rear spar. Z2118 had been retired from flying at that time and was down in the structural test department and was used for a series of tests which involved a 1000 lb bomb (full of sand I might add) which I

A Firefly 1 of 812 Squadron about to touch down on the deck of HMS *Vengeance* against a Pacific backdrop in late 1945 — just too late to see action. *(K. Brown)*

A pair of Firefly FR1s of 816 Squadron from HMS *Ocean*. The squadron provided air cover for the British withdrawal from Palestine in May 1948, and the following year, as part of the 13 CAG in HMS *Triumph,* escorted HMS *Vanguard* on its return journey from South Africa with the Royal Family on board. *(Lt/Cdr J. G. Corbett)*

accidentally dropped in the middle of a bunch of technicians – you should have seen them scatter! We also had a jettisonable fuel tank full of water and some large steel blocks to represent the weight of guns and ammunition. A lot of strengthening cropped up as a result of these tests. Z2118 was also used for some of the work on the power folded wing, which was put into production later.

'A word about Z1835, a very early Mk I which had been converted to just about every mark of Firefly in its time. Around 1946 it was still fitted with the early, low type pilot's hood and was unpainted. I was told that it had been prepared for a race. (An air race was being held at Folkestone during 31 August/1 September 1946 with the Lympne High Speed Handicap race. Qualifying speed was 260 knots and taking part were the Seafang, Fury, Vampire and Hornet.) I recall that when I saw it in 1949 the deck hook had been faired into the fuselage. The last recollection of Z1835 was when they were doing some trial installations of some Morris lightweight radiator which involved a very complicated piping system. Initially all the pipes went in bar one, so the fitters took them all out again. This time they had two left over that they could not get in, so they took them all out again and had another go – winding up with one out again, but a different one from the first try! I don't ever remember the aircraft flying with these radiators, though they may have done later.'

This may well have been a trial installation of the piping for the ducted radiator scheme mentioned earlier.

Acting on interest from another source, Major Wright of the Fairey Board of Directors asked the Design Office to provide some details of a twin-fuselage Firefly vis-à-vis the Twin Mustang. This was in August/ September 1950 and four versions were looked at, (a) a ship-borne anti-submarine aircraft, (b) a ship-borne fighter-bomber, (c) a shore-based fighter and (d) a long-range fighter with six 20mm cannon. Power plants were to have been two Merlin 35s but utilising the same radio and radar as fitted to the Firefly Mk 5. This seemed

a bit strange because the Merlin 35s, although developed from the Mk 24, was a training aircraft engine rated at 1250 bhp. The performance was consequently down, 290 knots at 11,500 ft. The Design Office decided to forget the idea.

On 14 June 1951 the Firefly situation at White Waltham was:

MB757	Mock-up Mk 7 – due to go to Boscombe for observer hood trials
TW695	Flight testing Fairey propeller
TW735	Flight jettison trials of stiffened pilot's hood
WB256	Static discharger trials – to Eglinton, 12 June 1951
WB 257	Down with electrical snags – awaiting some modifications
VT477	Aileron booster twin-jack scheme
WD857	Cloud collision warning scheme – to Ford 9 June 1951
WJ215	Contractors trials
WJ216	Being erected
PP534	TMk 3 in for Modification 1205 at Hamble

When the Technical Department asked about the disposal of Fireflies at White Waltham on 24 February 1952 they listed:

TW735	FRMk 4
TW695	Interim Mk 4
MB757	Mk I
VT477	FRMk 5

The three former ones were all non-standard after their various trials and were condemned to scrap. Interestingly the company still referred to the Mk 7 mock-up as a Mk I. VT477 had completely non-standard wings due to the aileron hydraulic booster controls, but it was suggested that by changing the wings and bringing it up to date with modifications required, it could be utilised by the FAA. By now Firefly work was at a low ebb with the company heavily involved in new and more exciting work: the GR17/45, which became the Gannet, the Fairey Delta 1 and 2, Gyrodynes and helicopter work.

Chapter 3
Into Service – and Combat

ESPITE the setbacks in the Firefly programme due to control problems and accidents the Admiralty had placed the utmost urgency on getting the aircraft into squadron service. Captain Eric Brown had more to do with the introduction of the Firefly into FAA service than any other officer, and I can think of no one more qualified than he to describe those early days.

'The third aircraft, Z1828, flew on 26 August 1942 and this was followed in September by the fourth, Z1829, originally intended as a structural test specimen but completed for flight testing as a replacement for the second aircraft (Z1827 which had crashed).

'It was the arrival of this fourth machine at Arbroath, the base of the FAA Service Trials Unit that gave me my first opportunity to examine the new naval debutante. The date was 1 February 1943, and the Firefly had been sent to Arbroath, together with a prototype Firebrand and a Barracuda II, for some practice on the dummy carrier deck prior to deck trials aboard HMS *Illustrious*. As I knew that the Firefly would shortly pass into the STU's care, I examined the aircraft with particular interest.

'My impression was one of beautiful proportions; a careful mating of smoothly-cowled Griffon engine blending with cleanly-contoured fuselage and aesthetically pleasing elliptical wings. All the similarity to the preceding Fulmar was confined to the general

Firefly F1 Z1881 W of 1770 Squadron at Grimsetter. The cannon were still without fairings at this time, early 1944.

configuration, with its tandem-retracting main undercarriage members. All the elegance of the Fulmar remained, but this had, in some indefinable fashion, been infused with an air of pugnacity; its ground stance seemed more business-like, an impression strengthened by the quartet of 20 mm Hispano cannon barrels protruding from the wing leading edges. One retrogressive step by comparison with the Fulmar that I noted, though, was the situation of the forward cockpit which was marginally aft in relation to the wing leading edge. This, in itself, was a fairly minor point, but when coupled with some very obtrusive metal framing and decidedly restricted canopy headroom, plus a shallow raked windscreen, forward view was obviously deficient and bid fair to become a critical shortcoming at high angles of approach incidence.

'By the time I was nominated as Firefly Project Officer in May 1943, the Service Trials Unit had transferred to Crail, on the northern mouth of the Firth of Forth, the first pre-production aircraft, Z1830, had left the Hayes line in the previous January, and delivery tempo was building up rapidly. Indeed, the Firefly in which I made my first flight on 4 June was Z1839, the tenth aeroplane off the production line.

'At this stage I was most interested in the landing characteristics of the Firefly, for my immediate task was to carry out a series of deck landing and catapult trials aboard *Illustrious*. Speed was reduced to 175 knots in the circuit at which cruise flap setting was selected, the wheels coming down at about 155 knots and full flap being applied below 125 knots. The initial approach in lightly loaded condition was made at some ninety knots on land – or about ten knots higher without flap – reducing to eighty-five knots on finals, and such was the power available from the Griffon that, in the event of a mislanding, the Firefly would climb away easily on climbing power, the use of full take-off power being unnecessary. The drill was to open the throttle to +9 lb boost, increase the airspeed to ninety knots, raise the undercarriage and retrim.

'The Firefly handled well on the approach, but view was seriously impaired by the previously mentioned windscreen and canopy faults. Furthermore, at the critical point at which the throttle was cut for touchdown, the stick had to be pulled back to counteract the tendency for the heavy nose to drop. This was

obviously to be particularly important on the carrier, as the arrester hook was mounted midway between the wing trailing edge and the tailwheel. The touchdown itself had a nice solid feel to it and once on the ground/deck the Firefly ran straight and steady, and the brakes could be applied reasonably fiercely without fear of nosing over. During the take-off for my third flight, the open canopy suddenly detached itself just after the unstick, draping itself around the leading edge of the port tailplane where it severed the main spar, producing violent stick flutter from the blanked-off elevator. I completed a very shaky circuit and landed at a high rate of knots, and from that moment, the jettisoning characteristics of the canopy were suspect and became the subject of wind tunnel testing.'

Readers might like to recall the rumours circulated about the difficulties Staniland had in opening the canopy in Z1827, but, in fact could it have been the canopy that came adrift and caused the failure of the tailplane?

'The trials aboard *Illustrious* took place on 8/9 June with a replacement aircraft, Z1844, and were very successful indeed, although they did highlight the deficiency in forward view during the approach. It was found that the best approach speed for a deck landing was 78–80 knots, a curved approach being necessary to obtain a reasonable view of the deck. The combination of poor forward view and the jettisoning problem promptly led to the introduction of a taller windscreen which improved the view in rain so much that the wind-driven windscreen wiper could be deleted. The new screen, which featured the minimum of framing, necessitated a raised canopy with the incidental advantage that the pilot was afforded more headroom.

'The next stage was to get the Firefly aboard a smaller carrier, and this was accomplished with HMS *Pretoria Castle* on 8 September. On the following day, however, I had a somewhat hairy experience when the Firefly was launched from the catapult at sixty-five knots into a wind speed of only eight knots over the carrier deck, with the unnerving result that the aircraft dropped to within fifteen feet of the sea! Having sorted this one out and still feeling decidedly shaken, I came in to land, checking that the arrester hook green light was showing the hook to be lowered, and landed on nicely, getting a ''roger'' from *Pretoria Castle*'s batsman all the way. The next thing I knew was violent contact with the crash barrier, which smartly wiped off the undercarriage, and the Firefly slithering along on its belly in a shower of wood splinters from the shattered propeller. The Firefly slid on to the catapult track and came to a grinding halt. As soon as I clambered out of the cockpit I could see that the hook had not lowered despite the fact that the green indicator light was still glowing on the panel! Investigation revealed that only one of the two hook unlocking latches had released, although this had activated the hook signal light. In spite of this failure there should never have been an accident as the batsman, whose responsibility it was to check that under-carriage, flaps and hook were all down, should never have given the final ''cut'' signal to land. Thus, a technical fault had been compounded by human error.

'As a result of this incident, a modification was introduced to the hook release mechanism and I was back on *Pretoria Castle* with another Firefly, Z1880, on 22 November for a two-day series of sidewind catapult launches and landings at weights up to 12,160 lb. These trials went well and so it was decided to test the Firefly in a further series of low windspeed trials, again on *Pretoria Castle*, in December, with the primary object of ascertaining the suitability of the new two-seat fighter for the ''Woolworth'' carriers, the small escort carriers which were being received from the USA. In the event, no particular problems were encountered, although the anticipated limit was reached when that arrester wire pulled out to its maximum and the retardation was so violent that the propeller tips clipped the deck. Although the Firefly could not be considered above average for ease of landing on a carrier, it was a good average, and so deck landing clearance was given to the first operational unit, No 1770 Squadron.'

When Eric Brown took over the Firefly project he was already an experienced naval pilot. He had trained as a fighter pilot and was aboard *Audacity* for the perilous Gibraltar runs. After a spell with the Service Trials Unit he went to Boscombe Down but after a short stay was posted to the Aerodynamics Flight at the Royal Aircraft Establishment, where he later became Chief Naval Test Pilot. Part of his job there was the collection, transfer and flight testing of German aircraft after the war in Europe was over. He then had a spell of exchange duty with the Flight Test Division of the United States Naval Air Test Centre at Patuxent River, Maryland, where he added to his experience in jet flying. His post-war positions included being Commanding Officer of 804 Squadron equipped with Sea Hawks; Commander (Air) at RNAS Brawdy and a spell in the Directorate of Naval Air Warfare before taking up a new career in civil helicopter operations.

Towards the end of 1943 Firefly Z1883 was sent to the Naval Air Fighting Development Unit (NAFDU) at RAF Wittering for tactical trials. The report, issued that October was not unkind. Layout of the aeroplane and its equipment was considered good, 'the layout generally inspires a pilot with confidence' they said. The view from the pilot's cockpit was considered acceptable in all directions except forward: 'It is considered that the view generally would be improved if a ''blister hood'' were provided, which would obviate opening the hood.' For flying characteristics it stated: 'The Firefly is very simple and straightforward to fly, although aileron control during take-off is not good. The landing characteristics are good and it is anticipated that no difficulty in deck landing will be experienced. In the air, controls are good, although frequent change of rudder trim is necessary. The ailerons remain light at all speeds up to 260 knots. The cruising speed is high, about 175 knots and +4lb boost, but the top speed is not impressive, being only 275 knots at 15,000 ft. Climb and speed of the Firefly are inferior to that of modern Axis fighters such as the FW190 and Me109. It is believed, however, that the Firefly with flaps in the cruising position will out-turn these enemy aircraft.' It is an interesting fact that during comparative dogfight trials in the USA, the Firefly with cruise flaps could out-turn all the conventional fighters, including the much vaunted Zero. The report summarised: 'The Firefly will be at its best as a close-escort fighter, against enemy long-range fighters, e.g. Me110, Ju88, on reconnaissance flights or, as is thought, as a night fighter.'

A naval report for March 1945 had the first Firefly squadrons all marked down in support of the British Pacific Fleet, and these were:

No 1770	Formed up – HMS *Indefatigable*
No 1771	Formed up – HMS *Implacable*
No 1772	Formed up – HMS *Indomitable*
No 1773	Form up 1 July 1945 with Barracudas, then Firefly
No 1774	To form up
No 1775	To form up
No 1790	Forming up at Burscough

1770 Squadron aircrew, taken in early 1944. Major Cheesman, the CO, is centre front row in the uniform of the Royal Marines. The officer fourth from the right in the front row is Lt Levitt, who was the first pilot to shoot down an enemy aircraft using the Firefly. The 'character' third from the left on the back row is not a squadron officer but Mr Allcock, a representative, identifiable by his cap badge, which is the logo of the Fairey Aviation Co! *(Crown Copyright)*

No 1791   Forming up at Lee-on-Solent
No 1792   Form up

In fact Nos 1773, 1774 and 1775 never did form up, the end of hostilities ending the requirement. The story of the three night fighter squadrons is told in the next chapter. We need now to go back to 1943 when the squadrons started to receive the Firefly.

The first Firefly squadron, No 1770, formed up on 1 October 1943 at Yeovilton, supposedly with twelve Fireflies, but the CO, Lt-Cdr P. Godfrey RNVR, found himself with thirty-two officers, 110 ratings and no operational Fireflies (one Firefly had been delivered to Yeovilton on 27 September but wasn't ready). Fireflies arrived in dribs and drabs and it was 24 February 1944 before the squadron were all airborne together. In the meantime squadron training got under way. On 7 October S/Lt Waters with observer S/Lt Hollywood in Firefly K had engine trouble on take-off and crashed the other side of Yeovilton village, both escaping, but the Firefly was burnt out.

In January 1944 the squadron moved to Grimsetter in the Orkney Islands. Grimsetter proved to be one of those drab wartime Nissen-hutted mud camps which for some reason officialdom seem to find ideal for use as airfields. Lt/Cdr Godfrey relinquished command in February due to ill health and the squadron was taken over by one of those rare breeds — a flying marine. Major V. B. G. Cheesman – known throughout the navy as 'Cheese' – already had a bone to pick with the Japanese. As a Walrus pilot on the cruiser HMS *Cornwall* he had the misfortune to be aboard on Easter Day 1942 when Japanese aircraft attacked and sank both the *Cornwall* and *Dorsetshire* in the Indian Ocean. Surviving the air attacks, and the sinkings, he was then subjected to strafing runs while in the water. Lt Cheesman and other survivors were picked up at dusk the following evening by the destroyer HMS *Enterprise*. In the Firefly Cheesman saw the ideal foil with which to present his feelings to the Japanese! On 6 February Lt 'Ben' Gunn left to conduct deck trials aboard HMS *Ravager* where he did over forty landings. He then went on to *Pretoria Castle* with another Firefly flown by Lt Underwood to complete over 120 deck landings between them.

The new CO immediately made himself popular by getting the squadron moved to Hatston (on 15 February) where life was more bearable, made more so no doubt by the presence of WRENS and fresh eggs! Despite rain, snow and gales the squadron gradually worked up with its new aircraft. The Firefly proved popular with its crews, it was sturdy, was a good weapons platform and had oodles of power for the young naval aviators. In fact, on 19 February S/Lt Stott came back from a training flight minus eight inches of two prop blades, the result of playing leapfrog over Atlantic rollers! On 18 May 1944, the squadron flew out to embark in the navy's newest and largest carrier, HMS *Indefatigable*. Commanded at that time by Captain Q. D. Grahame CBE DSO the ship received twelve Fireflies without mishap off Scapa Flow. The ship then steamed to the Clyde to embark the other squadrons that would make up the air group, 820 and 826 with Barracudas, and 894 with Seafires. With her full complement of aircraft *Indefatigable* spent the next two months working up to a full operational standard. No 1770 squadron found itself acting as escort fighter to the Barracudas, with a secondary role of strike/ reconnaissance fighter. Major Cheesman was not altogether happy with these roles and pestered the Admiralty to allow them to use the R/P (Rocket Projectile). This would make them even more versatile than they were, being true strike aircraft. It was not long before he got his way!

The work-up was for a new series of strikes against the German battleship *Tirpitz*. The very name seemed more daunting than any other enemy warship and was talked about with awe. She had been a thorn in the Allies' side for some time and when she moved into the Norwegian fjords presented a constant threat to the convoys going to Murmansk in Russia. It was decided to remove the threat once and for all. A reconnaissance flight on 23 January 1942 had detected her in Aasfjord some fifteen miles east of Trondheim. On the night of 28/29 January an RAF force of nine Halifaxes and seven Stirlings made a bomb attack but no hits were made and no losses suffered. Twelve Albacores were launched from HMS *Victorious* near the Lofoten Islands on 9 March but again no hits were made and two Albacores failed to return. The RAF tried again on the night of 30/31 March with thirty-three Halifaxes but had no success and lost five of their number. A month later, 27/28 April, thirty-one Halifaxes and twelve Lancasters went but failed to register a hit and lost five Halifaxes again. The same force returned the following night with twenty-three Halifaxes and eleven Lancasters, losing two more Halifaxes for no hits. The next attempt was by one-man torpedoes. A British smack disguised as a Norwegian trawler moved into the entrance of the fjord and hoisted the torpedoes up and over the side, but the hawsers holding them rubbed through and the torpedoes sank to the bottom of the fjord. The mission was abandoned and the smack sunk in the entrance of the fjord. In September three midget submarines, X5, X6 and X7 penetrated the German defence screen and eventually managed to damage her. It was not enough to hold *Tirpitz* though and as word spread that she was almost seaworthy the Russians had a go with fifteen heavy bombers on the night of 10/11 February 1944 but to no avail.

The Commander-in-Chief of the Home Fleet was aware the *Tirpitz* was ready to slip anchor as soon as repairs were finished. He planned a series of comprehensive strikes, aiming to get the first attacks in before the smoke screens hid her. Codenamed 'Operation Tungsten', it was probably the most carefully planned, briefed, rehearsed and carried out operation by the FAA during World War II. The Barracudas of No 8 and No 52 Torpedo Bomber Reconnaissance (TBR) Wings from *Furious* and *Victorious* respectively, rehearsed the attack with their supporting fighters against a specially built dummy range at Loch Eriboll in Sutherland. On 30 March 1944 the Home Fleet's Second Battle Squadron, with heavy cover provided by *Duke of York, Sheffield, Anson, Jamaica* and *Royalist,* and under a screen of twelve destroyers, set off with the carrier squadron, comprising *Victorious, Furious, Emperor, Searcher, Fencer* and *Pursuer,* to attack *Tirpitz*. The Force reached the fly-off position 120 miles north-west of Kaafjord in the early hours of 3 April. At 04.30 hours No 8 TBR Wing was launched and with the rest of the carrier aircraft formed up – forty-two Barracudas, twenty-one Corsairs, twenty Hellcats and ten Wildcats. *Tirpitz* was just getting under way when the force struck an hour later. Complete surprise gave the Barracudas fourteen direct hits resulting in 128 crew killed and 270 wounded. A further strike was made by nineteen Barracudas of No 52 TBR Wing an hour later, increasing casualties aboard *Tirpitz* to 438 killed or wounded. A second strike planned for 24 April had to be cancelled due to bad weather. *Tirpitz* was out of action for three months, which lessened the pressure on Allied shipping, but did not remove the threat. The Germans moved in thousands of smoke canisters and fifty-two light flak guns to supplement the awesome firepower of the ship and other flak already in position. On 15 May *Victorious* and *Furious* flew off twenty-seven Barracudas, twenty-eight Corsairs, four Seafires and four Wildcats in an attempt to make another strike but low cloud caused it to be abandoned. Another strike for 28 May was

One of the observers in 1772 Squadron, S/Lt Val Bennett, was also an artist and made a number of watercolour paintings of Firefly operations — in particular of 1770 to which he was attached at one time. Many of them depict scenes where it was not possible to take cameras, and he would ask crews for their recollections of events. In this scene, the Fireflies of 1770 are diving into a fiord to attack *Tirpitz*. *(V. M. G. Bennett)*

also cancelled. Keeping up the pressure, another strike was planned, 'Operation Mascot', for 17 July with aircraft from *Furious, Formidable* and the new carrier, *Indefatigable.* The Fireflies of No 1770 were to lead in some forty-four Barracudas while eighteen Corsairs and eighteen Hellcats provided fighter cover. The Fireflies were to go in first to suppress the flak! Major Cheesman was strike leader and remembers that day:

'All squadrons were airborne, formed up and speeding at 200 knots for the coast. It was our job, in the Fireflies, to lead in the striking force of torpedo bombers and ordinary bombers, onto the target for the attack. At sea the sky was clear, but to reach the target, we were to cross mountains climbing to 6000 ft, and we were not to know the nature of the weather the other side. When we had flown 100 miles the coastline came into view, but we remained at sea level until the last possible moment and then zoomed straight to 8000 ft for our passage over the mountains. What cruel looking terrain that was – all white, cold, barren and desolate, an engine failure here meant ''out harp and halo and hello St. Peter''. Then we were in snow! Instrument flying through cloud and snow over a high mountain range, under icing conditions, and looking for a battleship tucked away in some well protected fjord, was like looking for your grandmother's wedding ring in the Sahara Desert at night! We had been advised that the Germans had transported many thousands of smoke canisters up to Norway to meet such an emergency by blotting out the whole fjord with smoke and thus depriving an enemy of their target. Consequently, it was imperative that we should get there before the smoke screen could become effective. At times like this life can seem fraught and difficult – here I was with eighty aircraft following me, still in cloud and rushing along at 200 knots with nil visibility – a hole in the clouds, and there below on my port bow, a patch of water surrounded by mountains, and what is more, a ring of smoke forming around its shores. This is it! Target, port bow, three miles – attack-attack-attack. Down we screamed, all eighty of us, while all around us burst the shells of the anti-aircraft guns. Within seconds all hell was let loose, bombs, torpedoes, shells, tracers and bullets, from above and below as we dived for our targets. Within minutes it was all over, and forty minutes later we found that postage stamp on the sea, which we called home. Only seventy-four returned to land on, the cost of assuring the safe passage of convoys to Russia for a bit longer.'

Damage to the *Tirpitz* was minimal due to a heavy smokescreen but on 24 August the Barracudas got two hits but one failed to explode. Although there were a number of raids the element of surprise achieved at the April strike was never repeated. It was perhaps fortunate that there was no enemy fighter opposition during the strikes on *Tirpitz*, the aircraft losses being restricted to flak and other causes.

On 2 August S/Lt Evans had the dubious distinction of being the only observer in the FAA to write-off a Firefly – he started the engine while one side was jacked up on the compass base!

After the raid on *Tirpitz* the force moved towards the Leads of Norway for 'Operation Offspring'. The Fireflies of 1770 escorted Avengers in to lay mines on 9/10 August, and then proceeded to attack targets of opportunity, including some coastal shipping. One Firefly was lost, S/Lt Davies with observer S/Lt Bennett ditched about six miles out from Storholm lighthouse.

'Operation Goodwood', the next series of strikes against *Tirpitz* began on the morning of 22 August. A force of thirty-one Barracudas, twenty-four Corsairs, eleven Fireflies, ten Hellcats and eight Seafires took off but most were forced back by low dense cloud. The Fireflies and Hellcats however, pressed on, and found *Tirpitz* clear. The Hellcats were carrying bombs so Major Cheesman (in DT677 4A) led his Fireflies in first to quell flak sites, losing two in the process. Returning to the carrier the two squadron commanders had their aircraft re-fuelled and re-armed, offering to go again. In the afternoon eight Fireflies and six Hellcats went out alone. Unencumbered by the bombers the aircraft flew all the way at 210 knots and again arrived with the target clear. Before the smoke screen dropped intense flak opened up but Lt/Cdr Richardson, leading the Hellcats, did not hesitate, and paid the ultimate price. Major

Cheesman had, as always used his eight Fireflies as a diversionary force by attacking every flak site they could see, but to no avail – and they were lucky to escape the rain of lead unscathed. That fourteen fairly lightly armed fighters should take on the mighty *Tirpitz* and all its supporting gunfire must rank as one of the classic raids of the war for courage and sheer audacity!

After a day's respite, it was business as usual. *Indefatigable, Furious* and *Formidable* on the morning of 24 August launched thirty-three Barracudas, twenty-four Corsairs, ten Fireflies and ten Hellcats for yet another go at the mighty battleship. The Barracudas were slow climbing over the mountains and the force arrived to find the *Tirpitz* shrouded in smoke. The Fireflies were first in, attacking any flak sites, the Barracudas bombed blind through the screen, and amazingly got two hits – but the intense flak had claimed six of the attacking force. The last raid of 'Operation Goodwood' was something of an anti-climax. *Indefatigable* and *Formidable* launched twenty-six Barracudas, seventeen Corsairs, ten Fireflies, seven Hellcats and seven Seafires, the latter for diversionary attacks, but the Barracudas, this time leading the force, went up the wrong fjord and made the attack half an hour late. On arrival, *Tirpitz* was wreathed in smoke but the Barracudas followed the Fireflies down and scored two hits but, two of the attacking aircraft were shot down. The force returned to the Clyde and 1770 flew ashore to Ayr for a spot of well deserved leave. The *Tirpitz* was eventually damaged beyond repair on 12 November 1944 by a force of RAF Lancasters operating out of Russia using 12,000 lb 'Tallboy' bombs. On 17 November 1770 flew to Dale in Lancashire and on 21 November rejoined *Indefatigable* off Bardney Island, North Wales. The journey to join the British Pacific Fleet had begun.

Meanwhile, the second Firefly squadron, No 1771, had formed up at Yeovilton on 1 February 1944 with ten Fireflies, the CO being Lt/Cdr Ellis DSC, DFC, RN. An initial work-up started and by 15 February the squadron had sixteen Fireflies, some of these being reserve aircraft. The squadron left Yeovilton for Burscough on 3 March 1944 with fourteen aircraft, two following later. On 28 May the squadron was engaged in formation flying and on returning towards the airfield a general mêlée started with everyone trying to get on someone else's tail. Unfortunately, S/Lt Williams with observer S/Lt Sunderland in Z1906L, spun in off a turn and crashed into a field eight miles north of Burscough. Both crew were killed and the aircraft burnt out. The squadron flew aboard HMS

Trumpeter, near the Isle of Man on 30 June for deck landing practice. No problems were encountered and two months later 1771 joined *Implacable* off the Isle of Arran. *Implacable*'s other squadrons were 801, 880, 887 and 894 with Seafires, 828 and 841 with Barracudas, although 841 was absorbed into 828 later. During October strikes were made against shipping and shore targets along the Norwegian coast.

No 1771's first operational flight was 18 October 1944 when the squadron was instructed to search Tromso Sound, Malavgen, Nord and Bali Fjords for the *Tirpitz.* Eleven Fireflies took off led by Lt/Cdr Ellis and eventually found *Tirpitz* in Tromso fjord. A detached flight operating about forty miles to the south attacked Bardufoss aerodrome. Led by Lt Donaghey, the flight strafed hangars, barracks and parked aircraft, including Ju52s. On the return flight they attacked a German seaplane base at Sorveisen in Solberg Fjord, Lt Donaghey destroying a He115 and S/Lt Lumsden damaged a Blohm and Voss Bv 138. On another date it was the Fireflies of 1771 that found the Blohm and Voss Bv222V2 Wiking at Sorveisen and set it on fire. During these operations along the Norwegian coast the captain of *Implacable*, in order to confuse the enemy of her position, plied back and forth between Norwegian and home waters. It was

operations again on 26 October with an anti-shipping patrol between Meloy Island and Sandnessjoen but little was seen. The following day, during a similar patrol the squadron found a U-boat on the surface being escorted by a destroyer. In attacking, S/Lt Waters with observer S/Lt Weir in Firefly 4H were shot down and killed. A second strike was laid on and Lt Donaghey hit the U-boat ammunition locker and it was eventually left floating on its side.

On 27 November Fireflies of 1771 and Barracudas of 828 attacked a convoy just south of Sandnessjoen. The SS *Korsnes* and *Rigel* were driven ashore and lost, while *Spree* was severely damaged, three smaller ships were also damaged. Only minor damage was sustained by the attacking aircraft – S/Lt Gill in Firefly Z1887 receiving a hit in the starboard wing. Moving back into home waters 1771 disembarked to Hatston until 5 December when they again joined *Implacable* for more operations. On 8 December 1771 were out on an armed reconnaissance flight in the Hangesund area when they found and attacked some enemy shipping near Lervix, without loss. Back at Hatston later the squadron started training with a new weapon, the R/P, and were told that they were going to use them – on the Japanese. On 1 May 1944, the third Firefly squadron, No 1772,

Fireflies of 1772 Squadron at dispersal, Burscough 1944. Aircraft N was Z1978. *(Author's collection)*

The revised coding on Firefly squadrons, shown here as 4B and actually Z1984 of 1772 Squadron, came in on 1 October 1944. Note the spinner colours as mentioned in the text. *(Author's collection)*

Crews of 1772 Squadron at Burscough pose with one of their Fireflies, Z1946 Z. *(V. M. G. Bennett)*

The fateful day when three Fireflies were written off in a runway exercise. *(V. M. G. Bennett)*

had formed up at Burscough under Lt/Cdr A. W. Gough. The squadron quickly took to their new aircraft and training began in earnest. The only marking carried, apart from standard FAA camouflage, was an individual letter aft of the roundel, which the author was told was yellow. After a FAA directive the letter was prefixed by a '4', so that Z1979 of 1772 became 4Z, painted in aft of the roundel. No 1770 had their 4 before the roundel and the letter after it. The Firefly squadrons did not normally carry any specific marking but 1772 became the exception. They identified individual aircraft by using coloured spinners. The squadron was composed of three sections of four aircraft so each section had one main colour, i.e. white, blue or yellow. So, the flight leader would have an all-white spinner, his number two had a white spinner with a red tip, his number three had a white spinner with a red band halfway along the spinner and the number four had a white spinner with a red band round the rear of the spinner. This was repeated in the other flights with their colours. This was continued until 1772 got the later type of Firefly just prior to going to the Far East when all spinners were supposed to be black.

Working up, 1772, like any other had its share of accidents, probably the most serious being 29 July 1944 when Lt/Cdr Gough with Lt Wright as his observer, suffered a mid-air collision with Lt Sloan and observer Lt Baker. Gough managed to crash land but Sloan and his observer were killed. One of the exercises for all the crews was an oxygen climb to maximum altitude. On 4 August S/Lt Davidson with S/Lt Palmer as his observer, took off in Firefly Z1968 4M for such a climb. After attaining 33,000 ft they, being young and full of life, decided to do a really fast descent. Davidson pushed the nose over with full power on and down they went, the speed building up rapidly until they were doing well over 400 knots and, as they were now in what amounted to a terminal velocity dive, the controls locked solid. Davidson at last managed to pull out by using the elevator trimmer and it says much for the Firefly structure that nothing was torn off. On the ground they worked out the correction factors for compressibility and atmosphere and this gave a true airspeed figure in the dive of over 600 mph! The other young bucks of 1772 were so impressed that most of them had a go too, S/Lt Jobbings tearing off his undercarriage fairings in the process.

On 25 October the squadron lost three Fireflies all within a few minutes, even though there was no flying or casualties! It was a day when all flying had been cancelled due to bad weather. However, Gough was one of those 'press-on' types and decided to practice carrier procedure for a squadron take-off, with the aircraft ranged at the end of the runway as though on deck. All the aircraft were manned with the engines running, Gough acting as Flight Deck Control Officer (FDO), was to marshal them forward and wave them off in rapid succession. The idea being to start the run at full throttle until half way along the runway, throttle back and then taxi back to dispersal. The visibility was shocking, down to less than 200 yards and further hampered by the long nose of the Firefly. The first three Fireflies were waved away in rapid succession but the third, 4Z, no doubt carried away by enthusiasm did not throttle back in time and overtook 4M swiping it with his port wingtip causing 4M to ground-loop and collapse on its undercarriage. Careering up the runway he repeated the process to 4J with his starboard wing – finally ground-looping and losing his own undercarriage! The exercise was abandoned! On 1 November Lt/Cdr L. C. Wort DSC RNVR took over as the new commanding officer of 1772. After deck landing training aboard HMS *Empress*, 1772 embarked in HMS *Ruler* on 20 January 1945 and sailed for Australia.

Back on 21 November 1944, 1770 had re-embarked in *Indefatigable* and sailed for the Indian Ocean. On the way there was practice flying and using R/Ps. Major Cheesman recalls this period.

'We found this additional weapon to be most satisfying, but of course we had to get used to firing them by means of the Gyro Gunsight and this meant many practice runs before we were capable of using them in action. However, I was determined to find the opportunity of demonstrating our strike power to our Admiral, who was Rear Admiral Sir Philip Vian, and this we were allowed to do one day on passage from home waters. In order to make this demonstration sufficiently effective to the Admiral, I managed to have a marker buoy dropped some 500 yards off the port bow of the *Indefatigable*, which was carrying the Admiral's flag at that time, so that we were able to pounce on it with our rocket and cannon as the ship sailed past. Afterwards Admiral Vian sent for me and told me that this was one of the most impressive demonstrations of strike power from one squadron he had ever seen in his life.'

Impression of 1770's Fireflies attacking enemy shipping with rockets around the coast of Miyako. *(V. M. G. Bennett)*

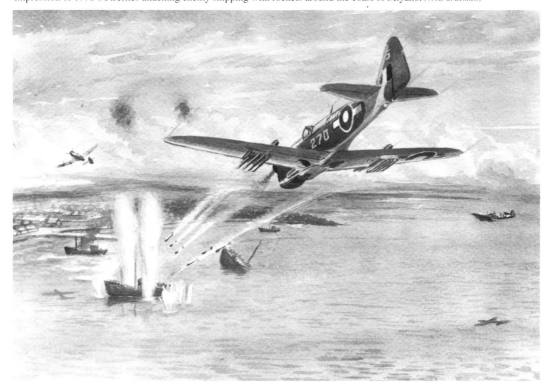

A flak-damaged Firefly of 1770 makes it back to *Indefatigable* and is pushed aft quickly to make room for the ones behind. The British Pacific Fleet coding seen here came in around May 1945. *(Imperial War Museum)*

They disembarked to Puttalam, Ceylon, on 10 December and proceeded to put in a lot of weapon training, especially with R/Ps.

Rear Admiral Vian had decided to make strikes against the Japanese held oil refineries in Sumatra before going on to Australia. His force consisted of one battleship, a cruiser squadron and ten destroyers with a smaller force of oilers and screening destroyers. He had three carriers with over 170 aircraft, *Indefatigable* with 1770 (Fireflies), 820 (Avengers), 887 and 894 (Seafires) and 888 (Hellcats); *Victorious* with 849 (Avengers), 1834 and 1836 (Corsairs); *Indomitable* with 857 (Avengers), 1839 and 1844 (Corsairs).

On the morning of 4 January 1945, Major Cheesman, with S/Lt Wilkey as his observer, took off in Firefly DT943 4A to lead the attack for 'Operation Lentil' – the strike on Pangkalan Brandon. He now recalls that eventful day.

'The form-up, needless to say, with some 400 aircraft in the sky was a tricky business, but thanks to the practices we had and rigid flying discipline, the whole air group was airborne within minutes and on course for the target. Despite low cloud and sea mist we pressed on and suddenly emerged into brilliant clear sky, just what we wanted. As we approached the target area instructions were passed over the R/T, "Starboard thirty, target thirty miles, formation B for Baker – GO", and the squadrons deployed into attack formations. There were barrage balloons all around the target as I looked for a lead in. "Bandits, left thirty up, ten miles" and our fighter cover wheeled away to intercept the Japanese fighters. Things hotted up, "Bandits right ninety, level and closing", the R/T was full of sightings as I lined up and dived. "Attack-attack-attack" I called as we swept down between the balloons. Down we went, over 300 knots and then I let my rockets go at a cracking plant. As soon as they were on their way I switched to guns and opened fire with the cannon. The lads in HMS *Cornwall* were avenged as the plant went up in an enormous explosion. A Jap fighter got on my tail but I took avoiding action and tried to get him, but he slipped away. The whole place was aflame with smoke, flak and chaos as scores of aeroplanes wheeled around the sky. The first Firefly ''kill'' went to Lt Levitt, our senior pilot, who shot down an Oscar, and another Jap type later. The Japanese took forty per cent of their fuel from this refinery but it never operated to capacity again until after the war.'

The force withdrew to Ceylon, and, after a little reshuffling emerged as the new British Pacific Fleet (BPF) – still under Rear Admiral Vian. The BPF consisted of carriers *Indefatigable, Indomitable, Victorious, Illustrious,* the battleship *King George V,* three cruisers and ten destroyers, all sailing for Australia. Rear Admiral Vian decided to make one more strike before leaving the area. Under the new arrangement all the aircraft were given a fleet code, thus Cheesman's Firefly DV120 4A became 270, and the 4-plus individual letter disappeared. On 24 January the force struck at Pladjoe refinery. The Fireflies and Avengers were already in their initial dives before the Japanese flak opened up. Once again the Fireflies devastated their target. During this action 1770 shot down two more Oscars. The next strike, 'Operation Meridian', was planned to knock out another oil refinery, this time at Soengi Gerong near Palembang. The Fireflies had been detailed to fire at the balloons as they flew through but two Avengers were still lost to them. Three more Oscars fell to the guns of 1770, the effects of cannon being most dramatic compared to the normal machine guns. These three strikes did incalculable harm to the Japanese war effort, with resulting shortages of aviation fuel on all fronts. At a cost of twenty-five aircraft lost in action the BPF had reduced the Jap aviation fuel output from Sumatra by thirty-five per cent. A not insignificant part had been played by the FAA's newest type – the Firefly.

Most of the BPF arrived off Sydney, Australia, on 10 February 1945. It was unsure at this stage which American fleet they were to join. General MacArthur wanted the BPF for his forthcoming amphibious campaigns in Borneo and Mindanao. Admiral Nimitz, Commander-in-Chief Pacific, equally wanted the BPF, and referred to it as 'his most flexible reserve' and hoped to use it for his forthcoming landings on Okinawa. It was not until the beginning of March 1945 that the Joint Chiefs-of-Staff decided that Nimitz had the greater need of the four British armoured carriers

and their 238 aircraft. American carriers only had wooden decks and suffered considerable damage if hit by a kamikaze aircraft. The Americans were amazed later in the Pacific when one kamikaze crashed on the flight deck of *Indefatigable* and she was operational again within an hour! Before commencing operations however, the British had to adopt US Navy operating procedures for such things as signals, tactics and carrier procedure techniques.

The BPF was included as Task Force 57 into Admiral Spruance's American 5th Fleet, arriving at Ulithi Atoll in the Caroline Islands on 19 March. On this same day three American carriers, *Intrepid, Wasp* and *Franklin* were damaged by enemy action and withdrawn from 'Operation Iceberg', the planned invasion of Okinawa. Task Force 57 left Ulithi on 23 March with orders to keep enemy airfields in the Sakishima Gunto group of islands out of action while the Americans secured, first the Kerama Retto, some fifteen miles from Okinawa, and then Okinawa itself. The Sakishima Gunto group of islands lies some 450 miles south of Japan and slightly south-west of the main Ryukyu islands. On the islands of Miyako, Ishigaki and Mihara were six airfields, which were in a favourable position to act as staging posts for Japanese aircraft based in Formosa to pass through en route for Okinawa, or to support operations in and around Okinawa. The BPF planned to mount the heaviest possible series of strikes against these airfields in an effort to deny their use to the enemy. Operations were planned for two days of heavy strikes, then withdrawal to refuel and replenish while the US Navy continued the pressure and then return for two more days, and so on.

On 26 March 1945, from a position about 100 miles south of the Sakishima Gunto the first strikes of 'Operation Iceberg' were launched. The Fireflies of 1770 were given the task of destroying the enemy flak positions and went in hard with rocket and cannon, also attacking Hirara airfield and its installations. Avengers bombed the runways and buildings, while Corsairs and Hellcats provided escort or target CAP (Combat Air Patrol). Fleet CAP was flown by the Seafires which did not have the range for strikes. The following day the fleet aircraft attacked those targets again. Although nineteen FAA aircraft were lost over the two days, twenty-eight Japanese aircraft had been shot down. The first replenishment period took three days due to a typhoon warning, but 31 March found the British aircraft making more strikes at the Sakishima airfields. After an initial rocket attack 1770 provided a target CAP. April Fools' Day found the Japanese reacting strongly to the British and American thrusts. Enemy bombing and fighter attacks persisted throughout the day with one kamikaze getting through and crashing at the base of the island on *Indefatigable,* only for her to be operational again within the hour. The Fireflies, because they had observers, also found themselves on air-sea rescue work, either in the search mode or as escort to rescue craft. The attacks continued throughout 2 April and the fleet gratefully withdrew that evening to replenish.

The next series of strikes began on 5 April, continuing until 7 April. The Fireflies found themselves on CAP and ASR work between the ship and targets. These jobs were not popular, patrols were frequently over three hours duration and very tedious, only one body was found floating in the water. While the BPF was replenishing on 8 April the US Navy carrier, *Hancock,* was put out of action by kamikazes, and it was believed these aircraft were based on north Formosa. Admiral Spruance requested the BPF, who only had one more series of strikes to do before returning to Australia, to strike at the kamikaze bases to

alleviate the situation. Dawn on 11 April found the carriers in their launch positions but bad weather delayed the strike for twenty-four hours. Although the weather had improved for 12 April, Japanese air raids started to come in before the first strike was launched. Fierce air fighting broke out above the fleet with the Seafires drawing first blood. At 07.15 the Seafires had cleared the way for a launch and twenty-four Avengers and twenty fighters were quickly flown off. The Fireflies of 1770 were split, a few on CAP, but the majority under Major Cheesman made rocket and cannon attacks on harbour installations. Two other Firefly crews were detailed to escort a US Navy Mariner flying boat to pick up some ditched aircrews near the Sakishima Gunto islands. The Fireflies were flown by Lt Ward with observer S/Lt Stott, and S/Lt Miller with observer S/Lt Thomson. Over Yonakumi Shima island they spotted five Japanese Sonia dive bombers heading for Okinawa, intercepted them, shot four down and left the other smoking!

Enemy attacks on the fleet persisted throughout the day and in a major attack that evening, one Val,

A pair of 1772 Fireflies airborne from Schofields in Australia, March 1945, still with the earlier coding. 4A was MB380 and 4B was MB381. *(V. M. G. Bennett)*

A Firefly of 1771 Squadron comes to grief on the return from another mission, and has just hit the barrier. *(Author's collection)*

five Oscars and two Tonys were shot down for no loss. At first light on 13 April the fleet was put on the alert by an early morning attack by four Vals but it was soon over and the first launch made. Avengers attacked Matsuyama and Shinchitu airfields while the escorts destroyed twelve enemy aircraft on the ground. The Fireflies destroyed a radar station at Yonakumi with rockets and then strafed small water craft close to Iriizaki. Later in the day 1770 put up a 'Jack' patrol – this was a US Navy innovation, devised to provide a last ditch stand against any kamikaze that slipped through the net. The aircraft was held at 3000 ft within ten miles of the destroyer screen and controlled by visual fighter directors using a local air defence R/T frequency. It was late in the day when the fleet heard the sad news that President Roosevelt had died. After accepting her last aircraft for the day the BPF withdrew to replenish.

At the refuelling rendezvous on 14 April the BPF was joined by *Formidable*, but *Illustrious* left for Leyte to effect some repairs. In view of American losses over the last few days the BPF was asked to

return to Sakishima Gunto islands for the next series of strikes, arriving on 16 April. Strikes were flown off against Ishigaki and Miyako on that day with Fireflies making rocket attacks on a radar station on Miyako. Further attacks were made on this island the next day but Ishigaki was quiet and left alone. Three strikes were made that day but little enemy activity was seen and the fleet withdrew that evening to replenish. Returning on 19 April four strikes were laid on against both Miyako and Ishigaki with Fireflies making constant rocket attacks, providing CAP and ASR cover. It was during one of these operations that Lt Taylor of 1770 attacked and silenced a coastal gun which allowed a Walrus to pick up a ditched crew. After this series of strikes the BPF left to go to San Pedro Roads at Leyte, arriving on 23 April after thirty-two days of operations.

But what of the other Firefly squadrons? After their series of skirmishes along the Norwegian coast 1771 had received R/Ps and trained up with them during January 1945. The same month Lt/Cdr MacWhirter took over as the new CO. On 12 March the squadron embarked in *Implacable* and sailed, via the Mediterranean for Australia. On getting there, flying training was carried out to acclimatise the crews. Operating from the shore base at Nowra it included carrying out weapon training at Jervis bay. The squadron flew aboard *Implacable* on 24 May and sailed for the Admiralty Isles.

No 1772 had boarded HMS *Ruler* on 20 January for passage to Australia, although some of the squadron went in HMS *Activity,* arriving off Sydney on 16 March. The squadron flew ashore to Schofields two days later and for the rest of the month and most of April were committed to a heavy weapon training programme. The squadron's activities were not without their lighter side – on 21 March while on a training flight the Fireflies were 'interfered' with by some boisterous Royal Australian Air Force Boomerangs. Not to be outdone, the next day 1772 flew across to the Boomerang base at Menangel and beat it up. The Boomerang boys, rising to the occasion, took off to teach the Firefly lads a lesson. There then followed a dogfight all over the sky but the Boomerang boys, thinking the Firefly easy meat, had bitten off more than they knew and the Fireflies came off best in nearly every case! On 24 April four complete crews were seconded to 1770 aboard *Indefatigable* for combat experience, while the rest of the squadron went off on a jungle survival course at the Australian HQ Training Centre at Canungra, Queensland.

Meantime, at San Pedro Bay, the BPF heard that its services were required in Borneo, but pressures on the US Navy off Okinawa forced Admiral Nimitz to ask for their assistance again to cover operations off Sakashima. Air strikes by the BPF resumed on 4 May, mainly against Ishigaki with 1770 attacking the airfield and other installations. The following day the Fireflies made rocket attacks against Miyara airfield, strafed static aircraft and shot up a blockhouse. Replenishment took place over 6/7 May, but bad weather on the 8th delayed the action, the Fireflies being airborne again on 9 May, making rocket attacks. The fleet returned to action on 12 May after two days replenishment, 1770 making rocket strikes against a radio station between Hirara village and the airfield of Hirara on Miyako. All the runways at Miyako, Ishigaki and other strips were found to be serviceable and bombed again. Although the Japanese repaired the runways each night, mainly with enforced labour, the continuous daily strikes by the Allies were having the effect required: no enemy aircraft could stage through for Okinawa. On 13 May three strikes were made against Miyako and one against

Ishigaki. Targets hit included barracks, runways, oil storage areas and barges. The Fireflies attacked a radio station on Ishigaki which they left burning. That evening the force withdrew to replenish over the next two days. It had been decided that the last strikes would be flown on 25 May, after which the BPF would return to Australia for a spell of well earned leave, to refit and prepare for a new series of strikes in July. Meantime, the morning of 16 May found 1770 attacking a camouflaged radio station near Nobara airfield on Miyako. During the afternoon the Fireflies went out again making rocket strikes against shipping and suicide boats around the coast of Miyako. Only three strikes were laid on for the next day, the Fireflies attacked barges at Osaki on the Miyako coast, and after escorting the bombers, returned to strafe the remains on their way back to the *Indefatigable.*

After replenishment over 18/19 May the Fireflies resumed operations on the 20th. One section went to Henna Saki, where their rockets wreaked havoc with a radar station, while the other section attacked the airfield and barracks at Hirara. The enemy seemed to get supplies and reinforcements through and despite the constant strikes the Japanese were always there to hit back. The work continued, 1770 attacking a radar station at Nobara with rockets on the 21st, both in the morning and afternoon. Everyone was now keyed up and after the next replenishment there were only two days of strikes before sailing to Australia. The morning of 24 May was dull with drizzle but a few raids were laid on, 1770 using its Fireflies to attack storehouses and motor transport north east of Hirara airfield. On the last day, 1770 attacked a suicide boat base north of Hirara, leaving boats and buildings burning. That evening the BPF sailed for Australia.

The BPF had done well: 5335 sorties flown from five fleet carriers had delivered 950 rockets, almost 1000 tons of bombs and half a million rounds of ammunition. Ninety-eight enemy aircraft were destroyed in combat and more than that on the ground. The FAA lost twenty-six aircraft to enemy action, 61 in accidents and seventy-three to kamikaze attacks and a hangar fire in *Formidable.* All this was achieved on twenty-three operational flying days, forty-one aircrew lost their lives.

On arrival in Australia 1770 was disbanded and its older squadron members, including Major Cheesman, sent home. The remainder reformed in Queensland but before forming up the Japanese surrendered and the squadron finally disbanded on 31 September 1945. During the time that they had been formed, 1770 had been on almost continuous operations, losing only six crews in action. Its

A good study of Firefly DK438 277/N of 1771 Squadron, with no rocket rails or drop tanks. Note '77' repeated on the forward engine cowling and the name *'Lucy Quipment'* under the exhaust manifolds. *(G. Gill)*

Johnny Mortimer's Firefly of 1771 comes to rest at the edge of *Implacable*'s flight deck. *(D. I. Carter)*

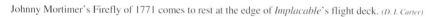

members were awarded one DSO, nine DSCs and ten were Mentioned in Dispatches, two post-humously. Their Fireflies were now handed over to 1772 who needed time to bring the squadron up to strength plus spare aircraft. With a wealth of experience from the crews seconded to 1770, the squadron were informed they were to replace 1770 aboard *Indefatigable* for the next round of operations against the Japanese.

Meanwhile, to keep up the pressure on the Japanese, Task Force 111/2 was formed up under Rear Admiral E. J. B. Brind, with orders to neutralise any remaining enemy aircraft. This force consisted of *Implacable* with 1771 (Fireflies), 828 (Avengers), 801 and 880 (Seafires), the escort carrier *Ruler* with 885 (Hellcats), four cruisers and five destroyers. The force sailed from Manus on 10 June with orders to strike at Truk in the Caroline Islands. The American Task Force 58 had already hammered this stronghold and there were few worthwhile targets. Two days of strikes were made on 13/14 June with the Fireflies of 1771 attacking shipping in Dublon harbour, and secondary targets of radio and radar sites. During the two days *Implacable* flew 113 offensive and 103 defensive sorties, before returning to Manus to join up with the BPF.

Due to defects and refit requirements, the only carriers available were *Implacable, Formidable* and *Victorious. Indomitable* was refitting and *Indefatigable* had been delayed in Australia by a breakdown of her air compressors. The US 3rd Fleet had meanwhile sailed and from 10 July made a series of devastating raids on the Japanese mainland. On withdrawing to the replenishment area, it was joined by the BPF. This was the first time that the two carrier forces had actually met and to acquaint the 50,000 American sailors with the outline of British aircraft, a flypast was arranged of the Firefly and Seafire. This was to avoid confusion with the Japanese Judy and Tony. The US part of the Task Force reciprocated with a flypast of the SB2C Helldiver!

Operations against the Japanese re-commenced on 17 July with eight Fireflies attacking Matsushima airfield and rail targets north of Honshu. This was the first time British aircraft had flown over Japan. The following day, the US force struck at the Yokosuka naval base, but for political reasons the BPF were excluded from this operation. The reason given was that the Fireflies and Seafires did not have the range to escort the bombers. The real reason, of course, was that they wanted the people back home to see that it was the US Navy hitting important Japanese naval bases on Japan

itself, without the help of any Allied effort. As a gesture the British were allocated targets well to the north east of Tokyo and eight Fireflies of 1771 attacked Konike airfield. The force retired to replenish on 20 July and were joined by *Indefatigable* with her air group. Bad weather now hampered operations until 24 July when the US Navy again picked the important targets and allocated secondary ones to the British. For the first time two Firefly squadrons would be operating together, even if striking at different targets. No 1771 attacked shipping in the Inland Sea area near Nagoya, while others strafed a destroyer in Ono Bay. Fireflies of 1772, with long range tanks fitted, went on an early morning strike to attack Tokushima airfield and encountered heavy flak. Just before lunch the Fireflies of 1772 went out again, first as escort to Avengers, and then to strafe Takamatsu airfield in Shikoku, just off Japan. S/Lt Goodsell and observer S/Lt Banks were shot down on this raid. It was a day of low cloud and poor visibility but six Avengers, two Corsairs and two Fireflies of 1771 found the Japanese escort carrier *Kaiyo* and left it with a broken back and on fire. This attack was particularly significant as it was the only strike by FAA aircraft against an enemy carrier in World War II. Despite the poor weather, some 416 offensive sorties had been flown with a further 100 CAP sorties.

Bad weather again the next day prevented a maximum effort but some strikes were laid on – 1771 again attacking shipping near Habu in the Inland Sea area, while 1772 went off to escort Avengers. The bad weather prevented the Avengers getting through to the target, so 1772 went off and shot up harbour installations at Ajiro Saki in Shikoku, several coastal vessels being sunk in the process. Later in the morning another strike was laid on with 1772 escorting Avengers, after which they attacked parked enemy aircraft and flak positions on Tokushima airfield. S/Lt Scott was hit by flak but managed to get back to the ship, and an Avenger ditched, but S/Lt Kingston and S/Lt Roberts orbited the crew until a friendly submarine picked them up. The force sailed to the replenishment area that evening.

The Inland Sea was the principal target area on 28 July and 1771 started the ball rolling by setting fire to a vessel in Sato Bay. At 05.50 hours, most of 1772 went off as usual to escort the Avengers, after which they attacked Harima shipyard in OO Bay on Honshu. One of the crews left behind, S/Lt Kingston with S/Lt Bennett as observer, was launched at 07.40 hours in Firefly MB502 276, to patrol and look after two ditched Corsair pilots. At

11.45 hours 1772 were launched again to repeat the earlier escort and strike. This time a 7000 ton tanker was set on fire, two smaller vessels attacked and a lugger sunk, but not without loss: Lt Stevens, a Canadian, and his observer S/Lt le Grange, were shot down over the target and not seen again. Lt Stevens had been the senior pilot and very popular, but the squadron were cheered to hear that Don Banks, believed lost in action on 24 July, had been picked up by a submarine after he had been adrift in his dinghy for two and a half days. Bad weather prevented flying on 29 July but cleared enough to allow flying the day after. The enemy airfields in the Tokyo plain area were fog bound and aircraft were routed to coastal targets. No 1771 took their Fireflies to Maizuru harbour, making cannon attacks on the submarine depot at Jingei. Launched at 05.35 hours, 1772 had escorted some Avengers to their target, the weather being ten tenths cloud all the way, the Avengers bombing blind through the overcast. Lt/Cdr Wort took 1772 down below the cloud base and strafed Susuka airfield. At 11.45 hours 1772 were launched again to escort Avengers and afterwards went and attacked shipping in Yokkaichi, near Isewan on Honshu. That evening the force withdrew to replenish, but due to typhoons and the dropping of the atomic bomb on Hiroshima, operations were not resumed until 9 August.

On this day Corsairs alternated with Avengers in strikes on the dwindling Japanese navy. No 1771 attacked shipping in Konega Bay and left some burning, other 1771 Fireflies attacked Matsushima airfield shooting up enemy aircraft, and one Firefly observed for the fleet bombardment of Kamaishi. Matsushima was also attacked that day by 1772 who shot up rows of transport aircraft, S/Lt Roberts received heavy treatment from the flak but managed to get back to ship. Over fifty enemy aircraft were destroyed on the ground that day, the Fireflies doing their fair share. 10 August was to be the last full day of operations with FAA aircraft roaming at will over Honshu and attacking targets of opportunity. No 1771 went out escorting Avengers and then attacked Koriyama airfield, while other 1771 Fireflies attacked a destroyer and a factory. After escorting their Avengers to the target 1772 attacked various targets, some strafed Koriyama airfield, where there was still very accurate flak, S/Lt Roberts with observer S/Lt McBride, being shot down in flames. Other 1772 Fireflies strafed shipping, mainly destroyer escorts in Onagawa and Okachi Wan, north of Sendai on Honshu. Some Fireflies received flak damage and S/Lt O'Neil and observer S/Lt Darby, both New Zealanders, had to bale out. They were captured by the Japanese, but

after the surrender were freed and rejoined *Indefatigable* in Tokyo Bay.

Over these two hectic days the enemy had lost more than 700 aircraft to the fast carrier force. The FAA lost thirteen aircraft and nine crews. The CAP, usually over 100 aircraft strong, shot down any Japanese aircraft venturing anywhere near the fleet. The BPF were asked to contribute two more days of strikes but the weather on 11 August was too bad. Many of the BPF vessels, including *Implacable* with 1771 aboard, had to leave for Australia for attention and repairs. This left only one carrier – *Indefatigable,* with 1772 aboard. Operations resumed on 13 August with aircraft going out to hit targets of opportunity. An early morning CAP was 1772's first task and later went out on an armed recce over the Taira area, strafing three trains and a coastal vessel. During the afternoon 1772 went out as Avenger escorts and strafed the marshalling yards at Taira, north of Tokyo. The Avenger target was obscured by cloud and the Fireflies tried to lead them to the diversionary target, a factory, but the bombers did not show up. There was no news of the expected surrender so after replenishment, operations started again on 15 August. The Avengers, going out on another strike, were intercepted by a dozen or so Zeros but the CAP Seafires shot down eight for the loss of one of their own. The Fireflies strafed Kizarazu airfield and returned to the ship. At 07.00 hours all further strikes were cancelled pending the unconditional surrender of Japan, the actual signing not taking place until 2 September 1945 in Tokyo Bay.

Flying was curtailed for a few days but 22 August found 1772 airborne on a practice sweep with eight Seafires, who complained of the high cruising speed of 200 knots! On 27 August the Fireflies were given a new task – that of locating prisoner of war camps on Shingu and Nagoya. Sweeps were made over these islands but none were located. On 28 August a section of Fireflies found a PoW camp at Yokkaichi, which they photographed, another was located at Arimatsu around the same time. During these sweeps, often over three hours duration, 1772 would overfly Japanese airfields where now resided what remained of the Japanese air strength. Hundreds of enemy aircraft were lined up, grounded forever. A typical sweep would take in the airfields located at Akendgahara, Kumozu, Susuka, Mitsubishi, Okazaki, Meiji and Kamezaki. Another sweep was made on 29 August and on the following day 1772's Fireflies started dropping essential medical supplies by container. (This was interesting because during September/October

1945, a Firefly MB692 was attached to the Airborne Forces Experimental Establishment at Beaulieu to flight test containers that could be dropped to either small units behind enemy lines, or, as in this case, medical supplies.) The first such drop was made at Yokkaichi, where the crews had the pleasure of seeing their supplies being collected by the POWs. On what must have been one of the last sweeps of the squadron, 1772 on the morning of 2 September 1945 flew over Yokkaichi POW camp, and as they circled an American B29 arrived and dropped supplies. It was all over! The BPF now returned to Australia where during September both 1771 and 1772 were disbanded. The only Firefly unit left in the Pacific was 1790 Squadron, also in Australia.

What an enviable record for a new fighter. Despite being classified as mainly suitable for escort duties, the Firefly had shown that even in its most unenviable tasks as a supportive and flak suppressive aircraft it had really come out with flying colours as the Fleet Air Arm's most formidable all-weather strike aircraft – due in no little way to the courageous crews that flew her!

Chapter 4
Nocturnal Fireflies

FLEET AIR ARM pilots had always done night flying as part of their training and fighter pilots were no exception to this. Until 1941 there had never been much need for night operations by fighters. A number of events were to change the way of thinking within the Admiralty, these were:

1 The introduction of the monoplane with its much higher performance and deck approach speeds. Any operation of these aircraft, and especially single-seat fighters, was considered totally unsuitable for night work.
2 The introduction of Air Interception (AI) radar into RAF night fighters.
3 The ability of German Focke Wulf Condor aircraft to shadow a convoy at sea during the hours of darkness.

Until these events there had been no urgent need of carrier-based night-fighter aircraft. Now, suddenly, there was need for an aircraft to fill this gap. Just being introduced into the fighter squadrons of the FAA was the Fairey Fulmar, and suggestions were made that this two-seater was ideal to install the new AI equipment, which, with specially trained crews would give protection to the convoys at night. The Fulmar, while lacking speed, had a good endurance, a battery of machine guns and room in the rear cockpit for the AI equipment and operator. It would do until a more specialised aircraft could be found. Trials began in 1941 with a Fulmar fitted out with AI Mk IV. It must be remembered that these were early days and the equipment fairly rudimentary. The conditions for an actual interception were pretty remote because the radar power was low and as such the 'returns' were not clear. It was however, a start, and plans went ahead to (a) form a special night fighter training unit, (b) try the Fulmar operationally from carrier decks at night, and (c) build up some experience by having FAA aircrew fly night operations with RAF units using AI, (d) find a more suitable night-fighter.

The training unit, No 784 Squadron, formed up at Lee-on-Solent on 1 June 1942 as a naval night-fighter training squadron. At this time of course,

the Firefly was still on the secret list and none had been issued to the front line squadrons. Consequently, Fulmars were introduced, six initially, but after the squadron moved to Drem on 18 October 1942, the Fulmar strength increased rapidly. There was considerable interest within the FAA about the new night-fighter role and there was no shortage of volunteer crews. Training got under way and after the first few courses had passed out some went to interim postings pending the forming of the first Firefly night-fighter squadron, while others gained experience operating with RAF units.

In October 1942 the Naval Staff agreed that: 'Naval night-fighting has reached a stage where an operational development unit has become necessary. There is need for an efficient naval night fighter at a very early date. It is hoped that the Firefly will fulfil this need, but this aircraft is fitted with an entirely new design of AI (AI Mk X) set with a novel form of presentation, and some operational experience is urgently necessary if the Staff are to state correct requirements in time for them to be embodied in the production design. Failure will inevitably lead to many early teething troubles and the necessity for extensive modifications.'

In the interim it was decided to form a Naval Night-Fighter Interception Unit at Ford to work with the RAF FIU based there. A draft Admiralty Fleet Order was raised on 10 April 1943, to form a Naval Night-Fighter Interception Unit, to be No 746 Squadron with the following objectives:

1 To develop and adapt night-fighter tactics for naval aircraft and to advise the Admiralty on the operational use of night fighting and interception equipment.
2 To carry out such services, operational and tactical trials of night fighting and interception equipment as directed.
3 To visit naval night-fighter units to obtain first hand information on their experiences, and to ensure that they were brought up to date with the latest approved tactical information about their equipment and its employment.
4 To maintain close liaison with the RAF Fighter

Interception Unit at RAF Station Ford, and the Naval Fighter Direction Centre at RNAS Yeovilton, in order to be acquainted with the latest developments of their work as they affected night fighter interception.

5 To advise the Admiralty on amendments to Admiralty manuals and publications in so far as the tactics of night fighter interception were concerned.

The new unit, while having its own CO, Major L. A. Harris DSC RM, would actually come under the control of the RAF FIU's CO. At this time of course the Firefly was still on the secret list and had not yet joined any front line squadrons. No 746 Squadron formed up at Lee-on-Solent on 23 November 1942 and moved to Ford in December. Initial equipment was three Fulmar night-fighters equipped with AI Mk IV and three Fulmar target aircraft. Fireflies started to arrive in May 1943.

With this shift to include the Firefly in the night-fighter role, urgent meetings were held with Fairey to discuss the equipment and its layout. The first thing they discovered was that with putting the equipment in the rear cockpit its weight upset the C of G range. To get over this they inserted a fifteen-inch extension forward of the pilot's cockpit. The radar scanners were mounted in a nacelle projecting forward from the leading edge of the wing just outboard of the fuselage. On 9 February 1943 the Director of Contracts at the MAP informed Fairey that the Admiralty had a requirement for 100 Firefly night fighters. They wanted fifteen delivered by 1 October 1943 and the remainder at twelve per month. They would be known as the Firefly NF Mk II, production of which was to be drawn from Firefly orders already placed. Fairey sent their revised programme back on 26 February, with the first fourteen machines which had already been put aside after the initial talks being Z1831, Z1833, Z1836, Z1840, Z1841, Z1845, Z1865 and Z1868 to 1870 inclusive. To these they added, indiscriminately, the required eighty-six, Z1894 to Z1898, Z1971 to Z1976, Z2045 to Z2052, Z2055 to Z2060, Z2092 to Z2095, Z2121 to Z2126, DT926 to DT930, DT950 to DT961, DT992 to DT998, DV112 to DV116, DV135 to DV146 and MB450 to MB459 inclusive. This was just the beginning. Other orders for the NFII followed until there were well over 300 on contract. Only thirty-seven were to be completed and some of these were eventually converted into the NF1.

In March 1943 NFII Z1831/G underwent brief trials at Boscombe Down to test its suitability as a night-fighter, with special reference to the longitudinal stability. The interest was due to the fifteen-inch bay being inserted forward of the pilot's cockpit. Handling trials showed that the old problem was there, longitudinal stability was below the standard required. Further trials were made with the C of G moved forward and this

The first Firefly NF Mk 1 Z1831/G showing the small windscreen which so limited forward vision and the port radar nacelle mounted on the inner wing. Note the anti-spin strakes on the fin. The longer nose is most marked in this side view.

(Imperial War Museum)

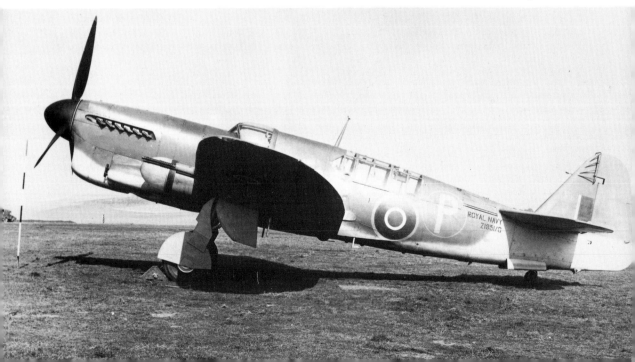

showed a marked improvement, but still not good enough. The aircraft went back to Fairey for some recommended modifications. At the end of April 1943 Z1831/G returned to Boscombe for further trials, but with the C of G moved forward and the length of the radar nacelles protruding from the wing leading edge reduced. It was decided after handling trials that, although the longitudinal stability was now satisfactory for night flying, the directional stability had deteriorated due to the engine move. Though just acceptable for Service use the report suggested an increase in fin area might help, both to improve the existing problem and to cater for any other modifications introduced which might produce adverse effects. During August and September 1943 NFII Z1840 underwent handling trials for Service clearance of the night fighter version of the Firefly. Three modifications had been incorporated to make Z1840 representative of the production NFII:

1 Tailplane incidence increased by two degrees
2 Metal covered elevators introduced
3 Re-designed pilot's cockpit canopy

Flight trials showed that the longitudinal stability problem greatly improved. Spin tests showed standard recovery after two turns and all the night flying trials were successful.

But all was not successful when the NFII started to be flown by the Service. Lt/Cdr Jimmy Kneale was CO of the first Firefly night-fighter squadron and he had this to say:

'It was apparent from the beginning that the lengthening of the fuselage had adversely affected the deck landing capability of the Firefly NFII, an opinion confirmed after a crash landing during trials on HMS *Ravager*. Considerably more serious problems were experienced with the arrangement of the transmitter and receiver aerials in separate radomes. Notwithstanding the efforts of experts from the Telecommunications Research Establishment (TRE) at Malvern, the required synchronisation of the scanner dishes was difficult to achieve. In addition, the Service trials disclosed that the mountings of the radomes close to the fuselage and propeller seriously interfered with the signal reception. These shortcomings, together with the realisation that the NFII could not be conveniently produced by the initially hoped for minor modifications to the FR1 assembly line, led to the abandonment of the project in June 1944. It is a measure of the misplaced

early optimism regarding the NFII that orders for 328 of these aircraft were placed. In the event only thirty-seven were built, some of which were converted back to FR1s whilst NFIU retained its quota as targets for AI interception exercises and for communication purposes.

'Fortunately by mid-1944 an alternative variant of the Firefly FR1 had emerged, whose speed of development and production was in stark contrast to the abortive attempts to salvage something from the time and resources wasted on the NFII. The key to this progress was the availability of an American centimetric radar set, designated by the US Navy as AN/APS-4 (Army-Navy/Airborne Pulsed Search) or ASH (Air-Surface H) as it was more commonly known. The FAA had first become aware of the potential of this set for single-engined aircraft during a visit by a section of the NFIU to Quonset Point, Rhode Island, to investigate what the US Navy was doing in the field of air interception radar. The NFIU representatives were at Quonset Point from mid-August to the end of October 1943. They were led by Major L. A. Harris DSC RM with Lt J. H. Kneale, RNVR (later CO of 1790 Squadron), Lt P. Twiss DSC RNVR (later Chief Test Pilot at Fairey) and Lt J. O. Armour RM (later CO of 892 Squadron) as pilots, and Lt J. Flooks RNVR, who at that time was the FAA's most experienced AI operator. During their visit to Quonset Point the NFIU section was attached to the US Navy's similar specialist unit known as Project Afirm, and both units worked closely together in evaluating both ASH and an improved AI set which had just become available for service trials and designated AN/APS-6.

'Because of the US Navy's own urgent requirements there was no early prospect of the FAA acquiring any of the APS-6 sets, but in mid-1944 ASH sets were released and installed in Firefly FR1s for evaluation by NFIU. Although inferior to APS-6 in several respects, including the lack of blind-firing capacity, ASH was nonetheless a more than adequate substitute for AI Mk X. It had the virtue of being compact, with most of its 200 lb weight contained in a transmitter/receiver pod which could be easily attached to the fuselage of a single-engined aircraft. Although orginally designed for air-to-surface use, it had an acceptable AI performance. Through the fortuitous timing of its

Note the short nacelle housing and the bulbous transparent cover of Z1875. *(Westland Aircraft Ltd)*

The first production Firefly NF1 with the revised shorter nose, ASH 'bomb' below the nose, revised higher windscreen and hood, and a flame deflector plate above the rear three exhaust stubs. *(Imperial War Museum)*

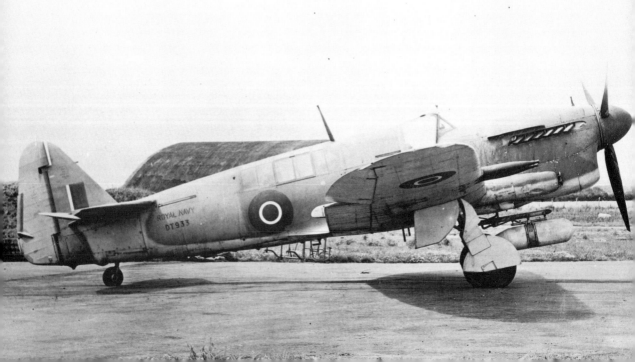

availability by mid-1944, ASH rescued the Firefly night-fighter project from the consequences of the failure of the NFII. The fitting of the container pod, below the aircraft's engine, and the installation of the operator's set, required only relatively straightforward modifications to the FR1 assembly line to produce the Firefly NF1, some six months later than the NFII variant.

'By the time FIU and NFIU had returned to Ford at the end of August 1944 it had already been concluded that Fairey Aviation could go ahead with the production of NF1s to equip the FAA's first specialist night-fighter squadrons. Within its known limitations, in comparison with APS-6 and other contemporary centimetric radar, the ASH installation tested by NFIU had performed satisfactorily with no serious servicing problems, and it was anticipated that by the end of 1944, sufficient

NF1s would be available to form the first night-fighter squadron. Before that was possible an unexpected opportunity arose to try out the Firefly NF1 in an operational role. Following the over-running of the V1 flying bomb launching sites in France and Belgium by the advancing Allied armies, the Luftwaffe had adapted a number of Heinkel IIIs to release V1 flying bombs from points off the Norfolk coast. From the third week in July the Heinkels of the Third Gruppen of Kampfgeshwader 3 had started this activity, initially in daylight, but as this got unhealthy they came over at night. About the end of the first week in September the unit moved from Holland to bases in Northern Germany. For this series of raids its crews were joined by others who were not so usefully employed. Towards the end of October the unit was transformed into the First Gruppen of Kampfgeshwader 53 and by the

Illustrations showing the layout of the ASH radar system, as fitted to the Firefly NF1. The lower one shows the correct angle of the ASH nacelle – not parallel to the thrust line, as usually depicted in illustrations.

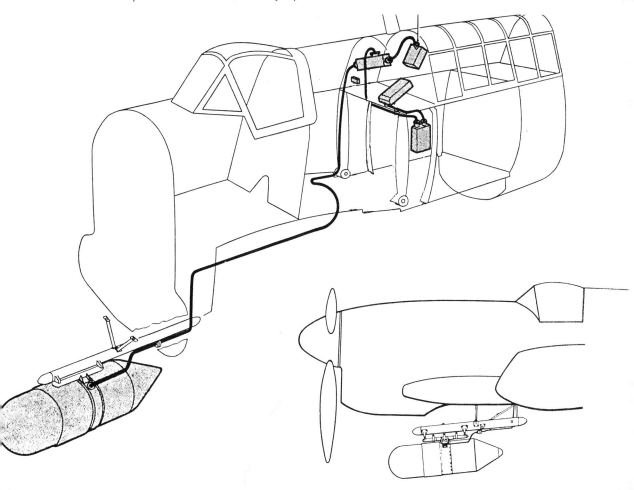

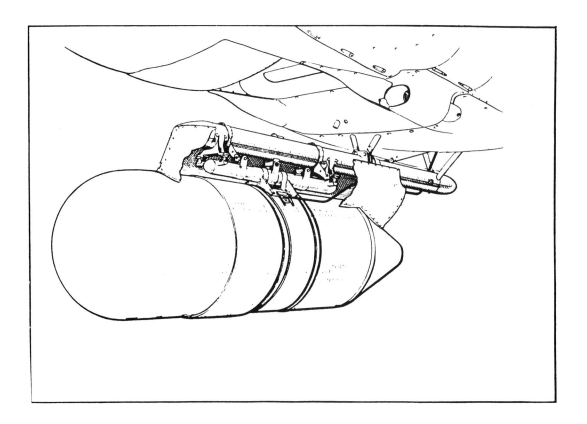

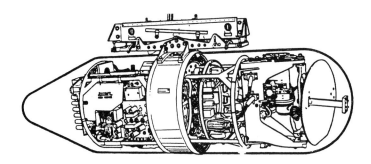

Illustrating the ASH nacelle itself, and beneath what the interior looked like with the scanner in the domed front.

middle of November all three Gruppen of this unit were in action over the North Sea. Operations from the new area began on 16 September with about fifteen Heinkels taking part and launching nine bombs. The tactics generally employed were to cross the North Sea below 100 feet so as to avoid early detection by the coastal radar stations, then climb to about 1000 feet to release the V1 followed by a rapid turn and dive to return to Germany at low level. These tactics made interceptions by night fighters both difficult and hazardous, especially after a few early losses caused the Heinkel IIIs to restrict their sorties to night when low cloud cover provided additional security from the RAF's night fighters. More launchings were made on most nights during the month and on a number of nights in October, November, December and January.

'Apparently the Luftwaffe lost forty-one launching aircraft during this four month period plus four in ground accidents. Launchings started to dwindle during November and by January had virtually ceased. This was not due to their losses or shortage of flying bombs, but to Allied air supremacy. Towards the end of October 1944 it became customary for FIU to send an aircraft to RAF Coltishall to supplement the resident night-fighter crews whenever a Heinkel III sortie was expected. For this purpose FIU used ''retired'' Beaufighters, the reason being that they had a much lower stalling speed than the Mosquitos generally used on operations and these were more capable of coping with the Heinkel's tactics. Permission was also obtained from the RAF for NFIU to participate occasionally in the anti-Heinkel operations from Coltishall, using the few Firefly NF1s it had for evaluation trials. Because the Heinkel IIIs came over in very small numbers, and rather more night fighters were scrambled to meet them, it was often a matter of chance which of the defending aircraft were best placed to be direct on to targets identified by the coastal radar. This fact, together with the few occasions when NFIU Fireflies were scrambled to join the RAF night fighters, meant that the opportunities for actual combat were very limited.'

Limited they may have been, but the experience to any naval night-fighter crews was of inestimable value. No amount of training could match the experience gained under actual combat conditions. This was a significant time for the FAA and the night-fighter programme in particular. The following details are as recorded by the pilots involved. On the night of 25/26 October 1944 Lt J. H. Kneale positioned his Firefly, MB419, to Coltishall, and with his AI operator, Lt J. C. Harrison, was scrambled but had R/T failure and had to return to Coltishall. Two

Early in 1944 three detachments of Fulmar night-fighters were attached to different carriers for convoy protection. This is B1 Flight, commanded by Lt Mike Howell, attatched to HMS *Campania*. *(Lt/Cdr M. B. W. Howell)*

Firefly NF1 MB564 of No 746 Squadron in 1945. This was the type 746 used for their night interceptions of flying bomb-carrying Heinkel IIIs in late 1944. *(Lt/Cdr J. H. Kneale)*

nights later they went back but there was no activity by the Heinkels. The next night was 14/15 November when they were scrambled again but no contact was made due to severe weather conditions. The difficult circumstances under which they operated was exemplified when two RAF Mosquitos strayed into the 'Diver Strip' gun belt and were shot down. There was no activity again on the night of 21/22 November, but that evening MB419 was flown to Coltishall by another crew, Lt M. Howell with Lt Lester as his AI operator. They were scrambled and Lt Lester managed to home in on a released V1 but the scan disappeared off the screen and it was almost certain it had gone into the sea. Lt Mike Howell says: 'With the Firefly we hadn't the turn of speed to actually catch a flying bomb, but if we could have got close enough for a few seconds to have a crack at it with the cannon we might have been lucky. The alternative was to catch the parent aircraft, the Heinkel III, either before it released the bomb, or afterwards, which would have made the Luftwaffe a little more cautious.' They had another scramble in the early

hours of the following morning but failed to make contact.

Lt Jimmy Kneale went back in DT933 on the night of 24/25 November and was scrambled but was disappointed when they were not directed on to a target. There was no activity on the night of 9/10 December when they returned in their usual aircraft, MB419. However, on 12/13 December he was scrambled with Lt G. L. Davies DSC, as his AI operator and they were directed onto a target. He recalls the trip: 'Only on one occasion was a Firefly NF1s cannon fired after a long ASH controlled pursuit in low-lying thick cloud which prevented any visual identification of the target. In the absence of a blind-firing facility this was no more than an opportunist attempt, and no results were claimed.' Two nights later they went back but there was no activity that night. Lt Howell also made some more sorties but all were inconclusive. Three days later Lt Howell flew Sir Alan Cobham to Staverton and back in Z1845; he continued with 746 for a while and carried out night deck landings on HMS *Pretoria Castle* during March 1945. In May he became CO of 732 Squadron, the first

Hellcat night-fighter squadron based at Drem. It should be mentioned, to put this limited NFIU activity into perspective, that the RAF had few successes against the night launching Heinkels, and suffered some losses which were attributable to the hazards of these operations.

It was now clear, following NFIU's service trials and anti-Heinkel sorties that the NF1 was a generally satisfactory night-fighter, with a bad weather capability which was only limited by the lack of a blind-firing device. Accordingly, efforts were renewed to obtain APS-6 sets for the FAA, and this was successful only in that the Americans released sufficient Hellcats equipped with this more advanced AI for one squadron to be formed, No 892 under Major J. O. Armour RM on 1 April 1945.

In January 1945 a special flight was made up from 746 for service trials. No 746A Flight moved to Hatston in the Orkneys for ADDLs and pre-embarkation exercises prior to embarking pairs of Fireflies in various escort carriers, this particular flight becoming an operational sub-unit shortly before VE-Day. For the first trials it was decided to use one crew from 746 and one from 784. On 17 February 1945 two Fireflies and the necessary

personnel and equipment embarked in HMS *Premier* for one operation but they did not see combat and disembarked to Hatston on 29 February. While there the crews undertook interception and intruder exercises. They embarked in HMS *Searcher* on 14 March and stayed until 30 March. During this period they did night deck-landings and practice interceptions, the learning curve still being high. The two Fireflies were damaged and had to be replaced, one was damaged extensively in a deck accident and the other from a heavy landing in very rough seas resulting in it being written off. A further embarkation in *Searcher* took place from 5 April to 14 April with a session of other exercises. When they returned to Hatston the unit was disbanded on 20 April. Reports about the trials of Fireflies operating at night from escort carriers made the following observations:

'It is still considered that Fireflies with a full operational load should not be flown off from escort carriers with a wind speed of less than twenty-five knots. One Firefly was inadvertently flown off, in daylight, with a wind speed of fifteen knots. The aircraft was

A Firefly NF1, PP617, of 1790 Squadron, running up at Burscough early in 1945. This aircraft carries an unusual camouflage pattern, and note the angle of the ASH nacelle in relation to the thrust line. *(Lt/Cdr B. C. Lyons)*

not airborne at the end of the flight deck and dropped a considerable height, almost hitting the sea. Some form of acceleration is urgently needed if full use is to be made of Firefly aircraft operating from escort carriers. RATO trials should be undertaken, but the Firefly with ASV/AI sets and numerous weapon attachments has great potential as a night-fighter/intruder. There were no major airframe or engine problems.'

In March 1945, 746 was re-styled the Naval Night-Fighter Development Squadron, and its tasks re-defined as testing the suitability of naval fighters and their equipment for night operations. The squadron moved to RAF West Raynham on 23 August 1945 and was disbanded 30 January 1946.

At an Admiralty meeting on 27 March 1945 the disposition of the Firefly programme was reviewed and units listed as:

No 1770 Sqn HMS *Indefatigable* British Pacific Fleet
No 1771 Sqn HMS *Implacable* British Pacific Fleet
No 1772 Sqn HMS *Indomitable* British Pacific Fleet
No 1773 Sqn To form-up at Woodvale 1 July with Barracudas then to have Fireflies for light carrier duties as part of 9th CAG
No 1774 Sqn To form-up as part of 12th CAG
No 1775 Sqn To form-up as part of 10th CAG
No 1790 Sqn Forming up at RNAS Burscough, for BPF June
No 1791 Sqn Forming up at Lee-on-Solent, for BPF August
No 1792 Sqn Forming up at Lee-on-Solent, for BPF October
No 746 Sqn NFIU – ASH fitted Fireflies, with detached Flight for operational use afloat as NF
No 766 Sqn NOTU – at Inskip, mixed ASH and non-ASH Fireflies
No 784 Sqn NFS – Drem, strength to be twenty-four Fireflies
No 790 Sqn FDOS – Move to Zeals, some ASH Fireflies
No 794 Sqn SAF – St Merryn

It was pointed out by their Lordships that nothing short of eight front line squadrons equipped with the Firefly would be acceptable.

Certain FAA officers had for some time nurtured dreams of a naval night-fighter squadron operating from carriers, and it was some of these that got

themselves on the first courses run by 784 at Drem. Lt/Cdr 'Ben' Lyons was one:

'My involvement with naval night-fighters started on 14 May 1944 when I underwent a training course with No 784 Naval Air Squadron based at Drem, near North Berwick. Classroom instruction in the art of air interception was given in Anson aircraft fitted with Mark IV AI equipment and another aircraft acted as a target. This was mainly for observers, but pilots also did some Anson time. We flew AI Mk IV equipped Fairey Fulmars. The Mk IV AI was an early air interception set with 'A' scope presentation in the rear cockpit. The course lasted until 25 August 1944 and involved fairly intensive day and night flying, mainly on practice interceptions. During the course pilots and observers teamed up and usually flew as a crew. The course consisted of about six crews (on this course all the observers had previous experience of night fighting, which helped considerably). All the crews were apparently destined for the first Firefly night-fighter squadron. All of use were given interim appointments and later re-joined 784 at Drem, which had by that time been re-equipped with the Firefly NF1 carrying ASH, as were the Ansons. This course lasted from 1 October to 15 December 1944 and the main emphasis was on interception by day and night. We did some seventy hours of flying and included some deck-landing training (by day only) aboard HMS *Ranee,* an escort carrier operating in the Firth of Forth.'

The first naval night-fighter squadron, No 1790, formed-up under Lt/Cdr J. H. Kneale RNVR at Burscough in Lancashire on 1 January 1945. Initially it was six Fireflies and six crews, with the full complement arriving on 1 February, but crews continued to trickle in until May. Previous to joining 1790, all crews underwent a two-month course with 784 squadron at Drem in Fireflies. Some of the Fulmar crews that had operated as night-fighters from *Campania, Vindex* and *Nairana* joined, as did two pilots and five observers who had operational experience with RAF Mosquito squadrons. Lt/Cdr 'Jimmy' Kneale picks up the story:

'The squadron was required to have the capability of operating not only at night, but also whenever weather conditions seriously reduced the effectiveness of day fighters. The traditional Lancashire weather pattern at Burscough was therefore more of a bonus than a handicap to 1790's working up programme. In the first few weeks some problems did arise with the station's Commander Flying and met officers regarding the prudence and feasibility of flying in conditions which would have grounded most other squadrons. However, as 1790's aircrews demonstrated their ability to cope with adverse weather, it was tacitly agreed that the decision to fly or not would be left to the squadron CO or his flight commanders, depending on who was in charge of operations at the time. On one occasion this resulted in a situation which led Commander Flying to question the wisdom of this trust. In very marginal weather conditions two Firefly NFIs were despatched on a night intruder exercise which would take them several hundred miles away from Burscough. By the time they returned some two hours later the airfield was blanketed in thick ground mist, which affected much of the surrounding area. Fortunately the aircraft were being flown by 1790's two flight commanders, Lt B. C. Lyons RNVR and Lt P. A. Toynbee RNVR and they eventually succeeded in landing safely. Both received commendations which paid tribute not only to their airmanship but also to their calmness and patience in coping with a dicey situation.'

The experience of Lt Toynbee was to stand him in good stead on another occasion as recounted by his observer/AI operator, Lt 'Jock' Frazer:

'I remember on one night exercise when our "playmate" (target aircraft) had to return to base to change aircraft as his radar was unserviceable. Pat (Lt Toynbee) and I amused ourselves by doing ASV runs on shipping in the Irish Sea. Our "playmate" returned and we duly completed the interception exercise. It was a lovely clear night over the sea but the idiots in flying control did not tell us that the airfield had become fogbound. Our "play-mate" had enough petrol to divert and did so. We, who had been airborne much longer, had not. As an experienced AI operator I could tell Pat when we were over the airfield and by going down through the fog carefully we at last spotted Burscough's red identification beacon. Until we landed that was the only light we saw. We had two unsuccessful attempts at an approach with the tanks showing empty. Pat

suggested we have one more attempt and if that failed we would climb to 3000 ft, head out to sea and bale out. I was so busy keeping my eyes on the beacon that the thought of baling out didn't really register and I agreed. On the third attempt, thanks to Pat's skill we caught a glimpse of the runway lights and landed safely. We taxied to the squadron dispersal much relieved. I put my hand up to open the hood and found it jammed tight. I had to be let out by a rigger with a screwdriver. Then it hit me, five minutes earlier I had been on the verge of baling out . . . a few stiff gins restored my equilibrium

'Many of the other crews had interesting or amusing stories such as that of a crew on a night cross-country exercise. The pilot was Lt Alan Tallboys, a New Zealander who was a member of the Magic Circle. He would never play cards for very long but just for fun would deal you a full house and himself four-of-a-kind. His observer that night was Johnnie Miller. In a Firefly the observer had practically no forward vision and had to rely on the pilot to tell him what was coming up. And so –

Alan ''There's a railway line ahead.''

Johnnie (after a look at his map) ''You sure it isn't a road?''

Alan ''It could be, but there is a bloody great engine on it!'' '

The work-up at Burscough was based on the primary role of night-fighting with a secondary role of day reconnaissance. The purpose of course, was to build up the standard of interception techniques so that eventually a squadron would be capable of operating from a carrier at night. A high standard of controlling was imperative and night-fighter FDOs were specially trained. The limitations of the controlling radar were also an important factor as it was essential that the ship's radar be capable of controlling aircraft from heights of less than 1000 ft up to the operation ceiling of any attacking aircraft. Navigation played a very important part and after renewal of basic skills the crews were sent off on night cross-country and intruder exercises using the mapping facilities of their ASH radar. It was quickly realised that this mapping feature of ASH was amongst its most valuable properties, and would simplify night missions over enemy territory. It was expected that this would manifest itself in three basic ways:

(a) Intruder sorties over enemy airfields using 'search' mode to navigate to the target and AI on arrival to locate any enemy aircraft.

(b) Intruder sorties with the object of strafing enemy airfields and ground installations.

(c) The location of targets for other aircraft not equipped with radar capable of mapping.

Training continued and in the afternoon of 24 May 1945 the twelve Firefly NF1s flew in formation from Burscough to join HMCS *Puncher* in the Irish Sea for the final stage of 1790's working-up programme, deck-landing training. Although only one pilot, the CO, had previously deck-landed a Firefly, this was not considered a problem because all the remaining squadron pilots had some, in several cases considerable, experience of deck-landing other types of aircraft. What was not appreciated until it was too late however, was the unsuitability of virtually no wind conditions in the Irish Sea for a stream landing of twelve Fireflies on to the restricted deck of an escort carrier. On arriving above *Puncher* the affirmative signal to land on was given and the squadron prepared to do so by following the carrier procedure designed to get the aircraft down with the shortest practicable interval between them. Lt/Cdr Kneale landed on first and was concerned to note that although he had picked up the first wire, his aircraft had come to a stop unusually close to the barrier. Clearly the wind speed over the deck was too low for Fireflies landing in a stream at around eighty knots on to a small aircraft carrier. His concern escalated to alarm when, having taxied his aircraft forward of the barrier, the second Firefly, piloted by Sub-Lt E. B. Everett RNVR with observer Sub-Lt J. Cariss, slithered on its belly under the port wing and over the bow into the sea! Because of the low wind speed over the deck the landing approach had to be flatter than normal, and by a slight misjudgement Tom Everett's Firefly touched down on the round-down and had the hook torn out by the stern guard rail. With nothing now to slow its progress the Firefly continued up the flight deck at such speed that it crashed through all three barriers, wiping off its undercarriage in the process. Leaving behind a considerable trail of debris the aircraft was still travelling briskly when it disappeared over the

This series of four photographs illustrates the occasion when Sub-Lt E. B. Everett lost his hook on the round-down and slithered off the bows. Picture one shows Sub-Lt Everett bringing his Firefly in for a flat approach, everything out and down – in two the hook has been torn out and the Firefly is just about to touch down – in three the aircraft is about to enter the barrier, the tailwheel has gone and the rudder is damaged, propeller tips bent, note the full up-elevator as the pilot tries to keep control – and finally, having gone through the barrier, losing its undercarriage in the process, the Firefly slithers forward to go over the bows. *(Lt/Cdr J. H. Kneale)*

Is this a bad landing? 'No,' says Lt/Cdr Dixon-Child, who was flying it at the time. Landing an in-line engined aircraft on a carrier at night was made more difficult because of the glare of the exhaust, not seen in daylight. The US Navy practised a steeply banked curved approach, which meant that the pilot, instead of looking straight forward was looking at forty-five degrees from the fore and aft line of the aircraft. Dixon-Child wanted to adopt this approach method for 1792 Squadron, and is depicted here about to straighten up and touch down. However, the Captain of HMS *Ocean* decided it was too dangerous for inexperienced pilots. It was to be June 1949 before the US Navy approach was adopted by the FAA. *(Lt/Cdr S. Dixon-Child)*

bows. *Puncher*'s helm was immediately put over to clear as much as possible of the crashed Firefly. Both the pilot and observer managed to get clear and were picked up later by the rescue boat. Unfortunately, by then Sub-Lt John Cariss was dead, despite strenuous efforts to revive him. No blame was attached to Sub-Lt Everett, and he quickly recovered to complete many landings on *Puncher* by day and night.

In the meantime the remaining ten Fireflies had been instructed to return to Burscough, but this in itself was not without its dramas. Approaching the Lancashire coast the engine completely seized up on an aircraft crewed by Lt P. A. Toynbee RNR and Lt E. M. Frazer RNVR. The story of their adventures is told elsewhere. Nine Fireflies now remained to continue the journey to Burscough, where, to complete a day of disaster for 1790 Squadron, the engine of another Firefly flown by Lt J. H. S. Pearce RNVR failed whilst in the airfield circuit. The result was an emergency wheels-up landing on the grass alongside a runway with both occupants escaping unscathed. Lt Pearce continued with a naval aviation career and was awarded a DSC during the Korean War.

After the relatively incident-free work-up at Burscough, the death of John Cariss, and the loss of two aircraft with damage to a third was a depressing start to 1790's carrier-borne programme. However, the next day the remainder of the squadron flew out and landed on *Puncher* with no mishaps. It is perhaps a measure of the extent to which the squadron recovered from these set-backs that the following signal should have been sent to Admiral (Air) by Flag Officer Carrier Training on 6 June 1945:

'The high standard of carrier flying by day and night and interception exercises carried out by 1790 Squadron whilst in *Puncher* is most satisfactory. It reflects great credit on *Puncher*, NAS Burscough and 1790 Squadron.'

After embarkation leave and re-equipment with eighteen new Firefly NF1s 1790 flew to Sydenham Airport, Belfast, taxied round to a wharf and were embarked aboard HMS *Vindex* alongside by dockyard crane. HMS *Vindex* was a British-built escort carrier and at that time was being used to ferry aircraft, the flight deck being packed to capacity with Fireflies and Seafires. By the time the

Z1844 at Hucknall, with that well-worn look. The different type of glare baffle was the one adopted by the Admiralty for its Firefly NF1 aircraft. *(Rolls-Royce PLC)*

A close-up of the exhaust baffle on Z1844. When the engineer responsible for this attachment was testing it, he stated that he could walk round the aircraft when the engine was running at night and detect no indication of exhaust glare at all!

(Rolls-Royce PLC)

ship sailed 1790 had a full complement of eighteen pilots and observers, together with their own Air Radio Officer and Air Engineer Officer. In addition, the squadron had, uniquely, its own Fighter Direction and Deck Landing Control Officers. With such a depth of experience, less than half the squadron complement were Sub-Lts, 1790 had every expectation of performing well in what might still be a year or so of war in the Pacific.

HMS *Vindex* sailed on 26 May 1945 with a call at Port Said and then Colombo as 'Jock' Frazer recalls:

'Next stop was Colombo, then Trincomalee, in what was then Ceylon and is now Sri Lanka. There was a lot of high spirited nonsense in Colombo which ended with half the squadron locked up in jail for the night, and the other half trying to break them out! A full report of this followed us to Australia but by the time it had caught up with us it had been over-signed by six Admirals and was totally out of date. We had a telling off by the Captain but it was all rather tongue-in-the-cheek and under the circumstances all was forgotten.'

HMS *Vindex* arrived in Sydney on 12 August 1945 and three days later Japan capitulated – an event that produced very mixed feelings in 1790, in particular after all the training, one of being let down. The squadron moved to RNAS Schofields, about fifteen miles from Sydney and The Blue Mountains. There was now a considerable relaxation of effort and flying was only carried out to retain skills or for putting on immaculate displays of simulated carrier procedure at air displays. Lt 'Jock' Frazer found time to write one of his odes which went like this:

Odd ode to 1790 Squadron

The shades of night were here at last
As down the flarepath mighty fast
I hurled my mass of steel and flame
And just got off the ground in time,
To miss a tree of vast dimension
Just growing, with no fixed intention.

Then up and up into cloud
R/T booming very loud,
Controller shouting, 'Orbit now'
'And fly at Angles fifteen then'
I thought this was the one exception
When we should make a night interception.

Then on and on into the sky
Flying very very high
When all at once I hear a shout
And found my 'looker' baling out,
And by the position of the moon
Found I was flying upside doon.

Then down and down and round and round
To the four ale bar of the Rose and Crown
Hit with an almighty jar
And found myself against the bar,
So cheer up lads, lets have a beer
'Cos I'm bloody lucky to be here.

Although the war was over 1790 remained in being and became part of the 8th CAG commanded by Lt-Colonel P. Nelson-Gracie RM. The other squadrons in the CAG were 801 with Seafires and 828 with Avengers. On 9 November Lt/Cdr Kneale relinquished command to Lt 'Ben' Lyons who finishes the squadron story:

'The 8th CAG spent most of its time either disembarked at Schofields or aboard HMS *Implacable,* our parent carrier. Exercises at sea by day and night were a regular event. One night, a particularly black one with no horizon, I was on the final approach to *Implacable* when all her deck lighting – indeed all lighting – failed! Quite hairy. The defect was very soon rectified but the incident left me somewhat shaken. This was a very interesting period as, even though it was peacetime, we had the opportunity of evaluating 1790's potential for operating at sea as night-fighters. I believe we helped to establish night-fighters as necessary to the FAA. HMS *Implacable* and 8th CAG sailed from Sydney for the UK on 5 May 1946, but 1790 had one final flight. On 16 May 1946 I led the squadron for the last time – to Trincomalee, Ceylon, where all the Fireflies were put into storage – but that was not the last I saw of some of those Fireflies.'

To go back a short space of time. No 1791 Squadron formed up at Lee-on-Solent as a night-fighter unit equipped with twelve Firefly NF1s. They too embarked in HMS *Puncher* in June 1945 for deck-landing training, but after VJ-Day it was disbanded at Burscough on 23 September 1945.

No 1792 formed up at Lee-on-Solent on 15 May 1945 with Lt/Cdr S. Dixon-Child as CO. Equipped with 12 Firefly NF1s the squadron embarked in

HMS *Ocean* for a spell in the Mediterranean. Lt/Cdr 'Jesse' Hanks recalls the reason:

'In December 1945 I was appointed Assistant Operations Officer to HMS *Ocean* where the FAA was evaluating the relative merits of single-seat Hellcat night-fighters (892 Squadron) against the two-crew Firefly arrangement (1792 Squadron). This eventually came out in favour of two-seater operations and so established the practice of adding four Firefly NF1s (Black Flight) to each carrier for night operations. This two-seat/ single-seat argument was raging back and forth in the RAF, USAAF and USN at the same time, but eventually most people went for the two-seat arrangement, and in time side-by-side became the norm (so that the pilot had someone to speak to really!).'

After the war 1790 was, in effect, reassembled in two parts, one as No 784 at Drem as a night-fighter training squadron, and moving to Dale later. Another part formed-up as a Night Flying Unit (NFU) and was attached to HMS *Ocean* then in the Mediterranean. Freddy de Freitas was one of the observer/AI operators and fills in the background:

'I did the night flying course at Dale in March 1946 and one of the pilots was a Lt Buchan-Sydserff, whom I eventually crewed with. On the Fireflies at 784 was a special exhaust cowling, or fairing, which served both to reduce exhaust flame glare for the pilot, and cut down any exhaust indications to an enemy aircraft. We used ASH radar in the AI mode and it was rather tricky but could be good if you worked with a good FDO. In May 1946 I joined 816 Squadron which was part of the 20th CAG aboard HMS *Ocean*. The NFU became known as Black Flight. The rest of the squadron had Firefly 1s and centralised maintenance was just coming in at that time. However, because of our special exhaust fairings and the need for our radar to be very highly maintained, we usually managed to keep our own aircraft. To keep us on top line presented a problem because during this period the carrier could not spare much time for night flying, which called for considerable organisation, and we spent a great deal of time doing ordinary squadron flying. Our procedure was to do an NFT (night flying test) of about

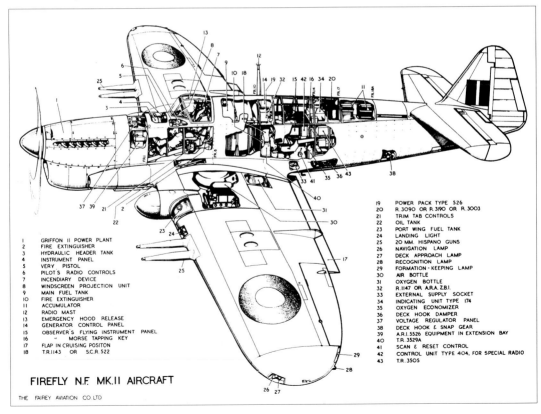

1	GRIFFON II POWER PLANT
2	FIRE EXTINGUISHER
3	HYDRAULIC HEADER TANK
4	INSTRUMENT PANEL
5	VERY PISTOL
6	PILOT'S RADIO CONTROLS
7	INCENDIARY DEVICE
8	WINDSCREEN PROJECTION UNIT
9	MAIN FUEL TANK
10	FIRE EXTINGUISHER
11	ACCUMULATOR
12	RADIO MAST
13	EMERGENCY HOOD RELEASE
14	GENERATOR CONTROL PANEL
15	OBSERVER'S FLYING INSTRUMENT PANEL
16	" MORSE TAPPING KEY
17	FLAP IN CRUISING POSITON
18	T.R.1143 OR S.C.R.522
19	POWER PACK TYPE 526
20	R.3090 OR R.3190 OR R.3003
21	TRIM TAB CONTROLS
22	OIL TANK
23	PORT WING FUEL TANK
24	LANDING LIGHT
25	20 MM. HISPANO GUNS
26	NAVIGATION LAMP
27	DECK APPROACH LAMP
28	RECOGNITION LAMP
29	FORMATION-KEEPING LAMP
30	AIR BOTTLE
31	OXYGEN BOTTLE
32	R.1147 OR A.R.A. Z.B.I.
33	EXTERNAL SUPPLY SOCKET
34	INDICATING UNIT TYPE 174
35	OXYGEN ECONOMIZER
36	DECK HOOK DAMPER
37	VOLTAGE REGULATOR PANEL
38	DECK HOOK & SNAP GEAR
39	A.R.I.5526 EQUIPMENT IN EXTENSION BAY
40	T.R.3529A
41	SCAN & RESET CONTROL
42	CONTROL UNIT TYPE 404, FOR SPECIAL RADIO
43	T.R.3505

FIREFLY N.F. MK.II AIRCRAFT

THE FAIREY AVIATION CO LTD

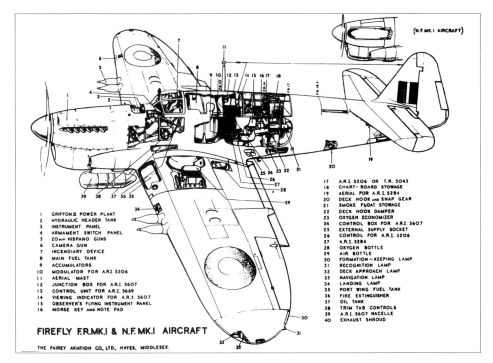

1	GRIFFON II POWER PLANT	17	A.R.I. 5206 OR T.R. 5043
2	HYDRAULIC HEADER TANK	18	CHART- BOARD STOWAGE
3	INSTRUMENT PANEL	19	AERIAL FOR A.R.I. 5284
4	ARMAMENT SWITCH PANEL	20	DECK HOOK and SNAP GEAR
5	20mm HISPANO GUNS	21	SMOKE FLOAT STOWAGE
6	CAMERA GUN	22	DECK HOOK DAMPER
7	INCENDIARY DEVICE	23	OXYGEN ECONOMIZER
8	MAIN FUEL TANK	24	CONTROL BOX FOR A.R.I. 5607
9	ACCUMULATORS	25	EXTERNAL SUPPLY SOCKET
10	MODULATOR FOR A.R.I. 5206	26	CONTROL FOR A.R.I. 5206
11	AERIAL MAST	27	A.R.I. 5284
12	JUNCTION BOX FOR A.R.I. 5607	28	OXYGEN BOTTLE
13	CONTROL UNIT FOR A.R.I. 5669	29	AIR BOTTLE
14	VIEWING INDICATOR FOR A.R.I. 5607	30	FORMATION – KEEPING LAMP
15	OBSERVER'S FLYING INSTRUMENT PANEL	31	RECOGNITION LAMP
16	MORSE KEY and NOTE PAD	32	DECK APPROACH LAMP
		33	NAVIGATION LAMP
		34	LANDING LAMP
		35	PORT WING FUEL TANK
		36	FIRE EXTINGUISHER
		37	OIL TANK
		38	TRIM TAB CONTROLS
		39	A.R.I. 5607 NACELLE
		40	EXHAUST SHROUD

FIREFLY F.R. MK.I & N.F. MK.I AIRCRAFT

THE FAIREY AVIATION CO. LTD., HAYES, MIDDLESEX.

one and a half hours followed by a night exercise of about two hours.

'We had a couple of other specialised roles, one was firing off ''Gloworms'', these were R/P fitted with flares on the head to silhouette small targets such as E-boats etc. We also did some long-range reconnaissance and then used ASH to try and vector strike aircraft onto a target. This was the forerunner of sophisticated techniques later used by AEW Skyraider and Gannet aircraft. Our set-up was that a flight of four Fireflies was attached to a front line squadron aboard a Carrier Air Group. When the CAG changed, the Black Flight was reformed and joined the new CAG. The first commission was in either late '45 or early '46, until in 1950, with the build-up in the Far East HMS *Ocean* went trooping and Black Flight joined 827 aboard HMS *Triumph* to be based on Singapore. For various reasons it could not operate there and eventually returned to Malta leaving the aircraft in *Triumph*.

'In July 1948 I was back in *Ocean* as Senior Observer for Black Flight attacked to 812 Squadron. Lt Buchan-Sydserff was Senior Pilot and we crewed up again. Both of us had odd names and the practice of putting names on aircraft was highlighted on one occasion because the first name on the fuselage was Buchan-Sydserff, then me with de Freitas but the Pilot's Mate was Naval Airman English! By now 812 had the Firefly Mk 5 while we still had the Mk I night-fighters. The reason was that the ASH was wing-mounted in the Mk 5s

and performance could not come up to the standard required. This enabled us to keep our own Mk Is. In 1949 trouble developing in the Far East led to us being transferred to *Triumph*, but it didn't work out. On passage we had a big deck park and could not night fly. In the Far East we spent part of the time working out of Hong Kong, part from Sembawang and also Singapore. We did very little night flying but in October I logged a couple of operations making R/P attacks on bandits in the Malayan jungle. Later the same month we were posted back to the Mediterranean leaving our aircraft behind. We had a very good safety record for a night carrier operation and I know of no serious accident at night. Hooks being pulled out and the odd propeller pecking the deck was about the limit. This I think was due to everyone involved – deck crews, batsmen and deck-handling parties being on top line for night operations. Due to the limitations of the wing-mounted ASH on later marks of Firefly the night operations quietened down for a time. After a while a Sea Hornet squadron was formed for AI work and eventually the art became known as ''All-Weather Operations'', and, in the fullness of time moved into the jet era with Sea Venoms and then Sea Vixens.'

The pioneering work of the people and units mentioned in this chapter were the forerunners of today's highly sophisticated all-weather naval aircraft and radar.

Chapter 5
The Firefly FIII/IV Enigma

THE EARLIEST indications of a Firefly Mk IV go back to 20 October 1941 when H. E. Chaplin, Fairey's chief designer, was on a technical visit to Rolls-Royce at their Derby factory. Chaplin was informed of a projected Griffon rated for high altitude work – the Griffon 61. During the meeting Rolls-Royce pointed out that although it could improve the performance of the Firefly if fitted, it would weigh 500 lb more than the Griffon IIB which was the production engine for the Firefly 1. They suggested that to cater for the extra weight it would be better to adopt the Mosquito-type leading edge radiators. When Rolls-Royce visited Chaplin at Fairey's Hayes factory on 5 November, he informed them that they had assessed the leading edge radiator idea and found it acceptable, and asked if they would provide details of radiator sizes, intercooler, weights of coolant and oil etc. The idea was also passed to the Admiralty who mulled it over, then shocked everyone by stating that they were anticipating the introduction of the Griffon 61 engine onto the Firefly production line by January 1944 – only eighteen months away! The aircraft would be of sufficient re-design to warrant a new mark number – the Firefly FIII. The radiator location however was still to be under the engine. Fairey were also trying to get the Admiralty interested in using contra-rotating propellers at this stage but it was felt to be too innovative to introduce at such an early stage of the programme.

In February 1942 talks were being held about a single-seat version of the Griffon 61 powered Firefly with leading edge radiators. The Admiralty, although interested, had not raised the idea or offered a specification. At a meeting in May it was pointed out that the interest in the Firefly lay with its potential as a two-seat fighter and the single-seat idea was to be shelved. The interest in the potential of the Griffon 61 remained, and in mid-1942 the Ministry interceded again to ask for performance figures for a two-seat and single-seat version of the Firefly capable of carrying a torpedo. The single-seat machine was dusted off and the Design Office at Fairey came up with the comparative figures:

	Single-seat	Two-seat
AUW	14,360 lb	15,070 lb
Wing loading	41.6 lb/sq ft	43.7 lb/sq ft
Speed at sea level	243 knots	236 knots
Speed at 19,000 ft	282 knots	273 knots
Service ceiling	34,000 ft	32,500 ft
Climb to 15,000 ft	11.5 min	13 min
Range at 6500 ft	750 miles	634 miles
Endurance	4.25 hours	3.60 hours
Take-off power	1980 bhp using a 13 ft 6 in three-blade propeller	

Not even the Griffon 61 could haul a torpedo-carrying Firefly fast enough for the Ministry and the idea seems to have been dropped as quickly as it was raised.

In October 1942 it was stated officially that the Firefly FIII would also be required as a night fighter, and that orders for 200 machines would be forthcoming.

Rolls-Royce had visited Fairey on 3 November 1942 to discuss the Mk III engine/radiator installation. It was agreed to carry out flight tests on a Firefly Mk I with a mocked-up leading edge to represent the radiator, intercooler and oil cooler installation. The aircraft earmarked for this work was Z1839, which at that time was at Boscombe Down on development work. Rolls-Royce also suggested that new fuel tanks be fitted in the wing leading edge to retain the original fuel capacity. The drawings for the mock-up leading edge conversion were issued to the Fairey shops on 26 November 1943, with plans to start flight trials within two weeks. This did not quite work out due to Z1839 being written off in an accident. It was decided to put the mock-up conversion on the original prototype Firefly, Z1826. Early in 1943 Rolls-Royce visited the Fairey design team to discuss a number of technical topics. It was mentioned that the tenth aircraft, Z1835, was still on the production line and earmarked for the Experimental Shop to make it suitable to take the Griffon 61 when it arrived. The aircraft would then go to the Rolls-Royce Flight Test Establishment at Hucknall about the end of April. By 23 April the engine was installed with a planned first flight date of 2 May. The Firefly FIII was delivered to Hucknall on

The prototype Firefly FIII Z1835 with a Griffon 61 and a different type of exhaust baffle. As this was an early production aircraft, it has the shallow windscreen and unfaired cannon. *(Author's collection)*

24 May 1943 powered by a Griffon 61. It flew a number of tests for fuel consumption and endurance figures until 22 July when it flew to Boscombe Down. Here, it was subjected to initial handling trials, performance measurements and other checks, such as carbon monoxide contamination. The results were disappointing – it was found that the Firefly FIII was totally unacceptable for Service use because of:

1 Poor directional control characteristics, i.e. it 'snaked' on the climb, the rudder tended to overbalance to port, and yawing in a dive caused violent sideslipping. It was suggested that the fuselage be lengthened 30 inches and the tailplane be raised six inches.
2 Longitudinal instability with flaps and under-carriage down.
3 Ineffectiveness of elevator at slow speeds, partly due to (2).
4 High drag from existing power plant installation.
5 Excessive heat and fumes from the engine.

The top speed at 18,300 ft was 300 knots – lower than expected. The aircraft returned, by road, to Hucknall on 18 September 1943. Here it was fitted with a two-speed two-stage Griffon 71 and flight tested until 29 May 1944 when it returned to Boscombe. It moved back to Hucknall on 18 August and was fitted with a Griffon 72, the pre-production engine of the Firefly Mk IV prototypes,

the production machines all being powered by the Griffon 74. By this time the Firefly FIII was dead and Z1835 was acting as one of four prototypes for the Firefly IV programme. Z1835 was despatched once more to Boscombe on 22 September 1944 where, after further trials it returned to Fairey.

Another scheme under discussion in August 1944 was that of using a 'commonised' airframe to suit the purposes of the Firefly 1 and III both in the day and night fighter roles. This had come about due to the AI, radio scanning equipment in general use, being superseded by an American ASH system. This was suitable for ground scanning, as used in the fighter reconnaissance mode, and also for radio location in the night fighter role. The ASH equip-ment could be mounted under the engine cowling on an outrigger bracket, a forward position being necessary to obtain a good upward angle. Fairey said they aimed to introduce the 'commonised' airframe in January 1945 on late production Firefly Mk Is, but these would be superceded by the FIII in March 1945. It was estimated that around 2000 modifications would be involved in producing the revised airframe and at the time, with numerous Firefly programmes under way, it was doubtful whether the programme could be met.

A meeting was held at the MAP at the beginning of November 1944 to discuss the future of the Firefly III. Boscombe Down had said that even with C of G improvements, the aircraft was unstable. It was decided that wherever the FIII was, it would be

The first interim prototype Firefly Mk IV Z2118, still with its Mk 1 tailplane and elliptical wings. Note the earlier type of air scoop beneath the nose. *(Westland Aircraft Ltd)*

A view of Z2118 at Boscombe Down, after being modified to have squared-off wing tips and the later style fin and rudder.
(Crown Copyright)

returned to Fairey for further investigation. Production was put back provisionally to October 1945.

Rolls-Royce now 'dropped a spanner in the works' by declaring that they too intended to commonise, and in this case it was the Griffon. They said they were considering the 'commonisation' of the single-stage Griffon 32 to power the Firefly 1, the Barracuda V and Seafire XV. They stated that as the Firefly programme was to be considerably extended, certainly well into 1946, by then they anticipated only having the single-stage Griffon in production. They thought that if the Firefly 1 went out of production in 1946, as was intended, then the engine change would not be justified. What they were saying was that they did not intend developing the two-stage Griffon if it was not required. Events were to change that line of thinking!

By 6 December 1944, the installation of the leading edge radiators project was going well, although no official approval had been received. As mentioned, earlier in the year Z1826 had been selected as flight test bed for the mock-up. Four initial flights were made, two by Colin Evans and two by Lt Shea-Simonds RNVR. The first, by Colin Evans was on 23 March 1944 and then again on 25 March

when he assessed general handling and stalls. It was flown on 24 March by Lt Shea-Simonds with wool tufts attached at the wing roots and flap area, and again on 31 March when he checked elevator and trim tab angles. The actual installation consisted of an extension forward of the chord of the wing roots, together with a loss of aerofoil shape. The extension was twenty-one inches at the fuselage side decreasing to zero just short of five feet outboard. The leading edge aperture was eighteen inches in span and 6.5 inches deep located close to each wing root and ducted to the under surface of the wing. The flight tests showed that the airflow remained good throughout the speed range, the only thing of note being the fact that the port extension had a tendency to stall before the right side. However, lateral control was maintained down to around eighty-five knots and the wing tips showed no signs of stalling. The idea of the new layout and installation was therefore sound and Fairey intended to carry on themselves and hoped to have a proper prototype flying within two months. Work on the commonised Griffon 32 installation was stopped and Fairey hoped that the project would not go ahead.

The death knell of the Firefly FIII was sounded on 16 December 1944, when, at a meeting between

A first-class and interesting underside view of the third Mk IV prototype MB649. It gives a clear indication of the leading edge radiator layout. *(Westland Aircraft Ltd)*

Fairey, MAP and Air Ministry officials, the decision was taken that all work on the aircraft in its present form should stop, and a new mark of Firefly be introduced. The meeting was to discuss the implications arising from the Boscombe Down criticism of the aerodynamic qualities of the first Firefly FIII Z1835. They also wanted to consider the changes recommended and see whether they could be implemented in selected aircraft to act as prototypes, and finally, to consider the effects on any production changes from the scheduled FIII. This meeting was of considerable significance as the outcome would affect the design layout and indeed, the very future of the Firefly. The proceeds of the meeting are therefore reported in some detail. The basic criticisms of the existing FIII layout which gave rise to the necessity for modifications were:

1 The very forward C of G range, though beneficial as regards longitudinal and directional stability, gave rise to high stick forces and a tendency to nose over on the application of brakes.
2 The disturbed airflow over the wing flaps and tail unit arising, it was thought, from the side radiator exits.
3 The high drag of the existing power plant installation and the fact that the aircraft was unpleasant to fly with the hood open due to heat and fumes from the engine entering the cockpit.

These troubles were all attributed to the annular nose radiator installation with its side exits for exhaust fumes and part of the cooling air. This had led Fairey to propose repositioning the radiators in the wing (as a centre section) leading edges either side of the fuselage. It was this proposal that formed the main subject of discussion at the meeting and it had to be considered in conjunction with the following points:

1 Restoration of the fuel capacity. The wing radiator installation involved the deletion of the wing leading edge fuel tanks, each of twenty-three gallons capacity.
2 Introduction of ASH equipment. Scheduled for the FIII but not installed in Z1835.
3 Improvement of directional stability.
4 Strengthening of undercarriage and arrester gear to meet the increase in weight from changing to Griffon 72.
5 Provision of flame damping exhaust system.
6 Provision for tail-down catapult launching.

On the subject of item 1, it was noted that the revised layout did not involve any change in the primary Firefly structure. Fairey had proposed that the ASH radar was to be carried in a nacelle positioned approximately mid-aileron span, balanced by a similar nacelle holding fifty gallons of fuel on the other wing. At a later date it was anticipated that there would be a requirement to have a semi-permanent wing fuel installation to cater for the increased rate of fuel consumption arising from increase of engine power.

The Director of Technical Development (DTD) ruled that, in the first instance, ASH should be carried under the fuselage in a similar manner to the Firefly FR and NF aircraft. A request was made to investigate rumours circulating that the under fuselage installation would give rise to 'blurring' of the radar images from vibrations of the ASH nacelle. It was agreed at the meeting that subject to approval from the Telecommunications Research Establishment (TRE) at Defford, and the Director of Armament Development, a wing ASH installation could be developed as a separate and later issue as it would permit the carriage, if required, of large under-fuselage armament stores. One problem that was aired was what effect it would have on the under fuselage mounted ASH response when production changed from a wooden to a metal propeller. This was before any final decision on the wing nacelle. It was felt in some quarters that a metal propeller would cut off the ASH view through the propeller disc completely. Trials conducted with a Firefly proved this to be untrue, but the nacelle was eventually moved to the wing anyway – whereupon, the pundits gleefully said that when the pilot fired his guns the vibration would make the set unusable and in this they proved to be partly right.

The original Firefly FIII Z1835 in a different guise, with a new nose job hiding a Griffon 72 with an experimental exhaust baffle. The tail has also been changed to bring it up to the prototype Mk IV standard. *(R. J. Carter)*

In the foreground, fully converted and painted up as such, is the old Firefly FIII prototype Z1835 as the second prototype Mk IV with another different air intake, only the retention of the original low windscreen spoils its shape. Next in line is a Firefly 1 F15 for Holland, and behind that Spearfish RN241, with another Firefly in the background. *(Westland Aircraft Ltd)*

On the question of directional stability, Fairey said they proposed to introduce a dorsal fin blending into the leading edge of the fin proper, the outline being similar to that on the Flying Fortress. This proposal was accepted, although the DTD ruled that if contra-rotating propellers were introduced later, they would have to review the situation. It was noted that Fairey were awaiting results of RAE tests on the existing Firefly 1 undercarriage before knowing what strengthening was needed. DTD stated that it would have to be to an acceptable standard before the first production aircraft was fitted with the Griffon 72. The first two machines, acting as prototypes, would be accepted in the unstrengthened state so that they did not hold up the programme. The flame damping exhaust system was to be of a readily removable form. The introduction of facilities for tail-down launching was deferred to a future meeting. The DTD then ruled that two prototype aircraft be prepared but three sets of prototype parts were to be produced. The first prototype was a conversion of Z2118, originally allotted as the second prototype FIII aircraft with the annular nose radiator installation. The power plant had already been delivered for this aircraft and a first flight date planned for March 1945. The second prototype was a conversion of Z1835 with a first flight planned for April 1945. It was agreed the prototypes would be in the

unmodified state, i.e. no ASH, restoration of fuel capacity, undercarriage or arrester gear strengthening, but that they were to be installationally representative of production aircraft.

Fairey now said that they considered production of the new Firefly layout could commence on the production line in November 1945, and would be well in hand by early 1946 with the changeover completed by May 1946. They stated that the sub-contractors, General Aircraft Ltd could not produce the change at such an early date, and it would be necessary for Fairey to modify components as required, but expected the sub-contracted components to start arriving in the fully modified state by March/April 1946. All this was based on full production drawings being available in May 1945 which, in view of prototype completion dates was very tight. In fact, both representatives from the Ministry considered the dates extremely optimistic and dependent on every phase of the changeover proceeding smoothly to plan, a happy state of affairs usually never realised. One would have thought that Fairey might have been a bit more realistic after the earlier production problems.

The Director of Technical Development then summarised what had been a long and protracted meeting. He stated that the Firefly FIII prototype (Z1835) revealed characteristics which made it quite unsuitable for Service use and that in the absence of a clear-cut diagnosis of the reasons for such characteristics it was difficult to envisage the steps required to correct the faults. It was however, readily apparent that the wing leading-edge radiator proposal showed great promise of effecting considerable improvement. He emphasised the need to complete the target dates for the prototypes on time, and for Fairey to complete wind tunnel tests on the changes required. The question of the tail-down launching requirement and the contra-rotating propellers would be reviewed in two months' time. He ruled that the revised radiator layout should not be associated with the nomenclature, Firefly FIII, but a new mark number be proposed via the normal channels.

The new aircraft was designated Firefly Mk IV, actual variants not being ratified until production orders were placed, i.e. FR Mk IV. The preliminary specification meeting was held on 13 March 1945. As expected, the first flight date slipped, first to March, then to April. In an effort to bring the programme back onto line it was proposed that two additional prototypes be made available and so MB649 and PP482 joined the team. The interim Firefly Mk IV prototype, Z2118, flew for the first time on 25 May 1945 at the Great West Aerodrome. Exactly one year later, the first production Firefly Mk IV, TW687, took to the air – the Firefly FIII/Mk IV enigma was over! After going through initial acceptance tests, Z2118 went to Boscombe Down on 27 July 1945 for its handling trials. Fairey were delighted with the first reports received from Boscombe and by late August realised the Firefly IV was a winner. The programme began to pick up. By 13 October the first two prototypes were flying at Heston, the third was at Hayes, due to go to Heston for final assembly, and the fourth was to go to Heston mid-November. Z2118 spent some time between the Fairey airfield and Boscombe as various little production snags were ironed out, eventually finishing this work on 24 October 1946 when it returned to Heston. By then the other three prototypes were flying. MB649 flew on 21 February 1946 with a Griffon 72 and went on to do the flame damper and hood release trials. PP482 also flew in February 1946 and became the weapons platform trials aircraft, eventually testing just about every armament the Firefly was likely to carry, and in all configurations. Z1835 had spent most of 1944 between Boscombe and Hucknall powered by the Griffon 61, then the 71 and finally, to become the second interim Firefly Mk IV prototype, the Griffon 72.

On 28 November 1945 Fairey provided projected FIII performance figures with those obtained on Z2118 powered by the Griffon 72.

	Firefly FIII	Firefly Mk IV
AUW	11,540 lb	11,560 lb
Max speed at 18,000 ft	301 knots	333 knots

Apart from the changes mentioned it was found from flight trials that the following modifications, which affected performance, were required:

1 Wing tips clipped from elliptical to square reducing the span to 41 ft 2 in.
2 Shorter Hispano Mk V cannon fitted.
3 High finish paint scheme, coupled with careful tailoring of cowlings and fillets.
4 Longer spinner fitted.

To check what effects these had the first three modifications, plus one or two others, such as removal of wireless masts, were flight tested on a Firefly and showed an increase in speed of seventeen knots.

The new aircraft was presented to the press, being reported in *Flight* on 8 November 1945 and *The Aeroplane* one day later. In June 1946 the MOS wrote to Fairey and asked them what was involved in installing contra-rotating propellers on the Firefly IV. They added that the main role of the Firefly Mk IV was to be night fighting and for this role it was desirable that the swing on take-off be avoided if at all possible. TW695 was chosen to do the flight tests and was delivered to Hucknall on 25 November 1946. Here it was fitted with contra-rotating propellers and test flown before reverting back to a single four-blade propeller. Throughout the next couple of years TW695 was back and forth between Hucknall, Boscombe and Heston. It was found, for various reasons, that contra-rotating propellers and flight decks did not mix. The Seafire 47 used them later but the relationship was not wholly successful.

The Firefly FR Mk IV was released to the Service for operations from shore bases only on 12 February 1947. Spinning and aerobatics were prohibited pending successful completion of trials, and maximum diving speed was limited to 370 knots.

The actual testing of production Firefly IVs from Heston was entrusted to Fairey's new post-war chief test pilot, Group Captain Gordon Slade, ably assisted by Peter Twiss DSC, Squadron Leader J. O. Mathews DSO DFC, Tim Woods of General Aircraft Ltd and Ralph Munday of Heston Aircraft.

Two of the test pilots at Faireys during the late war years and immediate post-war period were F. H. Dixon (left) and J. C. Evans, here seen with Z2118 displaying the early type of air intake. *(Author's collection)*

A wet start to the day as Fireflies are rolled out of the hangar at Heston for another day's flying. Both these Mk IVs were converted from Mk Is on the production line and have the second type of air scoop, with TW688 in the foreground.

(Westland Aircraft Ltd)

Firefly IV TW693 being flown by Peter Twiss still in its primer colours, although the serial has been added under the wings and the tail is camouflaged. It certainly looked different without the usual clutter under the wings. *(Westland Aircraft Ltd)*

The contra-propeller trials aircraft TW 695, seen here being taxied by Peter Twiss. Desite the engineering complexity of operating this arrangement it may have saved many lives in the long run by reducing torque problems. *(Flight International)*

The first production Firefly FRIV TW722, photographed at the end of 1946. It was eventually converted to a TT Mk 4 and survived until 1959. *(Flight International)*

The normal sequence for production aircraft was that an initial flight was made without the ASH nacelle and wing fuel tank, but still in its undercoat of paint. When a pilot was satisfied with any control adjustments or minor changes, the nacelles were installed and the aircraft passed through the paint shop to receive the high gloss finish before a final clearing test flight.

In 1948 Gordon Slade flew Firefly IV TW692 to Baghdad in Iraq for a series of so-called tropical trials. The story released was that Fairey and Rolls-Royce wanted to dispel the myth that there was difficulty in operating liquid-cooled aero engines in very hot climates and/or hot and high airfields. The real story, of course was that certain Middle East countries were expressing an interest in buying the Firefly IV. Slade flew out via Malta, Cairo and Habbaniya, giving demonstrations wherever he went. At Heliopolis, Cairo he demonstrated the Firefly before Air Marshal Sir Brian Baker, then Deputy Air Officer Commander-in-Chief, Middle East. The important ones of course were at Baghdad where he performed before HRH the Prince Regent of Iraq; Colonel Sami Fattah, Chief of the Iraqi Air Force; Wing Commander Fisher, Air Adviser to the

British Mission and various staff officers of the Iraqi Air Force. In spite of difficult climate conditions the Firefly gave an impressive performance, at no time indicating any problems due to the conditions. Unfortunately, like many other interested queries at that time, the Iraqis did not order the Firefly. In fact they may have had some quaint ideas of using them as strike aircraft – but in the old fashioned mode with a rear gunner! David Carter, an apprentice at Fairey around that time recalls being involved. 'Early in 1948 there was some scheme to install a flexibly mounted gun in the rear cockpit – it might have been for Iraq – and when any scheme of this nature was being considered, it was usually tried on any available aircraft by the largest and smallest men, or boys, in the shop. In my case, I've always been fairly hefty, even at the age of eighteen, and I found myself wrestling with a large cannon (unmounted) in the rear cockpit of Z2118. It never really came to anything, and anyway, there wasn't really room for the pair of us.'

With the release of the Firefly IV into service there were still lots of trials to be conducted, although with the war over the sense of urgency had relaxed somewhat. Delivery of the first production machine was 29 September 1947 but it was another year before the squadrons started to get them. Some twenty Firefly IVs were released from the factory in March 1947 and production continued apace. Intensive deck landing trials took place on HMS *Illustrious* throughout March by TW724, 725 and 735 when some 166 deck landings were made.

On 31 August 1947 Peter Twiss won the Lympne High Speed Handicap Race in VG979 competing against his boss, Group Captain Gordon Slade who was flying the Firefly Trainer MB750. He demonstrated the contra-prop Firefly TW695 at the October 1947 SBAC Display at Radlet.

The first unit to receive the Firefly IV was 825 Squadron in August 1947 as part of the 19th Carrier Air Group (CAG) with the Royal Canadian Navy, details of which are recorded elsewhere. The first FAA front line unit to equip with the Firefly FRIV was 810 Squadron, when they reformed at Eglinton, Northern Ireland on 1 October 1947. As part of the 17th CAG the squadron embarked in HMS *Implacable* for exercises and deck landing training. In August 1948 they joined HMS *Theseus*

for a cruise to South Africa. During 1949 the squadron embarked for a cruise to the Mediterranean, took part in exercises in home waters and with the British Army in Germany before being disbanded on 16 October that year. Earlier in 1948, both 812 and 814 squadrons re-equipped with the Firefly IV at Eglinton, and in August 816 accepted the Mk IV for training prior to going out to Australia. No 812 only operated the FRIVs for a short time before changing them for the Firefly 5. Meantime, 814 had taken its FRIVs aboard HMS *Vengeance* in August for a cruise to South Africa. In the New Year the ship sailed for the Arctic Circle for cold weather trials, and it wasn't long after this that the squadron handed over the FRIVs in exchange for the Firefly 5.

Second line units were, for the most part, the most prolific users of the Firefly IVs, these being Nos 703, 727, 767, 778, 781 and 799 Squadrons. Some of these were for refresher training, deck landing training, day and night fighter training in adverse weather conditions. The Service Trials Units had some of the more interesting tasks to perform when they had to assess the suitability of

Not all arrivals back on the flight deck were as one wished. Here, one Firefly has gone through the barrier into the aircraft park, damaging some others. The offender, 235/K, is VG973. *(Author's collection)*

A pair of Firefly FRIVs, TW734 and TW730 of 825 Squadron at RNAS Eglinton in 1948. *(A. E. Hughes)*

A Firefly FRIV 220/Q of 814 Squadron flying over St Helena without wing nacelles but with long-range drop tanks.

(Author's collection)

aircraft for specific roles. As an example, 703 Squadron reformed on 19 April 1945 at Thorney Island as the Naval Flight of the RAF's Air-Sea Warfare Development Unit, usually abbreviated to NASWDU. During the period 1947/48 Firefly FRIVs TW743, 744 and VG968 were used to conduct various tactical weapon trials. In May 1948, 703 moved to Lee-on-Solent where it took over the tasks of 778 Service Trials Unit, so becoming NASWDU/STU, at least until April 1950 when it simply became the STU. Among the many requirements to test the FR/NFIVs was its use in the dive-bombing role, two-seat strike aircraft, strike reconnaissance and general or sea recce. The dive-bombing and two-seat strike roles were still considered of prime importance by the Admiralty. During April to July 1948 trials were conducted at targets at Bracklesham Bay bombing ranges. The naval pilots conducting the trials remarked on how pleasant the FRIV was to fly with controls light and responsive. They reported that the FRIV was suitable for carrying out dive and glide bombing attacks with no dangerous characteristics. It was recommended that when using Gyro Gun Sight (GGS) any angle below fifty degrees would suffer from inaccuracy as it wasn't possible to depress the sight enough. In conclusion, it was stated that although not an ideal dive-bombing aircraft the FRIV was probably the best aircraft in general service for that role.

In 1950 a brief investigation was made into the possibility of using a Firefly IV as a photographic survey aircraft. The main requirements were:

1 That the aircraft should be capable of carrying an air survey camera and observer/operator.
2 An operating height of 30,000 ft.
3 Endurance of at least two hours at 30,000 ft.
4 A target area 160 miles from base.

All unwanted equipment was removed from an FRIV and, with a crew of two, 146 gallons of fuel in the main tanks plus two fifty-five gallon nacelle tanks, the take-off weight was 12,690 lb. From the flying that was done at 30,000 ft it was found that the minimum speed for continuous cruising was 145 knots at 2400 rpm. At full throttle this gave a fuel consumption of sixty-two gallons/hour and an endurance of 2.19 hours. However, nothing came of these trials but the query may well have come from Fairey Air Surveys.

By late 1950 most of the Firefly IVs had been superseded in service by the 'commonised' Mk 5. The discarded Mk IVs were used for a variety of trials to assess items of equipment for the Mk 5s.

During January 1951 for instance, TW695 spent some time with AS6 WD857 in trials to determine the feasibility of carrying sonobuoys in streamlined containers fitted beneath each wing. Preliminary handling trials were conducted using two wooden mock-up containers to determine the effect of handling and check performance characteristics. Then the real containers were substituted for proper trials. The tests showed that there was no adverse effects on the handling characteristics when the containers were carried, either when closed or open. The majority of tests included dives at up to 340 knots, although occasionally 350 knots were exceeded. It was found that there was a worthwhile reduction in drag compared to an aircraft carrying sonobuoys externally on racks, and this would have given a seventeen per cent increase in endurance for anti-submarine patrols. Firefly FRIV TW735 was used to check the flight jettison of pilot's bubble hood (Mod 868) during July and August 1951. Later that year some twenty-eight machines were earmarked for conversion to target towing duties. It was obvious the FAA career of the Firefly FR/NFIV, in its chosen role, was over. After a long and arduous propagation via the FIII, the Firefly Mk IV was in service only for a short time before being superseded by the Firefly Mk 5.

Chapter 6
Fireflies Down Under

O N 23 OCTOBER 1945 the Australian Embassy wrote to the British Admiralty to say that the Australian Naval Board were in the process of preparing a submission to the Commonwealth Government. This was a scheme for the establishment of a Royal Australian Navy (RAN) Air Branch. In order to obtain the required detailed information and guidance the Naval Board wanted to send to the UK Lt/Cdr (O) V. A. Smith DSC RAN. His functions were to explore those avenues which would give the Board the required information to set up such an organisation. He was to be accompanied by Lt/Cdr (O) G. M. Haynes DSO RAN.

This wasn't the first time the RAN had tried to form an air branch. After World War I, some tentative plans to form a RAN Fleet Air Arm were drawn up, but these lapsed in 1921 when the Royal Australian Air Force (RAAF) was formed. However, some RAN personnel trained as pilots and observers with the RAAF and in 1924 the Australian Government decided to provide the RAN with a seaplane carrier. Named HMAS *Albatross,* the seaplane carrier was launched in Sydney in 1928 and commissioned on 23 January 1929. It was designed to carry nine Supermarine Seagull seaplanes. The depression years of the 1930s meant cutbacks in naval spending but

Firefly FRIVs of 816 Squadron on the flight deck of HMAS *Sydney,* shortly after forming up as the 20th CAG. There is some variation in spinner colours, which suggests different flights. *(Royal Australian Navy)*

The FRIV aircraft were gradually replaced by the FR5 from 1949 onwards. This aircraft, FR5 VT500 201/K, was with 817 Squadron operating from the carrier *Sydney*. *(Royal Australian Navy)*

Albatross continued in use until 1933 when she was put into reserve. As part payment for the cruiser HMAS *Hobart,* she was handed over to the Admiralty in 1938. This action marked the end of the air arm but fourteen years later, with all the experience of World War II behind them, the Australian Government decided to form a new FAA capable of providing fleet fighter cover and anti-submarine protection.

The re-birth of the RAN Fleet Air Arm is acknowledged to have been launched on 28 August 1948, the day that the 20th Carrier Air Group (CAG) comprising 805 Squadron (Lt/Cdr P. E. I. Bailey) with Sea Fury IIs, and 816 Squadron (Lt/Cdr C. R. J. Coxon) with Firefly 5s, was commissioned at RNAS Eglinton, Northern Ireland. At Devonport on 16 December 1948 the First Lord of the Admiralty, Viscount Hall, handed over the carrier, HMS *Terrible,* to Australia. It was accepted by the Right Honourable Mr J. B. Beasley, High Commissioner for Australia, who re-named it HMAS *Sydney*. She had been laid down in April 1943 as a Majestic-class aircraft carrier for the Royal Navy and launched in September 1944 as HMS *Terrible*. Overall length was just under 700 ft with a beam of 80 ft, her peacetime complement was 1100 officers and men. At the end of the war she was laid up until acquired by the Australian

Government for the RAN. After embarking the 20th CAG she sailed from Devonport on 12 April 1949, reaching Australia the following month.

The Australian FAA eventually received 108 Fireflies and operated them successfully for over ten years. They were operated at different times by 723, 724, 725, 816, 817 and 851 Squadrons. Support ashore was provided by the Naval Air Station HMAS *Albatross* at Nowra, New South Wales. The airfield at Nowra, and its satellite at Jervis Bay were originally constructed during World War II for the RAAF. After the war Nowra lay disused until 1947 when renovations began in preparation for its being commissioned on 31 August 1948, ready for its new role.

In November 1950 *Sydney* returned to the UK for a second series of aircraft. These became the 21st CAG and consisted of 808 Squadron with Sea Furies and 817 with Fireflies. On returning to Australia it wasn't long before the Sea Furies of 805 joined them and they sailed for Korea. *Sydney* had been called upon to provide support for the United Nations command in Korea and was to be on station between September 1951 and January 1952. By the middle of November 1951 her aircraft had flown more than 1000 sorties over the mainland. Fuller details of her actions are contained in Chapter 11. Suffice to say that she spent sixty-

A well positioned Firefly AS Mk 6 WD884 flying near the NSW coast. The later methods of coding and putting 'NAVY' in large letters are well illustrated. 'RAN' is still stencilled above the serial number, which was usually arranged with the letters above the numerals. The crew's names are positioned just forward of the cockpit. *(Royal Australian Navy)*

A Royal Australian Navy Firefly fitted with a 'G' type winch Mk 2 for target towing work. The variable pitch windmill at the front of the nacelle provides the power to control the pay-out or haul-in of the cable. *(Royal Australian Navy)*

VX373 was the first of the Firefly Mk 5 trainer conversions, shown to good effect in this excellent picture. The old system of overall yellow had been discarded in favour of silver overall with yellow training bands around the fuselage and wings. One cannon was retained in each wing for operational training. *(Royal Australian Navy)*

four days on operations, flying some 2366 sorties with her aircrews winning three DSCs, one Bar to a DSC and one DSM. *Sydney* returned to Australia in February 1952.

It was in 1952 that the RAN were invited to participate in the 1953 Coronation Review Flypast at Spithead in the UK. No 817 Squadron with eight Fireflies joined *Sydney* for what was called 'The Coronation Cruise'. After leaving Australia, the first stop was at the Cocos Islands on 4 April 1953. By 13 April she had arrived at Aden where six Fireflies made a formation flypast. From Aden it was up the Red Sea where the aircraft flew ashore to Fayid on the 20th, re-embarking off Port Said the following day. The ship arrived off Tobruk on 23 April and the aircraft flew ashore to El Adem. Here the Fireflies made a formation flypast with the Vampires of No 78 Wing over the Australian memorial at Tobruk. On 28 April they were in Malta and a day later ashore at Gibraltar. The eight Fireflies flew ashore to Gosport on 4 May. A flight review of the flypast route was made on 30 May which included the Isle of Wight, Poole, Weymouth, Salisbury, Calshot and finally, Spithead. After a full flypast dress rehearsal on 13 June, 817 joined the rest of the units on the 15th to fly past the new Queen. There were seventeen Firefly squadrons in the flypast with 817 in tenth

position. This was not all the Firefly squadrons available as four were not taking part. Two days later 817 joined *Sydney* off the Isle of Wight and then it was off again – this time to the West Indies and flying ashore at Palisadoes, Kingston, on 8 July. That morning Lt/Cdr John Stenning in Firefly '200' was catapulted off at 09.00 hours for the 5000th launch since the original commission in 1948. After that it was through the Panama Canal and on to Pearl Harbor, where they arrived on 31 July. After that they took part in some exercises in Fiji before finally arriving back at Nowra on 14 August 1953.

When *Sydney* was involved in Korea it left a gap in the Australian sea defences, there being concern when *Sydney* was asked to return to Korea in 1953. To give cover, the Admiralty lent the RAN a light fleet carrier, HMS *Vengeance* in November 1952. She embarked Firefly AS6, Sea Furies and Sycamore helicopters. *Vengeance* returned to the UK in 1955 with personnel to form the first RAN Sea Venom and Gannet squadrons.

Operating the Firefly during the early days presented no problems but as new pilots came along there was an obvious need for a Firefly trainer. Pilots joining the Firefly units may have been flying nothing but nosewheel aircraft and a tailwheel aircraft was very different. It was decided to modify, if possible the Firefly 5. Four aircraft were selected, VT440, VT502, VX373 and VX375, with VX373 being the first conversion. The only conversion kits for the modification were those originally designed for converting the earlier marks of Firefly. Three sets were sent out from the Stockport factory in the UK but a lot of local redesign was necessary. This was done by the Fairey Aviation Co. of Australia Pty., a subsidiary of the UK Fairey Aviation Company. The fourth Firefly was converted by using this experience to produce a locally made kit. Apart from the four conversions to Firefly TMk 5, two other Mk 5s, VX388 and WB271, were converted to target towing and these became known as Firefly TT Mk 5. Four AS6 Fireflies were also converted to the target towing role, WB518, WD828, 840 and 901 and these became Firefly TT Mk 6.

By the late 1950s the Fireflies were suffering from general fatigue, corrosion and lack of spares. The roles were gradually being taken over by more modern types including jets.

The colours and markings of the RAN Fireflies followed those of the British FAA. In fact, on 29 July 1948, the RAN Liaison Officer wrote a memo to the Director of Air Equipment (Admiralty) outlining the required markings on RAN aircraft, in this case the Fireflies and Sea Furies of the 20th CAG. In this he stated:

1 Colours and markings to be in accordance with AFO 3/48.
2 Fin marking – a large letter K in black.
3 Service number to be three digit code applied to fuselage, for the twenty-five Sea Furies – Nos 101 to 124; for the twenty-five Fireflies – Nos 201 to 224 although the last aircraft from each batch is not required to have a code.
4 Aircraft serial number on aft rear fuselage – but not required on under-surfaces of mainplanes.
5 RAN stencilled on rear fuselage in place of Royal Navy.
6 Squadron badge allowed, i.e. 816 for Fireflies.

The fate of the 108 RAN Fireflies was as follows:

63 were sold for scrap
16 were reduced for spares and produce
 7 were used for firefighting
 5 crashed while at sea
 3 were lost in Korean operations
 2 were lost in mid-air collision
 2 were lost to some other cause
 1 was written off at Nowra

The mid-air collision in which two were lost was on 27 November 1956. VX381 of 805 Squadron was on a divisional form up subsequent to an

One of the conversions of an AS 6 to target towing, WD901 878/NW displays the new centre roundel marking of a kangaroo. Previous to this, the roundels had been standard red/white/blue. *(J. M. G. Gradidge)*

Full of atmosphere, and a delight to look at. Fireflies TT Mk 6 WJ109 907/NW and WB518 903/NW of 851 Squadron prepare to leave Bankstown and return to Nowra. Note the spinners. *(Royal Australian Navy)*

observer exercise when it was struck by WD887. The former aircraft lost five feet off its starboard wing and ditched in Jervis Bay.

When the Australian Government announced that it was accepting tenders for surplus Fireflies in 1966 it created quite a bit of interest. The outcome was that nine were eventually sold and one other, WB271, won a tender with an offer of A$400

(£160) made up from the ship's company of the carrier HMS *Victorious* and RAN personnel at Bankstown. This aircraft was ferried back to the UK and presented to the FAA Museum at Yeovilton. Of the others:

WD901 was purchased by Casula Auto Wreckers, Liverpool, NSW. Still coded 907/NW it was

Firefly FR5 VX385 205/K of 817 Squadron visits Fayid, Egypt, when *Sydney* was en route to the UK for the 1953 Coronation Fly Past. *(R. Dodd)*

This TT Mk 5 is actually VX388, the Firefly destined for the UK after being bought by HAPS in 1967. *(J. M. G. Gradidge)*

taken by road from Bankstown and placed at the entrance to the works. Eventually sold to Major W. Gabella of Fort Rucker, Alabama, USA. Crated by Skyservice Aviation, Camden.

WD826 was transferred to a naval apprentice training school at HMAS *Nirimba*, Schofields, about thirty miles north west of Sydney.

WD827 went to Blacktown Air League, Sydney. Acquired by Australian Aircraft Restoration Group (AARG) in 1973 as spares aircraft in project to get a Firefly airworthy. Loaned to RAAF Point Cook air base as display item but belongs to Moorabin Air Museum, Victoria, NSW.

WD828 was purchased by AARG in 1966 and after some basic refurbishment was flown to the Moorabin Aviation Museum on 18 February 1967.

WD833 was originally located at the gate of a naval establishment near Hastings, forty miles south of Melbourne. Sold to R. H. Grant Metals Ltd., Northcote, Melbourne and later sold to Tom King of Preston, Victoria. In 1974 sold to the Strathallan collection in Scotland who hoped to restore it. Sold in 1981 for £22,000 and moved to St. Merryn. Put in 1984 Christie's auction where bidding reached £48,000.

WD840 was purchased by Aircraft Engine Overhauls, Peakhurst, NSW, and flown to Camden Aviation Museum in 1967. Aircraft crated in 1968 and sold to R. Diemert of Manitoba, Canada.

WH632 went to Sydney Air League HQ 1965. Camden Aviation Museum then acquired it before selling it to R. Diemert of Canada.

WJ109 was preserved as a gate guardian at HMAS *Nowra* air base.

WB518 was purchased by C. Beltrame. Flown to Griffith in NSW and mounted on a 20 ft pylon as a memorial for the Returned Servicemen's League.

VX388 was purchased originally in 1967 by Historic Aircraft Preservation Society (HAPS) of the UK, who wanted to fly it back. It was estimated that it would take £5000 to refurbish it and fly it to the UK. Nothing ever came of this plan and it ended up at Camden Aviation Museum.

Chapter 7
Firefly Trainers

AT THE END of hostilities Fairey found themselves repairing and reconditioning Firefly 1s at the Stockport/Ringway factories, which the FAA really did not have a need for. At Hayes, work was already going ahead with new versions of the Firefly and there was a lot of experimental flying going on.

The Admiralty, in a meeting with Fairey at the end of the war, had intimated that there might be a requirement for an advanced trainer. They expressed an interest in a dual-control deck-landing trainer with a performance similar to the combat types in use at the time. Apart from the deck-landing training it would be used for advanced training, instrument flying, weapons training, but more importantly, it would ease the transition difficulties of comparatively inexperienced pilots, who were unaccustomed to powerful engines and speeds in excess of the normal training aircraft. Pupil pilots usually jumped from the cockpit of something like the Harvard or Master straight into a

modern high performance fighter with relatively high wing loadings, resulting in a high percentage of training accidents due to mis-handling. The advantages were obvious.

F/Lt Duncan Menzies, Fairey's senior production test pilot for the northern factories at Ringway, immediately saw the potential for such a trainer and the implications to the company. Visiting the Admiralty he was able to convince the Director of Air Warfare (DAW) and the Director of Air Organisation of Training (DAOT) that not only was the Firefly, when converted, the most suitable machine for the job, but that in terms of cost, it would be a cost effective exercise. As the Admiralty already owned the Firefly 1s that went into Fairey for repair or reconditioning etc., it would be an easy matter to convert a required number while still in the factory. The Admiralty were more than interested. Duncan Menzies then went to Hayes and got the Directors to agree to a Private Venture (PV) project for the Trainer.

G.6.3/Z2033 with the mocked-up rear cockpit. Only just visible are the anti-spin strakes on the fin. This is to stop the anti-spin parachute and/or its webbing, if deployed, from fouling the rudder or elevator travel. *(J. D. R. Rawlings)*

G.6.3/Z2033 at Heston, with the proper rear cockpit hooding fitted. This was for the tests to see whether the rear hooding would crack in high-speed dives. *(R. J. Carter)*

Soundings elsewhere had also indicated that sales might well not be limited to the Admiralty.

The Design Office came up with an adaption of the Firefly Mk I with the observer's cockpit replaced by a further single pilot's cockpit unit. To effect this conversion (Modification 5001) the rear fuselage top fairing was cut away from the decking at Frame 10, just forward of the rear cockpit, and replaced by a new structure designed to assemble to the top longerons and fair into the rear fuselage forward of the fin root. The fuselage was increased in width at the decking line and a new turtle back and side fairings fitted. A complete pilot's floor unit comprising floor structure, rudder bar, control column and standard seat was fitted but raised some twelve inches. The controls, equipment and

This detailed factory drawing illustrates the cockpit positions in relation to one another.

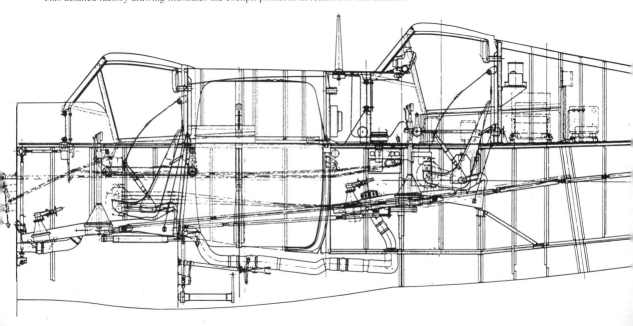

This picture shows to good effect the outline of the Trainer in its revised colours after visiting the naval base at St Merryn.

(Flight International)

With engine ticking over, Group Captain Gordon Slade, Chief Test Pilot at Faireys in the 1940s and 1950s, awaits the starter's flag to get away in the Lympne High Speed Handicap Race of 31 August 1947. Behind is Peter Twiss in the Firefly FRIV, a Firebrand and the Trainers competitor at one stage, the Spitfire Trainer G.AIDN, which later, ironically, was owned and flown by Sir Richard Fairey's surviving son, John. *(Author's collection)*

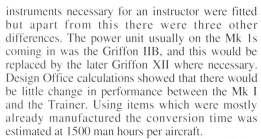

The front cockpit of the Trainer illustrating the bewildering array of instruments, switches, etc, facing a pupil pilot. As this is the prototype cockpit, there is no gyro gunsight fitted. In the T Mk 1, fitted with two 20 mm cannon, a gunsight was fitted in the front cockpit only for the pupil.
(Author's collection)

The rear, instructor's, cockpit, showing the paucity of instruments and switches, etc. Note the gyro gunsight; in the T Mk 2 these would be fitted in both cockpits.
(Author's collection)

instruments necessary for an instructor were fitted but apart from this there were three other differences. The power unit usually on the Mk 1s coming in was the Griffon IIB, and this would be replaced by the later Griffon XII where necessary. Design Office calculations showed that there would be little change in performance between the Mk I and the Trainer. Using items which were mostly already manufactured the conversion time was estimated at 1500 man hours per aircraft.

The Admiralty released MB750, which was being repaired at Stockport, for the trainer test programme. As work got under way the Admiralty said that they were worried about the effects of the airflow around the tail from the new layout, and they would like the Trainer cleared to do four-turn spins. So that the programme with MB750 was not delayed, Fairey pulled Z2033 off the repair line also, and this was to become the flying mock-up and spin clearance machine. Z2033 made its first flight as a mocked-up trainer on 29 May 1946 in the hands of F/Lt Sam Moseley. The rear cockpit mock-up was a light alloy-framed wooden structure. MB750 followed on 21 June 1946, again

piloted by Sam Moseley. Duncan Menzies had by this time moved out of test flying and was pilot in charge of service problems and liaison with customers. To facilitate test flying Z2033 became G.6.3, while MB750 was painted up in the company colours of silver and blue for demonstration purposes. As a company demonstrator, and because it was intended for use anywhere, MB750 had to be registered, and so became G.AHYA, although it never carried these markings, being marked up as F1. One of the initial worries of the pundits was that, with a rear sliding canopy, carbon monoxide fumes would float back affecting the instructor/ rear pilot. Flight tests removed that fear. Minor problems with dual control systems came up and one was with the flaps. Sam Moseley sorted it out:

'Dualisation of the Firefly flap control system posed some problems, which you will appreciate if you are familiar with the Firefly 1 flap control – a large lever moving through an arc in a gated quadrant. The problem was baffling the engineers and was solved by my suggestion that a motorcycle foot gear change mechanism be used at the cockpit(s) end(s) of the control. In fact, the system was first mocked up using a footgear change unit from one of my Rudge Whitworth motorcycles. As you may know, this consists of a drum with ratchets on its periphery, into which pauls attached to the operating lever engage. The beauty of the system was that it was much smaller and easier to use than the normal Firefly control, furthermore, as the operating lever always automatically returns to the same position, irrespective of the position of the drum and flaps, the control lever is always near to hand, a pointer indicating the actual position of the flaps.'

The Pilot's Notes for the Firefly T Mk I and T2 state, 'The flaps are operated by a short lever in a quadrant on the port side of each cockpit. The lever has three positions, up, neutral and down and springs back to neutral from the up or the down position when released.' It went on to say . . . 'To move the flaps one stage, the lever must be moved fully down once and released. To move the flaps two stages, two successive movements of the lever to down must be made. In a similar manner the flaps may be raised any number of stages by moving the lever up from neutral the required number of times.' So Sam Moseley's idea was incorporated into the Trainers.

On 14 August 1946 Duncan Menzies flew F1 to Heston (Fairey's Great West Aerodrome was taken over to become London's new airport, Heathrow) and spent two days demonstrating the new trainer to two Commanders, Humphries and Campbell, and two Captains, Fawcett and Willoughby of the naval training branch. F1 then went off to Boscombe Down for handling trials on 20 August, but was available to attend the 1946 SBAC Show at Radlet where Sam Moseley demonstrated it on 13 September. Returning to Ringway on 21 September Duncan Menzies then had approval to show off the new trainer to the FAA. He flew it round numerous naval airfields including the Advanced Flying School at Hinstock, the Operational Flying School at Lossiemouth, the Deck-Landing Training and Deck-Landing Control Officer Training station at Milltown, and the School of Naval Warfare at St Merryn where FAA pilots were allowed to fly it.

During the early part of the Trainer programme, some naval fighter pilots, by now residing behind desks in Whitehall, thought about the possibility of a dual Spitfire instead of a Firefly trainer. So, in the latter half of 1946 Duncan Menzies found himself sitting at the Admiralty opposite Geoffrey Quill of Vickers Supermarine, in the same office, at the same time and becoming good friends as they tried to convince the Minister that their aeroplane was best! However, Menzies knew that the Spitfire wasn't really suitable as a dual deck landing trainer and eventually won the order. Menzies, champing

One of the early conversions, still displaying the post-war colour scheme. Note that it carries a fin flash, which disappeared from naval aircraft later, and the broken style of stencilling used for the code numbers. *(J. D. R. Rawlings)*

The Firefly T Mk 3 observer trainer, seen here in use with 796 Squadron, differed very little in external appearance to the FR1. 272 is PP411 and 280 PP425. *(Author's collection)*

at the bit to get orders, got permission to demonstrate it again:

'It (MB750) was at that time F1 and partly owned by Fairey Aviation on a loan agreement. For insurance purposes F1 had to always have a Fairey test pilot in one cockpit when being demonstrated. I took it to SNAW (School of Naval Warfare) at RNAS St Merryn on 29 November 1946. They wanted to fly it themselves, i.e., two FAA instructors and no damned Fairey test pilot, which was quite understandable. With F1 this wasn't possible so I spent some hours on the telephone to Hayes and the Admiralty. The result was that St Merryn sprayed out F1, added service roundels, restored her old identity of MB750 and this allowed service pilots to fly her with no restrictions! I flew her back to Heston in that guise on 3 December and she stayed in those markings until sold.'

The following day Menzies flew to Hendon, picked up a Commander Bryant and flew first to Toussos-le-Noble, and afterwards French test pilots were allowed to fly MB750 at Les Mureaux. It was also demonstrated to the French Navy and visited Buc. Menzies flew back to Heston on 9 December but six days later he was in Holland demonstrating to the Dutch Navy, first at their Operational Flying School at Valkenburg and then at Coxyde. The last actual demonstration was on Christmas Day 1946 with Menzies returning to Heston on Boxing Day.

The aircraft was laid up in the early part of 1947 while various modifications were incorporated, including, I understand, Sam Moseley's suggestion for the flap operation. An Argentine Air Force pilot flew in on 15 May and on 3 June S/Ldr 'Wimpy' Wade flew an evaluation for the *Aeroplane*. On 22 July Menzies flew Group Captain Gordon Slade, Fairey's new chief test pilot, from Heston to Ringway in Fulmar G.AIBE, for the final conference with the Admiralty on Firefly Trainer production. Menzies' work with the Trainer was now done and his last flight in it was on 22 September when he flew it from Heston to Ringway. Just before that, Gordon Slade had entered MB750 in the Lympne High Speed Handicap Race, and came in third at 290.22 mph.

In the meantime Sam Moseley had been test flying the mocked up Trainer G.6.3. Built as FR1,

Z2033 was to lead an interesting life. First flown on 28 March 1944 by test pilot Colin Evans, it was delivered to the MU at RNAS Wroughton on 30 April. From there it went to No 731 Squadron at Easthaven, where, after a minor accident on 9 August 1945 it was delivered to Fairey's Hamble factory but was moved to Ringway on 8 October for repair/reconditioning. It was test flown on 1 April after repair by Albert Eyskens, a Belgian who did some test flying for Fairey before returning home in mid 1946. It was at this point that it was selected for modification to become the test mock-up trainer.

It was first flown in its new configuration on 29 May 1946 by Sam Moseley, after which he continued to do test flights in it when required. On 23 September he started spin trials, completing six that day. During September/October he flew more, mainly with trim in the aft C of G positions. After trials and modifications he achieved four-turn spins in April 1947 and the aircraft went to Boscombe on 8 August for service spinning trials. After returning to Ringway it again went to Boscombe in September for further spinning trials. It returned to Stockport in October, spinning trials complete and satisfactory. After languishing at the factory, Sam Moseley flight tested it on 28 May 1948 and delivered it to White Waltham on 5 June. While at White Waltham it was used to test a one-piece hood and dived to 370 knots without it cracking. Afterwards it was turned to another use. Ian Huntley, an employee at the factory remembers seeing it. 'I met Z2033 during 1948, when, very much sawn up it appeared as the prototype TTMk 1. It then had the raised second cockpit dummy removed leaving a patch with the original camouflage and part of the roundel showing. Below the patch were the remaining bottom portions of G.6.3 lettering.' In fact, Z2033 had become a target tower for Sweden, was registered SE.BRD and delivered to Stockholm by Peter Twiss on 15 February 1949. When retired from flying it was presented to the Skyframe collection at Staverton, where it arrived on 5 May 1964. After the demise of Skyframe, Z2033 moved to its new home at Duxford, where it is still to be seen.

MB750 continued to be used for demonstrations for a time but was eventually converted to a T Mk 2 and sold to Thailand. With few problems during the Trainer test flying, orders were received from the Admiralty to convert thirty-four Firefly 1s to the T Mk 1 configuration. These were usually aircraft in for repairs/reconditioning at Ringway where all the work was carried out. At least six of the thirty-four, DK429, 449, 453, DT933, MB465 and 496 were fitted with one 20 mm cannon in each wing. The first production T1 was MB473 which flew in its new guise on 23 July 1947. Thereafter Trainers came off the line at a rate of two or three a month. Some thought had already gone into ways of improving the trainers' capability and this resulted in the T Mk 2, equipped to operate as a tactical weapons trainer. All the T Mk 2s had two 20 mm cannon in the wings and had gyro gunsights in both cockpits. Again, all conversions were done at Ringway and all were ex-Mk 1s. The first T Mk 2 made its initial flight on 12 August 1949. Eventually some fifty-four were converted, and were cleared to carry 500 lb bombs, markers, flares, smoke floats, mines and various size practice bombs.

Two other trainers were conversions of the Mk 1, the F Mk 1A of which details are recorded elsewhere, and the T Mk 3. The operational training of naval pilots was not a problem but little thought had gone into the requirements of observer training. Fairey were approached by the Admiralty to see if they could squeeze yet another conversion out of the versatile Mk 1 design. The result was the Firefly T Mk 3, all of which were conversions of the FR Mk 1 but which differed from the other conversions in that they had no rear raised canopies. They were required to carry special equipment to train observers in the art of anti-submarine warfare. Conversions were done at naval air stations, but mostly at Fleetlands by Fairey work parties out from Ringway. Armament was deleted, the deck arrester hook removed and a few cosmetic changes in the cockpits were all that was required. The problem was that only one observer could be trained at a time. Although no actual figures have been released on the number of conversions the author believes it to be fifty. Most of the conversions took place during the period 1949 to 1951 with PP411 apparently being one of the first. Strangely enough, all the conversions were drawn from the PP serial range.

No 796 Squadron became the main user of the T Mk 3. The squadron had been re-formed after the war at St Merryn equipped with Barracuda IIIs. Its task was changed to the second phase of observer training in March 1950 with the Firefly T Mk 3s arriving in July. They were used until the Firefly T Mk 7 replaced them in June 1953. The T Mk 3 was used by other squadrons including the RNVR squadrons, Nos 1830, 1831, 1833, 1841 and 1844.

Other Firefly trainers included the T Mk 7 and the Australian T Mk 5, both recorded in their respective chapters.

Chapter 8
Canadian Fireflies

THE ORIGINS of Canadian naval aviation go back to the mid-war years. In August 1943 Captain H. N. Lay OBE RCN visited the UK to study the operation and administration functions of the FAA, with a view to advising the Canadian Naval Board on the desirability of setting up a FAA within the Royal Canadian Navy. He was allowed to visit various FAA airfields and establishments and talked to senior staff officers. The outcome was that he said that he intended to recommend the formation of a RCN FAA as no modern navy, however small, should operate without an air component.

After discussions at high level, it was decided that initially four air squadrons from the FAA would be allocated for manning by RCN personnel, but for ultimate transfer after the war. By the time

Firefly FR1s of 825 Squadron aboard HMCS *Warrior*. The colours were standard FAA of extra dark sea grey/dark slate grey on the upper surfaces with sky undersides and white spinner. The narrow deck is most obvious and left little room for errors. *(Canadian Armed Forces)*

negotiations had been finalised it was 1945 anyway and the Admiralty agreed to transfer two light carriers to the RCN. The first was HMCS *Warrior*, commissioned in March 1946 she formed an air group with No 825 Squadron with Firefly FR1s and 803 with Sea Furies. The other carrier, HMCS *Magnificent*, would not be ready until 1948 so the two squadrons forming her air group, No 826 with Fireflies and 883 with Sea Furies, were temporarily disbanded. In fact, 826 had re-formed at RNAS Easthaven, Scotland, on 15 August 1945, with a mixed complement of RN and RCN personnel. The squadron moved to Fearn for its work-up with Firefly FR1s, which replaced their initial equipment, Barracudas. Although a Canadian officer had assumed command by February 1946 drastic manpower problems forced the disbandment on 28 February, although it remained a RCN squadron on paper.

Manned jointly by the RN and RCN, 825 Squadron formed up at RNAS Rattray, Scotland, on 1 July 1945 with Barracuda aircraft. These were gradually replaced by Firefly FR1s, with sixty per cent of the maintenance ratings coming from Canada. On 24 January 1946 HMCS *Warrior* was commissioned and 825 became an official RCN Air squadron. The carrier arrived at Halifax, Nova Scotia, on 31 March, and for the next year the squadrons were under training either ashore at Naval Air Section Dartmouth, or afloat in *Warrior*, which, with the units embarked, visited the west coast during the winter of 1946. Formed into the 19th Carrier Air Group in April 1947 the squadrons took part in fleet exercises off Bermuda. Not long after this the 19th CAG turned its aircraft over to the 18th CAG and sailed for the UK in *Warrior*.

On 15 May 1947, the 18th CAG, consisting of No 826 and 883 Squadrons reformed at Dartmouth, Novia Scotia, to fly the aircraft formerly used by the 19th CAG. For the first seven months of 1948 the 18th CAG was put through its paces in a busy work up programme, and during the August/ September period was providing instruction at the Canadian Air Training Centre, Rivers, Manitoba.

No 825 meanwhile had re-equipped with the Firefly FR4 and was returning to Canada in June 1948 aboard the new carrier, HMCS *Magnificent*. A change took place on 15 November that year when both Firefly squadrons were joined together to form a new 18th CAG, the object being to centralize maintenance facilities for Firefly aircraft.

A meeting took place in the UK on 20 August 1948 to arrange a modification programme for Fireflies set aside for the RCN, and which they intended sending a carrier for early in 1949. There were eleven Firefly FR4s held in storage, and another six on order, which needed converting to Firefly Mk 5 standard, including the wing folding modification. Fairey said that given the go-ahead they would hope to have the work on the seventeen Fireflies completed by the first week in January 1949. Approval was given and the aircraft delivered to Ringway. They were all flight tested between December 1948 and February 1949, the first being VH138. The RCN returned to the UK in early 1949 and exchanged their Firefly 4s for the Mk 5s. For the next two years 825, and 826, operated from shore bases or *Magnificent*. In September 1949 the 18th CAG embarked in USS *Saipan* for practice in American deck-landing techniques. After taking part in some 1950

Caribbean exercises, pilots of 826 were sent to the United States to start ferrying seventy-five Grumman Avenger aircraft which were destined to replace the Fireflies.

There was another re-organisation in January 1951 when 825 and 803 became known as the 19th Support Air Group. All RCN squadrons were re-numbered on 1 May 1951, the new identity of 825 being Squadron 880, the original number reverting to the FAA.

Eventually the RCN acquired twenty-six Firefly Mk 1, three T1 and three T2 Trainers, twelve FR4 and eighteen AS5 (one being added at the last moment). Of the twenty-six Mk 1s, nine were sold to Ethiopia, four returned to the FAA, four were scrapped, five crashed in service and four went to Denmark. Five of the Trainers went to Ethiopia, one having crashed in service. Ten of the FR4s were returned to the FAA in exchange for the Mk 5s, two of the latter having crashed. Nine of the Mk 5s were written off in service, nine returned to the FAA and four were sold to the Dutch.

No Fireflies had been preserved in Canada, so when some of the Australian machines came on the

Preparing to catapult a Firefly FR4 from HMCS *Magnificent* in May 1948 during flying trials. *(Canadian Armed Forces)*

AS Mk 5 VH135 BD*K, which was later written off in an accident. Note the smaller fuselage roundel that came in later.
(Canadian Armed Forces)

market the Canadian Warplane Heritage organisation thought they would rectify the situation. The chance came when an advertisement appeared in the American *Trade-a-Plane* newspaper offering a Firefly for sale. This in fact was WD901, bought by Major W. F. Gabella. It had been shipped to the USA aboard SS *African Crescent* and taken by road to Charlesden Municipal Airport, South Carolina. Here it was converted for crop dusting and afterwards sat rusting until offered for sale. A syndicate from the CWH bought WD901 and spent C$50,000 putting it back into airworthy condition. It was flown to Toronto after refurbishment where it was fully restored. It was painted up as a Firefly of 825 Squadron with the code, BD*H and roundels using the maple leaf in the centre. Anyone wanting to see the standard to which this aircraft was restored should seek a copy of the American magazine, *Flying* for April 1974 when a magnificent two-page spread made up the front cover. Tragically, WD901/CF.BDH stalled and spun into Lake Ontario while being flown by syndicate member Alan Ness during the Canadian International Air Show, 2 September 1977. Alan Ness died as a result of the accident.

In 1978 CWH bought WH632 from Australia to replace their loss. After arrival in Halifax, Novia Scotia, it was moved to Shearwater, a Canadian Forces base for storage. Another Firefly had also been obtained from Australia and this was WD840.

In 1968 it was sold to Bob Diemert of Canada and crated to Vancouver, British Columbia. It was then loaded on a flat-bed trailer and driven across Canada to Manitoba. This in itself was no mean fact with Bob driving through the mountains at night so that he could go under bridges in the middle of the road when there was little traffic about. Unfortunately, by the time Bob bought the Firefly it had many parts missing including the engine and wing radiators. A replacement engine in running order could not be found so a decision was made to re-engine it with a Merlin 500 out of an Avro York. With no wing radiators available either it meant the full York engine arrangement could be fitted with underslung radiators, similar to the old Mk 1 Fireflies. The aircraft was stripped out and it became a seven-seater. The space occupied by the wing radiators was used to hold extra fuel tanks and it flew in its new configuration on 17 September 1972. Its next owner was Gene Fisher from the USA who was a member of the Confederate Air Force and had restored a B25 Mitchell to full flying condition. Gene went around the world after Firefly parts including the Failsworth scrap yard, but before he had restored it back to a Mk 6 it was sold to Don Knapp, the owner of a large 'warbird' collection who moved to Abilene, Texas, from Florida in 1990. Unfortunately Don was killed during a demonstration the same year at Dyess Air Force Base and at the time of going to press no decision had been made on the Firefly's future.

Chapter 9
Firefly Mk 5/Mk 6

Firefly FR/AS/NF Mk 5

THE STORIES of the Firefly Mk 4, 5, 6 and 7 are separate in their own right but of necessity interwoven. The first three marks differed only in the naval equipment carried although the Mk 6 and 7 did not carry guns. Even as the Firefly Mk 4 was being introduced into service the development of new equipment, new operating techniques and new operational requirements meant that it was obsolescent. Only the layout proved to be beneficial as Fairey developed a 'universal' airframe capable of rapid change. Externally the new aircraft was identical and virtually indistinguishable from the Firefly Mk 4 but the three variants planned for fighter reconnaissance, anti-submarine and night fighting, differed according to the equipment fitted in the pilot's and observer's cockpits. This became known as Modification 600.

There was discussion at one stage as to whether Modification 600 should apply to a Firefly Mk 4A – which the Ministry preferred, or go for a new mark. The change of equipment was considered sufficient to warrant a new mark of Firefly and thus was born the Firefly Mk 5. The only hiccup was the changing of the roles. The fighter-reconnaissance and anti-submarine roles could be swopped around in about half an hour, but to change either of these to the night-fighting role required the fitting of a flame damping manifold which could make the change a three-hour job. The final conference on the first production aircraft, VT362, embodying Modification 600 was

This picture shows a Mk 5 Firefly WB281 on flight test prior to the application of service markings and the fitting of guns.
(Author's collection)

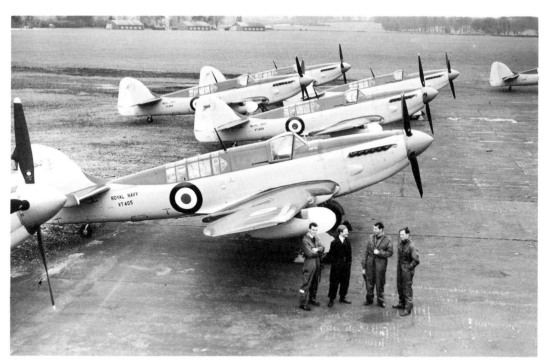

A new batch of Fireflies ready for delivery. In this picture, four can be identified as VT405, VT409, VT404 and VT406. The two pilots on the right are Gordon Slade and Peter Twiss. *(Flight International)*

held at White Waltham on 29 October 1947. First flight of the Firefly Mk 5 was on 12 December 1947 at White Waltham. Fairey had established its flight test centre there after the original flight test airfield, the Great West Aerodrome was absorbed into the new London Heathrow Airport. Heston was used for a short time but it was too small and too close to the Heathrow circuit. The decision to move to White Waltham was taken one day after Gordon Slade, Chief Test Pilot at Fairey, took off in a Firefly Mk 4 and narrowly missed a mid-air collision with a Constellation. The post-war period was in fact quite fruitful for Fairey as many other military contracts were cancelled and more orders were placed for Fireflies. Great interest was being shown in the anti-submarine operations. An out-standing order for Firefly Mk 4s was transferred to the new Mk 5 so that by the end of 1948 some 169 were on contract. Another order for seventy-five was signed bringing the total to 244 with deliveries to start from 1 April 1949. This was further increased on 10 August 1948 by another twenty-eight so that 272 were on order.

With initial production problems over the release of the Firefly FR Mk 5 to the Service came

on 21 June 1948. The actual release note remarked that the aircraft was a variant of the Firefly FR4, the only difference being the embodiment of some of the Modification 600 series which allowed conversion to the alternative roles of anti-submarine or night-fighting. The release of the anti-submarine role was held up due to problems with the wing-mounted ASH nacelle, but eventually cleared on 14 October 1948. Until a solution was found to the mounting problem of the nacelle, it was not to be fitted when deck-landing or gun firing. Modification 604 called for the fitting of a sonobuoy receiver, sonobuoys and radio altimeter. Trials had shown that up to twelve sonobuoys could be carried subject to a maximum releasing speed of 200 knots IAS and a minimum height of twice the IAS in knots. Two 250 lb depth charges could be carried simultaneously with sonobuoys. The October release note had also made the observation that the Firefly Mk 5 was not considered a suitable aircraft for night carrier operations because:

1 Rebound value of the undercarriage was far too high, and was in fact outside the limit accepted by the RAF for shore-based aircraft.

2 The hook damper was not sufficiently effective to overcome any bouncing with the problem of missing all the wires.

3 The pilot's view was a real problem. On the approach it was difficult to line up properly and when flared all sight of the deck was lost.

4 Controls – the Firefly Mk 5 proved to be sluggish on all controls at slow speeds.

It was felt that although the Firefly 5 could be operated safely at night, it was only suitable to do so by very experienced pilots of 'above average' deck-landing capability. Furthermore, it recommended strongly that all future aircraft designed for night carrier operations should be fitted with a tricycle undercarriage. It was hoped that before the squadrons became fully operational on the type that some of the problems that had come to light while operating the Mk 4 might be sorted out. On 15 January 1948 Lt/Cdr P. A. Hudson and Lt J. H. Westwood took Firefly TW738 to Defford for investigation into vibration problems. The AN/APS4 (ASH) failures in first line squadrons were becoming almost an epidemic. Although there was design allowance for deterioration of equipment, rough handling, heavy deck landings etc., there was considerably more vibration than anticipated when the guns were fired (the pundits had been right!). At the same time Firefly TW687

went to the RAE Farnborough for similar trials with the radios. The findings revealed the anti-vibration mountings for the ASH nacelle were just not good enough. Some better damped mountings were fitted to Firefly VT427 and Lt Elliott of the RAE carried out catapult launches and arrested landings to prove the change. There appeared to be no problems including those of distortion or structural damage and the modification was approved. All these trials involved the air side but ground maintenance was not forgotten. Although the Firefly was a well established FAA type it was always considered well worthwhile to carry out basic ground handling trials when an aircraft became available, especially a new variant. When Firefly TW689 became available between 22 April and 25 August 1948 such tests were carried out. These consisted of all forms of rough usage that an aircraft would experience during its normal service life. This involved manhandling, taxying, towing, wing-folding, slinging, continual removal of panels and cowlings etc, all interspersed between a flying programme to make it realistic. TW689 came through the tests satisfactorily with numerous small lessons learnt and improvements recommended.

Between 27 September and 21 December 1948 Firefly 5 VT393 was modified with a power-operated wing-folding modification. Some twenty-

VT393 undergoing RATO tests at the RAE Farnborough early in 1950. The rockets are firing and the aircraft accelerating along the runway. *(Crown Copyright)*

Firefly WB406 at Boscombe Down, fitted with target-towing gear for trials and clearance for service use. The nacelle holding the winch can just be discerned under the centre forward fuselage. *(Crown Copyright)*

Streamlined sonobuoy containers fitted to Firefly VT424 for acceptance trials. *(Westland Aircraft Ltd)*

Airborne on sortie training is VT393 202/GN of 737 Squadron, showing the code for Eglinton, Northern Ireland. *(B. J. Lowe)*

A squadron of Firefly 5s start to taxi out for take-off. Note the long-range tanks and rocket rails. *(Flight International)*

A Firefly WB382 237 of 810 Squadron. Note the way the upper dark sea grey demarkation line is extended in a wavy line along the rudder. *(J. M. G. Gradidge)*

nine flights were made to test the system thoroughly, the aircraft being a standard Mk 5 except for:

Mod 809 Power wing-folding modification.
Mod 809A Stabilising cross struts between port and starboard centre section hinge fittings. The selector valve was under the pilot's control with a latch pin indicator.
Mod 773B Centre section hinge top lug reinforced, aileron trim cable shortened, stabilisers preset.
Mod 735 Improvements to wing-folding pole attachments at wing tips.

The power wing-fold modification had been wanted for a long time and although it was a great help it was not completely independent because deck hands were still required to complete the operation. The basic installation comprised hydraulic wing-folding jacks fitted in the centre section and controlled by a three-gate lever in the pilot's cockpit.

On 10 February 1949 Fairey were advised of an order for fourteen more Firefly Mk 5s, followed by another ninety-two on 23 May – the total orders at that time standing at 444 machines.

As with all aircraft in service various modifications were tried and incorporated. Modification Arm. 737 for instance for the

Firefly was for a Light Series Carrier for the simultaneous carriage of R/P and sonobuoys up to a limiting speed of 304 knots and a thirty-degree dive, the flight test aircraft being VT393 during May/June 1949. Later VT428 carried out trials with American five-inch HVAR rocket projectiles but found no difference to the British ones. This aircraft also tested 20 mm cartridge case and link external guide shutes, and later still, 'G' type air/sea rescue containers under each wing.

These and the numerous other modifications presented few problems to the introduction of the Firefly Mk 5 and crews had no difficulty adjusting to their new mounts. Deliveries to the squadrons began in January 1948 and continued until May 1950 – but cutbacks and conversions to Mk 6 meant that 338 were produced as Mk 5s plus the 14 NF5s for the Dutch. The first units to get the Firefly Mk 5 were the Service Trials Units (STU) with 778 and 782 receiving their first ones in May 1948. The primary role of 782 was communications support for Flag Officer Flying Training (FOFT) HQ at Lee-on-Solent, and the Firefly Mk 5 was added for a special high speed flight.

In February 1954 703 Squadron formed a small unit called A Flight to test a new Ferranti Carrier Controlled Approach system which was being developed at the Air Signals and Radar

Establishment at Tantallon, about thirty miles east of Edinburgh. Operating as an independent unit, the Flight took six ex-825 Squadron Firefly 5s to Arbroath to conduct flight trials, each flight taking place at the sea end of the Firth of Forth and using the Bass Rock as a simulated carrier.

No 812 Squadron, which had been operating the FR4, changed them in July 1948 for the FR5. After embarking in *Ocean* in August they sailed for the Mediterranean, using Hal Far on Malta as a shore base. They returned to Culdrose in September 1949 to receive some updated FR5s and returned to Malta. That November they transferred to *Glory* as part of the 13th CAG and took part in fleet exercises and a couple of cruises. After that 812 went out to the Far East and operated during the Korean War, details of which are recorded in that chapter. The squadron left Korean waters in May 1952 after transferring its aircraft to *Ocean*.

No 814 Squadron operated its FR4s from Eglinton and *Vengeance* before changing them for the FR5 in 1949. It spent two months in the Mediterranean in early 1950 and made a visit to Norway in July. After another spell aboard *Vengeance* the squadron disbanded at Culdrose on 19 November 1950, only to receive the Firefly AS6 the next day.

When 737 Squadron received its Firefly Mk 5s in April 1949 it was to provide Part II of the Operational Flying School course as part of the 52nd Training Air Group at Eglinton. Later it also became responsible for the Anti-Submarine School and on 19 April 1950 X Flight was formed at Lee-on-Solent for special trials with search receivers that it was hoped would detect submarine radar. This unit spent two months at Gibraltar before going to Eglinton to become 744 Squadron. On 14 June 1950, 719 Squadron joined 737 to form the 53rd Training Air Group, still at Eglinton, where they operated until 1955 when the Fireflies were replaced by the Gannet.

A Firefly of 814 Squadron comes to grief while attempting to land on HMS *Vengeance*, September 1950. One pilot remembered that when he had a barrier crash, the observer was out of the cockpit and in the island before the pilot had removed his straps. *(Author's collection)*

No 804 Squadron, normally a day fighter unit, operated the Firefly Mk 5 from June to December 1949 as they had problems with their Seafires.

No 810, operating FR4s as part of the 17 CAG accepted their AS5s on 17 October 1949 at St Merryn, although they kept a few FR4s for a time. The AS5s were changed for the FR5 and the squadron operated in the Korean War for a time. After returning the squadron regrouped at Arbroath 29 June 1951 still with the Firefly Mk 5. They spent most of the year afloat, first in *Glory,* then *Ocean, Theseus* and finally back to *Ocean* in December for a second spell in Korea and disbanding on their return on 17 December 1953.

No 796 Squadron formed Part II of the Observer School and usually operated the Firefly T3, but used the AS5 from July 1950 to May 1952, eventually receiving the Firefly T7.

No 820 Squadron formed up with AS5s at Eglinton on 3 July 1951 but changed them for the Firefly AS6 that December.

No 821 Squadron reformed at Arbroath 18 September 1951 as an anti-submarine squadron operating the Firefly AS6. These were changed for the FR5 and the squadron operated in Korea for a time before being disbanded at Hong Kong on 25 May 1953.

No 825 had reformed at Eglinton on 12 June 1951 with AS5s, but the squadron role changed and they used the FR5 from November. The squadron operated out in Korea and reformed afterwards at Lee-on-Solent on 2 March 1953 with the AS5. 825 then joined HMS *Eagle* for cruises and fleet exercises and then joined HMS *Warrior* in the Far East, making rocket attacks against Malayan terrorists before being disbanded on 30 December 1954 at Lee-on-Solent.

The Firefly Mk 5 was also used by the RNVR squadrons, 1830 using them temporarily in 1953, and 1844 using them at Bramcote before changing over to the AS6. Some squadrons operated the AS5 and AS6 together until fully equipped with the latter.

Firefly AS Mk 6

With the emphasis very definitely on the anti-submarine role Fairey's were asked about fitting American sonobuoys to the Firefly AS5. Using WB251 Fairey carried out a series of flight trial installations of both British and American sonobuoy equipment. Following these preliminary trials the aircraft was sent to the RAE Farnborough for further trials, including various radio tests, prior to Service testing. The results from the trials indicated that substantial revision of the trial installation would be required for the production aircraft. This in turn necessitated further design changes to accommodate internal equipment but Fairey said they still hoped to start delivery of the modified aircraft in May 1950. An Admiralty note said that in view of the changes involved the modified aircraft should have a new designation – Firefly AS Mk 6. The second machine so modified should be fully up to the new Mk 6 standard so that it could undertake radio, catapulting and arresting trials before any CS(A) Release of the type could be given. The first modified aircraft was WB423 but the first true Firefly AS Mk 6 was WB505 which first flew on 23 March 1949 and was delivered to the FAA 26 May 1950.

On 17 November 1949 a technical meeting was attended by Fairey, MOS and Admiralty representatives to review the Firefly programme. Under discussion was the early introduction (into the Mk 5) of the GM4B compass and to look at the conversion of Firefly Mk 5s into Mk 6 aircraft. It was emphasised that despite Mk 5s still being delivered, the anti-submarine role was paramount and would take precedent over all other plans. As the meeting progressed it was suggested that there was little point in turning out fully equipped Firefly 5s which, in the present situation, would be stripped out and converted to the new AS6 and that time, effort and money could be saved by producing the Firefly aircraft to the bare minimum standard until the conversion standards had been agreed. The Director of Air Equipment (DAE) stated that all Fireflies produced from then on (November 1949) would in due course have to be converted, and suggested that conversion on the production line from the Firefly Mk 5 to an AS6 should commence immediately in the following steps:

Step 1 Removal from the Firefly Mk 5 production line of all equipment not required in the Firefly AS6, or that equipment which would not require repositioning in the Firefly AS6.

Step 2 Introduction into the Firefly Mk 5 production line of the GM4B compass, extra generator, Modification 940 the long-stroke undercarriage oleo, Modification 912 the new raised snap gear, Modification 926 the redesigned deck hook damper and A1271 radio with Aerial Type 62.

Step 3 Production of Firefly AS6 aircraft, less sonobuoy receiving gear and automatic plotting board.

WD857 at White Waltham in February 1951, where it carried out trials with mocked-up streamlined sonobuoy carriers. Note how close to the ground the open doors are. *(Author's collection)*

Formation study of Fireflies from 826 Squadron, 277/R being WB430 and VX423 is 273/R. 826 was embarked in *Glory* from November 1953 to March 1954, after which it returned to the UK to re-equip with the Gannet. *(P. Warner)*

Excellent deck study of Fireflies belonging to 812 and 814 Squadrons, embarked aboard *Eagle* in late 1952. Note the two tiers of rockets under the wings of the aircraft in the foreground. *(B. J. Lowe)*

Step 4 On finalisation of all the outstanding equipment in the completed Firefly AS6, an overriding proviso shall be that all aircraft off the production line shall be sufficiently equipped to fly away.

Everyone concurred and plans for implementation of the above scheme went ahead. One can only wonder at the effects these, and the many other changes to Firefly production schedules, had on the Fairey planning department. But things began to move and on 13 April 1950 the DAE requested Fairey to transfer 19 Firefly Mk 5 aircraft, serial numbers WB422 to WB440, from Fairey's White Waltham site to Stockport/Ringway for conversion to AS Mk 6. This number grew as the Admiralty sorted out the whereabouts of the Mk 5s. Some were already at Stockport for repairs and/or having the power

wing-folding modification put in. These were all transferred to the Mk 6 conversion programme. The nineteen previously mentioned had all been converted and delivered by 26 February 1951 when the last, WB439 was delivered to RNAS Culham. Eventually some 131 aircraft were in line to be converted under the programme. It was pointed out at a further meeting in January 1951 that despite the conversion modifications the Mk 5 was not having 'non-essential' modifications, of which there were always a number being introduced throughout an aircraft's Service life based on experience, and therefore the converted Mk 5s would not be to the same standard as a true-built Mk 6! In the light of this, the Admiralty informed Fairey on 11 January 1951: 'It has been decided until further notice to suspend the conversion of Firefly Mk 5 to Mk 6 and feed in is to be stopped after the seventy-fifth aircraft.' On

This picture, taken from a Firefly Trainer, shows Firefly AS6 WD907 282/FD, which at the time it was taken was on loan to the Scottish Air Division. Then there are two Harvards, one coded 238/AC, a Sea Fury Trainer 234/AC, a Vampire with its undercarriage down, and finally a Meteor T7. *(G. R. MacDonald)*

23 May 1950 the Firefly AS Mk 6 had been released for Service use – but for ferrying purposes only. The main difference between the AS6 and the earlier marks, the note said, was the deletion of guns and provision for carriage and operation of British sonobuoys. At that time the sonobuoy equipment was not available and as flight tests had not been carried out, the clearance was for ferrying only. Naturally, this put considerable restrictions on the operation of the aircraft, no flight deck operations, no spinning, no aerobatics, no armament stores to be carried etc. until completion of trials, which wasn't too long in coming. Standard Firefly 45 and 90-gallon drop tanks could be carried and jettisoned under the same conditions as for the Mk 5. The fuel nacelle under the port wing and the ASH nacelle (or alternative fuel nacelle) under the starboard wing were part of the airframe proper, and not considered as expendable stores, although provision was made for jettisoning in an emergency. There were nine essential modifications to be done also before the aircraft was finally released. Most of these were of a radio or electrical nature.

One of the problems associated with operating naval aircraft was that environmentally it was a disaster area. Continually flying at low to medium altitudes in a salt-laden atmosphere in a metal aeroplane created all sorts of problems. Paint finishes, however good, were quickly eroded and aircraft took on that well-worn look with paint flaked off, oil and carbon stains and general dirt. Consequently when the paint laboratory at RNAS Fleetlands came up with a revised finish for naval aircraft it created quite a bit of interest. It was decided to test the new finish out on the Firefly. At the end of June 1950 the Admiralty and Fairey were in discussion about how to conduct the service trials without interfering with the all-important anti-submarine programme. It was decided to apply the new finish to both wings of twelve Firefly AS6 aircraft and see how they behaved in service. The wings were to have:

(a) A primer of mist coat type
(b) A synthetic resin base
(c) Zinc chromate pigmented which it was hoped would have high water sensitivity.

The new scheme was to Specification SAA INT 28/1948 together with synthetic resin colour paint to AME 3A. In August the Resident Technical Officer (RTO) at Fairey wrote to the Admiralty to

The RNVR air squadrons provided a good back-up to the front line squadrons. This picture shows a Firefly 6 891/BR of 1844 Squadron, based at Bramcote. *(Author's collection)*

Maintenance work being done on three Fireflies of 814 Squadron while ashore from *Vengeance* with WD890 being 220/Q.

(Author's collection)

say that these Specifications were issued to the Dominions and the USA and he did not think that firms in the UK stocked them. He did say, however, that British firms were notified that a requirement existed for a self-glossy finishing scheme of a primer and finish for naval aircraft to replace Specification DTD 517A, the more usual finished applied to naval aircraft. He was proved to be wrong when both ICI and Docker Bros. came up with the required stuff, soon followed by Cellon and Lewis Berger. The intention now was that should the trials be successful (and they were) DTD 517A would be replaced by the new finish to a new Specification DTD 772. On 31 October 1950 the MOS informed all the RTOs at all the relevant manufacturers' plants of the proposed change. This was Addendum No 2 to DARD Technical Circular No 8 (Issue 2) for Camouflage and Identification Marking of Aircraft, and stated: 'Further to Addendum 1 to this circular, High Gloss Finish to Specification DTD 772 is now acceptable for naval aircraft as an alternative to Synthetic Resin Finishes and Primer of Specification DTD 517A. Where the primer is of the etching type, and is approved to Specification DTD 900, the metal surfaces of the aircraft need not be otherwise prepared than by degreasing. All surfaces carrying DTD 772 finish must be polished with the specified materials by the manufacturers before delivery.'

The twelve Fireflies selected for the special surface finish trials were WD899, WJ106, 108, 109, 110, 112 to 117 inclusive and were despatched to Anthorn mostly in June/July 1951. Some of the initial findings were disappointing as paint appeared to flake off quite easily, but when it was found that the flaking came from flexible joint areas the concern diminished. After a time it was found that the finish to DTD 772 was better than the previous one and became the accepted preparation.

As mentioned elsewhere in the text, and associated with changes to the later marks of Firefly, one of the main problems was the deck hook damper. If this wasn't sufficiently suppressed, each time a pilot put the Firefly down hard it bounced up again and missed the wire(s) and ended up in the barrier. In January 1951 there was a proposal to go for a trial installation of a new Fairey hydraulic deck hook damper and snap gear, in conjunction with the longer travel oleo legs. Deck landing trials were required to actually test the new arrangement so Firefly AS6 WD858 was fitted up and flew aboard HMS *Vengeance*. There was a reason for the choice as 814 Squadron, aboard *Vengeance*, were already

operating the AS6. Between 15 and 22 February 1951 around sixty flights were made, mostly by 814 pilots so that the qualities of the new oleo could be assessed by experienced naval pilots. It was agreed that although the change was not 100 per cent it was a definite improvement and should be incorporated. In May Fairey wrote to the MOS to say that the Modification 940 long-stroke oleo leg had been an interim measure to meet urgent requirements. They now wanted to rectify that with a proper change to Modification 1244 as this would help even further to dampen any landing rebound.

The first front-line squadron to receive the Firefly AS6 was 814 in January 1951. This became significant because, along with 809 Squadron (Sea Hornets), they formed the 7th Night Air Group, the FAA's first all-weather unit. They had come a long way since that Admiralty memo of 1943. The Group embarked in *Vengeance* in May 1951 for work up and training. Flying the AS6 814 completed some 927 hours of night flying, recognised that year by the award of the Boyd Trophy. They joined the 15th CAG aboard HMS *Theseus* in September and then spent some time ashore before embarking in HMS *Eagle* in June 1952. The following year was spent mainly on exercises in the Mediterranean and home waters and their Firefly AS6 aircraft were replaced by Grumman Avengers on 15 March 1954.

No 826 received its Firefly AS6 aircraft on 15 May 1951 to be part of the 13th CAG. Intended to join *Eagle*, the squadron instead embarked on HMS *Illustrious* in October for an autumn cruise in the Mediterranean. The squadron transferred to HMS *Indomitable* in 1952 for a spring cruise in the Mediterranean and a summer one off Portugal. An autumn cruise was spent aboard *Theseus*, but early in 1953 they re-joined *Indomitable* for a cruise to Malta when trouble flared up in Egypt. After short spells in *Illustrious* and HMS *Glory* 814 returned home to re-equip with the Gannet.

As recorded earlier 821 Squadron reformed at Arbroath as an anti-submarine unit with the AS6, only to lose them when they accepted the FR5 to operate in the Korean War.

No 824 received eight Firefly AS6 aircraft at Eglinton on 18 February 1952 and embarked in *Illustrious* in June for fleet exercises before joining *Theseus* in January 1953 for a spell in the Mediterranean. After a short spell aboard *Illustrious* the squadron reluctantly exchanged their Fireflies for Grumman Avengers.

Two squadrons of the RNVR operated the AS6, 1840 and 1844, before the RNVR was disbanded under the defence cuts of 1957.

How many Fireflies ended their days as instructional airframes with various naval units? Here WH630 has a Class II circle against the pilot's cockpit, with its identification number of A2385, and was at Yeovilton in 1956 where it was eventually scrapped. *(J. M. G. Gradidge)*

Firefly AS6 WD907 of the Channel Air Division based at Ford shows off its fine lines. *(Flight International)*

Second line units operated the AS6 in some numbers. The Trials and Development Squadron, 744 reformed on 20 July 1951 within the Naval Anti-Submarine School at Eglinton. Two of the squadron's aircraft were fitted with a new homing devise for finding sonobuoys in the water without the need of smoke markers. To test the equipment these two aircraft, WD871 and 872 flown by Lieutenants Cowton and Rayner, with observers Lt Edwards and Lt Pritchett respectively, flew from Lee-on-Solent to Malta on Friday 5 October 1951 via Bordeaux, Istres, Rome and then Malta. The squadron disbanded at Eglinton on 1 March 1954 but reformed the same day at Culdrose as the Naval Anti-Submarine Warfare Development Unit (NASWDU). The unit moved to RAF St Mawgan on 23 October 1954 to operate alongside the equivalent RAF unit. After various trials the Fireflies were withdrawn at the end of 1955 to make way for the Gannet.

No 751 Squadron reformed on 3 December 1951 as a Radio Warfare Unit which had been built up from a naval contingent at the RAF Central Signals Establishment at Watton. Trials were conducted in electronic counter-measures equipment using a variety of aircraft including the Firefly AS6, which was retired early in 1956. No 767 Squadron, the 'Clockwork Mouse' unit operated the AS6 only between March and December 1951. The name of 'Clockwork Mouse' arose due to the large number of aircraft operated to train Deck Landing Officers (Bats) and flew round the circuit continuously.

No 771 Squadron, a Fleet Requirements Unit with origins going back to 1938, operated the AS6 between October 1950 and December 1953. On 3 March 1952 Lt Goody USN with Lt Schoenberger USAF as observer, flew Firefly AS6 WD857 aboard *Illustrious* from the Service Trials Unit at Ford. Trials were to be conducted (between deck landing practice by a Vampire and Meteor) using ASV 19A (ARI 5384). During the next two days Lt Manuel RN with Lt Schoenberger as observer, carried out twenty-one flights while testing the new ASV installation, with Lt Goody doing another five. The trials were successful and WD857 left *Illustrious* to conduct some catapult trials – the last tests in the AS6 programme.

Although the Firefly AS6 had become standard equipment with the front and second line squadrons of the FAA, it wasn't long before the continuous development of anti-submarine equipment was placing the task beyond the capability of a single operator and obsolescent aircraft, and as such the Firefly AS6 could only be regarded as a stop-gap until something better came along. In late 1948/early 1949 Fairey had proposed a three-seat interim anti-submarine Firefly converted from a production Mk 4 or 5 aimed only as a stop-gap until the new GR17/45 (Gannet) came along.

Chapter 10
Danish Tugs

IN THE early summer of 1951 the Royal Danish Air Force (RDAF) placed an order with Fairey for two Firefly target towers. The Admiralty released Z1842 and Z2020 to Fairey and these eventually became 625 and 626 in the RDAF. Although this three numeral code was officially preceded by the number 64, i.e., 64–625, it was never applied to the aircraft. Both aircraft were delivered from storage at RNAS Abbotsinch to Ringway on 7 March 1951 for overhaul and conversion to the target towing role.

Firefly TT Mk 1 625 was completed in September that year, test flown and delivered on 6 October. No 626 came out of the factory during

October and was delivered to Vaerlose on 26 November 1951. Both were painted yellow overall with serials and fleet numbering in black, with RDAF markings in national colours.

The two Fireflies were operated successfully until 1952 when the Royal Canadian Navy presented four Firefly Mk 1s to the RDAF under the Mutual Aid Military Assistance Program. When delivered the RCN Fireflies were still in their Mk 1 configuration and not converted for target towing duties. The four Fireflies were MB579 (630), PP413 (627), PP457 (628) and PP460 (629), with the last three being written off in accidents. Conversion of the Fireflies for target

Firefly TT Mk 1 No 625 of the RDAF airborne on a sortie over Denmark. Note the early flat pilot's hood and the en route position of the winch windmill to reduce drag. *(Royal Danish Air Force Official)*

One of the ex-Royal Canadian Navy Fireflies, No 630, at the refuelling stop at Esbjerg airfield, 23 July 1958. Note the later style pilot's hood. *(Jens Lovmand Hvid)*

towing was done at the RDAF workshops at Vaerlose from kits supplied by the Fairey company.

On 17 January 1955 Lt Moller, with winch operator Warrant Officer Lund, in Firefly 627, made a heavy landing at Ronne Airport, Bornholm and damaged it beyond repair. Another heavy landing accident wrote off 629 on 14 January 1957 when Lt Larsen, with winch operator Sgt Lyngbye, landed at Vaerlose. Lt Krag and winch operator Sgt Christensen were taking off in 628 on 20 February 1957 when the engine cut and the Firefly was written off in the ensuing forced landing. All the crews escaped unharmed.

While being operated by the RDAF, the Fireflies were frequently used over the gunnery range off the north-western coast of the island of Romo, which is the southernmost of the three Danish North Sea islands, themselves just off the Jutland coast. When on these missions the distance was too great for the aircraft to fly to the range, carry out a detail, and then fly back to base afterwards. Refuelling stops were made at Esbjerg, a grass airfield, where fuel was pumped into the Firefly by a wobble pump attached to a forty-gallon drum.

In May 1959 the three remaining Fireflies, 625, 626 and 630, were sold to the Swedish civil target towing company, Svensk Flygtjanst, who put them on the Swedish register as SE-CHL, CHM and CHN respectively but only used them for spares.

Chapter 11
Combat Again – Korea

AFTER THE END of the Second World War on 27 November 1945 the USA, USSR and UK signed the Moscow Agreement proposing a four-power trusteeship for Korea. By 1947 those powers still had not reached agreement on how best to carry out their plan. In 1948 the Government of the Republic of Korea was formed and recognised by the United Nations (UN) General Assembly as the lawful Governing body for Korea. Unfortunately the country by that time was split into two zones, the northern one controlled by the Russians and the southern one controlled by the Americans. By the end of the year the Russians had set up the northern zone with a communist satellite government and withdrawn their occupation forces. In June 1949 the southern zone became the Democratic Republic of Korea (ROK) and after recognition by the UN Assembly the Americans withdrew their forces.

The ROK military force was built up purely for defensive purposes and was in no way able to carry out any form of offensive action. This was entirely different to the North Korean forces who were built up mostly with aid from Russia and later, China, into a powerful offensive command. With the situation in their favour the North Koreans crossed the 38th Parallel at 04.00 hours on 25 June 1950. Utilising T34 tanks they swept southwards against the lightly armoured ROK forces. Their objectives were Kaesong and Chunchon. To support this attack more North Korean marines and infantry stormed ashore on the east coast near Kangnung and by 09.00 hours that same morning Kaesong had fallen. The following day the UN Security Council condemned the attack and called upon the North Koreans to cease fire and withdraw north of the 38th Parallel. On 27 June the UN Security Council had received no answer to their request and called on all members of the UN to support the ROK. The same day President Truman ordered American air and naval forces to give support. Remote from America and Europe, it would be some time before any such support could reach the war zone

and stem the flow. The North Koreans, realising this, moved swiftly southwards seizing the Republican capital, Seoul, and advancing to within fifty miles of the south coast port of Pusan. Although there was little hope of immediate help to the hard-pressed South Koreans, UN naval help was much more quickly to hand. The Royal Navy Far East Fleet, some twenty-two ships in all, were spread over a large area but as luck would have it, some of them were actually cruising in Japanese waters when the invasion took place. The Commander-in-Chief of the Far East Station at that time, Admiral Sir Patrick Brind KCB CBE, had decided that the majority of the Fleet would sail in Japanese waters that summer to avoid the heat of Singapore or Hong Kong. Within five days of the attack, the light fleet carrier, HMS *Triumph,* the cruisers *Belfast* and *Jamaica,* destroyers *Cossack* and *Consort* with frigates *Black Swan, Alacrity* and *Hart,* were at action stations off the Korean coast, a prime example of the high state of training and readiness the British ships were in at that time. HMS *Triumph,* commanded by Captain A. D. Torlesse, had on board the 13th CAG consisting of No 827 Squadron commanded by Lt/Cdr B. C. Lyons RN with twelve Firefly FR1s, and 800 Squadron with twelve Seafire F47s.

Plans to combine a British and American force, Task Force 77, took place under Rear-Admiral Hoskins USN who was to be in tactical command aboard his flagship, the carrier USS *Valley Forge.* The two fleets rendezvoused on 2 July and sailed north carrying out reconnaissance and anti-submarine patrols. At dawn the following day twelve Fireflies and nine Seafires were launched to attack Haeju airfield with R/Ps. No enemy aircraft were seen but hangars and buildings were damaged for no loss to the striking force. At 11.00 hours the next day twelve Fireflies and seven Seafires flew off to attack a railway bridge between Haeju and Youau. Two hits were recorded on the bridge and then aircraft attacked targets of opportunity including some troops. A number of things quickly became apparent. The Fireflies (and Seafires) were all showing their age

A Firefly FR1 of 827 Squadron is 'waved off' from the approach to HMS *Triumph*. Note the Union Jack painted on the deck and the UN identification stripes on the Firefly. *(Imperial War Museum)*

and credit must be made to the maintenance mechanics and fitters who kept them flying. Another problem was that the Fireflies only had a limited range of about 130 miles radius. Rather than set up a shore base near the centre of operations it was decided to use the FAA base at Sembawang on Singapore. HMS *Unicorn*, with her workshop and stores ashore became the replenishment carrier for the rest of the war. During these early days of the war the Fireflies provided anti-submarine patrols with the Seafires giving cover with CAPs. HMS *Triumph* returned to Sasebo on 22 July for some urgent repairs, and the CAG took the opportunity of transferring twelve spare aircraft from *Unicorn*. Returning to the west coast two days later the squadrons found themselves yet again restricted to CAP and anti-submarine work, while the aircraft from *Valley Forge* attacked targets in support of UN troops retreating through south-west Korea. This was still done with enthusiasm and on each of the four days

of operations the ships' aircraft did forty-two sorties. A Seafire was shot down by a B-29 crew and this prompted the authorities to put markings on each aircraft so that they would be identified by UN forces. This consisted of black and white stripes around the wings and rear fuselage similar to those used by the Allies after the D-Day landings. The operations with the US 7th Fleet came to an end on 30 July when *Triumph* sailed for Kure to carry out some much needed maintenance.

This took ten days, after which she proceeded to the Yellow Sea for a solo blockade patrol. This was due to an American carrier, USS *Philippine Sea* joining Task Force 77 and releasing *Triumph* for roles more suited to her complement. The blockade was to prevent the enemy from supplying his forward areas by sea and the interdiction of any suspicious surface craft. The Fireflies were used principally for coastal surveillance, the length of their beat representing something like the distance between the Thames

Estuary and the Firth of Forth. Seafires provided CAP and extended aerial reconnaissance. Targets were few with an enemy sea force unable to match what the UN forces could provide. What they had moved mainly by night and lay up under camouflage during the day. In a rare appearance, a pair of IL-10 aircraft of the North Korean air force attacked the British destroyer HMS *Comus* but failed to register a hit. It did make everyone realise that they could not drop their guard, even for a second. A small group of enemy ships was detected in the Taedong estuary on 16 August and six Fireflies with six Seafires, all armed with R/P, damaged a coaster, a minesweeper and a medium-sized freighter.

A third patrol started on 26 August. On 29 August a Firefly failed to pick up a wire on landing and went into the barrier. In doing so, the propeller broke and half a blade flew off and hit the operations room, shattering the glass and fatally wounding Lt/Cdr I. MacLachlan DSC RN

the Commanding Officer of 800 Squadron. The squadron's senior pilot, Lt T. D. Handley RN succeeded him and in doing so become the last CO of a front-line Seafire squadron. On 1 September the last reserve aircraft, twelve Fireflies and fourteen Seafires were transferred from *Unicorn* to *Triumph*. Most of these were in poor condition having been held back in the hope that they would not be needed. The Seafires in particular suffered from heavy usage, and damage to the rear fuselage from heavy landings only aggravated the work of the maintenance crews, made more difficult by the poor condition of the replacement aircraft. *Triumph* steamed for the Sea of Japan on 7 September to begin a series of strikes against the enemy's railway system. During the next two days the Fireflies of 827 and Seafires of 800 Squadron made rocket and cannon attacks against targets between the old border and Wonsan. One train was destroyed, rolling stock set on fire, three tunnels blocked by firing rockets into both

A pair of Firefly FR5s of 810 Squadron returning to HMS *Theseus* after a strike against enemy targets. The ship below is the Canadian destroyer *Nootka*. *(Imperial War Museum)*

entrances and a coastal vessel were all targets for *Triumph*'s aircraft.

The enemy had been stopped, and held at the Pusan perimeter, but it had been a close thing. The fact that the UN forces had air supremacy and control of the sea lanes meant that supplies and communications allowed a turn to the offensive. The overall UN commander was General MacArthur of World War II fame and he ordered an amphibious landing at Inchon, South-West Korea, well behind the enemy front and a direct threat to his communications and supply routes. This was launched on 15 September 1950, followed the next day by a UN breakout from the Naktong Line near Pusan, but it was the 25th before the North Korean resistance faltered and fell back. UN forces re-took Seoul three days later. At dawn on 15 September the Fireflies and Seafires from *Triumph* provided air cover for the assault convoys as they moved up the west coast of Korea. They were also called on to provide blockade patrols to prevent any interference from an enemy sea force that might attempt to stop the landings. To cut down the time spent on patrol six Fireflies were fitted with two 45-gallon drop tanks which gave them around two hours' patrol time. Air support for the actual landings was provided by the American carriers. Fireflies spotted for HMS *Kenya* and *Jamaica* when they bombarded shore targets but this was the only contribution by FAA aircraft to the actual landings. No opportunity was lost to attack small surface craft, including junks and coastal freighters.

The value of off-shore air and naval forces was amply demonstrated when two divisions of American marines and infantry were put ashore at Inchon. This was under the guns manned by the crews of 261 British, American and Canadian warships. These landings have been ranked as one of the most successful amphibious landings in history. Within five days the American troops had reached the outskirts of Seoul. The combined effect of the UN break-out through the Pusan perimeter, and the seaborne attack at Inchon was too much for the thinly stretched North Korean army. As quickly as it had advanced southwards, it now retreated northwards, beyond the 38th Parallel. The story goes that on the withdrawal of *Triumph* on 20 September she had only two serviceable Fireflies and a single Seafire, eight other aircraft were flyable but not fit for missions over enemy territory. Lt/Cdr 'Ben' Lyons says: 'All 827's Fireflies were old, and although the maintenance crews did very good work, they were just about on their last legs. In fact, when *Triumph* withdrew

from the line, our engineering officer declared all of them unfit to fly in peacetime.' When *Triumph* left for Hong Kong on 25 September 1950 she went with the admiration and praise of the US Navy Commander, Far East, Admiral C. T. Joy. He had been most impressed by the dogged and determined manner in which the small British carrier had carried out its tasks with obsolete piston-engined aircraft. It was perhaps unfortunate that the first carrier to partake of the action in Korea was still equipped with the oldest operational aircraft still in front-line FAA service. Only the effort put in by all concerned allowed the proud record of not missing a single operation between 3 July and 20 September 1950. At Hong Kong, *Triumph* was relieved by HMS *Theseus* and she sailed for the UK, arriving in November 1950. Her aircraft were disembarked and this signified the end of another era, the withdrawal from front line service of both the Seafire and Firefly 1.

HMS *Theseus* arrived in the war zone early in October with the 17 CAG aboard under Lt/Cdr F. Stovin-Bradford RN, the ship being commanded by Captain A. S. Bolt DSO DSC. The most noticeable difference was the aircraft used by the 17 CAG, which consisted of twelve Firefly Mk 5s of 810 Squadron commanded by Lt/Cdr K. S. Pattisson RN and 21 Sea Fury FB11s of 807 Squadron under Lt/Cdr M. P. G. Smith RN. *Theseus* became part of Task Element 95.11 whose role was to blockade the enemy-held west coast and prevent any supplies or amphibious forces from getting through. The carrier's first operational patrol was between 9 and 22 October 1950, with strikes against Chinnampo and Haeju. The previous day a Firefly had gone through the barriers, wrecking itself and two others in the deck park. No 810 Squadron was thus reduced to nine aircraft even before operations started. Fireflies attacked a railway bridge on the 10th destroying two centre spans and then attacking road bridges. By now the North Koreans were in full flight northwards and it became difficult to determine where the front line was. A UN line was set up just north of Pyongyang to Wonsan and the aircraft from *Theseus* attacked the port of Chinnampo which the UN command wished to open up as a supply port. On 13/14 October the Fireflies carried out highly accurate dive-bombing and rocket attacks against some of the dockside buildings and stores. Over 16/17 October other strikes were made on Chinnampo, Sariwon and Mongumpo but operations were then suspended again for a few days while the position ashore was clarified. Bad weather restricted operations on 18/19 October but

Deck landing was always a hazardous occupation, and if you did not get it quite right you ended up in the barriers, like this Firefly FR5 WB382 206/R of 812 Squadron aboard HMS *Glory*. *(G. A. Genks)*

aircraft roamed the Shinanju-Chougju province before *Theseus* withdrew and returned to Sasebo. The Fireflies had flown 120 operational sorties, the Sea Furies 264.

After four days replenishment in Sasebo, *Theseus* sailed on 27 October for a second series of operations which ran from 29 October to 3 November 1950. This was a short and uneventful patrol to cover some minesweeping operations in the Chinnampo Estuary. Six Fireflies had to be left ashore this time as there were problems with the catapult. Two days later hordes of Chinese 'volunteers' raced across the border and proceeded to attack UN forces. *Theseus* meantime had been ordered to Hong Kong as it was deemed unnecessary to have an aircraft carrier on station in the Yellow Sea. The crossing of the border by the Chinese became a major offensive and the UN forces, under extreme pressure, began to retreat. *Theseus* was immediately recalled to provide badly needed air support and from 5 to 26 December 1950 operated at very high pressure attacking enemy positions, vehicles, bridges, etc. in an effort to help UN forces find time to regroup and stem the flood. During this period the Fireflies flew 207 sorties out of an Air Group total of 630. Because of the effects of operating around the

clock on aircrews and aircraft it was found necessary to organise alternating patrols of 9/10 days and then a similar number off for replenishment and rest while the US Navy carriers had a go. The enemy offensive slowed, and finally halted. There were other operating problems, for instance *Theseus,* in need of a hull clean, could only make about twenty-two knots. The Firefly FR5, fully loaded, needed twenty-one knots down the deck when being catapulted, but a fully laden Sea Fury required twenty-eight knots. To alleviate the problem it was decided to use the Fireflies as bombers and arm the Sea Furies with rockets giving them a lighter load. The weather was frequently foul, consisting of sea fog, intense cold and frequent gales. There was also the added threat of isolated enemy aircraft getting through to attack aircraft, such as on 11 December when MiG 15s attacked the ship's helicopter while airlifting some stragglers from the Chanyan area. The attack came just as the Sea Fury cover had left to be relieved and the new cover had not arrived and they were extremely lucky to get away with no damage. As the year drew to a close the 17 CAG were awarded the Boyd Trophy, presented each year to the FAA unit of outstanding merit.

January 1951 saw the launch of a new offensive by the Chinese/North Korean armies and by the middle of the month the UN forces had been pushed back to a line south of Suwon and Wonju. The enemy were held at this point with the UN forces fighting back hard and gaining ground. *Theseus* rejoined the fray and on 7 January she was operating off the west coast in support of the US 25th Division. Strikes were co-ordinated by airborne forward controllers flying in unarmed Harvard trainers, known by US forces as 'Mosquito Flights' and was a highly dangerous occupation. Bad weather now hampered flying and through 12/13 January the carrier experienced blizzards with ice and snow on the flight deck. The catapult started to play up again and became unserviceable during the morning of the 14th. Fortunately some aircraft were already airborne so the Sea Furies could have room for a free take-off, at the expense of drop tanks and external armaments. The Fireflies were launched by RATOG with full loads and attacked enemy positions in the Suwon-Inchon area. The US carrier USS *Bataan* arrived during January and this allowed *Theseus* to withdraw to Sasebo on 16 January for a well earned rest and some maintenance. During this period the Fireflies had flown 102 sorties out of a total of 301.

The next series of patrols was from 26 January to 3 February 1951 when *Theseus* relieved *Bataan*. Weather conditions were much improved and some 408 sorties were flown of which the Fireflies did 151. Four Sea Furies were lost during this patrol, three to enemy action and one crashing in the sea. On 2 February *Theseus* set a new record when sixty-six operational sorties were flown in one day. The following day they withdrew again for rest and replenishment. Bad weather yet again hampered operations during the next patrol period of 14 to 23 February. This resulted in 380 sorties, of which Fireflies contributed 137, much of these being for reconnaissance or anti-submarine patrols. On the 14th Petty Officer Airman J. F. Wigley was killed when a Firefly landing on inadvertently fired one of its guns, this being the third occurrence that day. The patrol ended and *Theseus* withdrew; her next series being from 5 to 13 March. Some 118 sorties were flown by the Fireflies providing close support for the army, bombardment spotting for HMS *Kenya* and some CAPs. Rail and road bridges were attacked on a daily basis but light flak was now increasing as they were brought in to protect the enemy supply routes. On 12 March, Lt D. L. James flying Firefly WB408 was badly damaged by flak but managed to get down at Suwon airfield. Not so lucky was Lt C. G. Cooles RN with observer F/Lt D. W. Grey RAF when they were shot down the following day in Firefly WB269. The number of sorties flown in the next patrol, 23 March to 1 April, went up to 339, of which the Fireflies did 144. The nature of the work remained the same but Lt/Cdr G. R. Coy's Firefly was hit by a 40 mm shell on one patrol and although severely damaged he managed to land back on *Theseus*.

The next session was to be the last for *Theseus*, running from 9 to 19 April with Fireflies flying 146 sorties out of 393. Targets tended to be the same, bridges, rail installations, rolling stock, supply depots, road transport etc along with armed reconnaissance and bombardment spotting. One Firefly and five Sea Furies were lost or badly damaged. Rear Admiral Scott-Moncrieff DSO RN took over command of the task group on 14 April and *Theseus* transferred her affections back to the west coast. Some 94 sorties were flown over 17/18 April before she withdrew. During the seven months that *Theseus* had been in the Far East she had flown 3,489 operational sorties on eighty-six operational flying days. Her replacement, HMS *Glory*, arrived on 22 April and she sailed for the UK three days later.

Embarked in *Glory* was the 14 CAG consisting of 812 Squadron commanded by Lt/Cdr F. A. Swanton RN with twelve Firefly FR5s, and 804 Squadron commanded by Lt/Cdr J. S. Bailey RN with twenty-one Sea Fury FB11s, plus a Dragonfly rescue helicopter. The first operational patrol was on 28 April when fifteen aircraft were launched and a Sea Fury was lost to unknown causes. The new air group quickly found its feet and found themselves on similar types of strikes or patrols as their predecessors, losing another Sea Fury on 2 May. The usual bad weather intervened but between 13 and 15 May the Air Group flew 155 operational sorties, and lost another Sea Fury. In each case the pilot was rescued. Lt R. Williams flying a Firefly was hit by ground fire on the 18th and had to ditch in shallow water about seventy miles ahead of the carrier, rescue for the crew being effected soon afterwards. HMS *Glory* now withdrew to replenish and the USS *Bataan* took over.

The ship was back in the operational area by 3 June, and the following day a Sea Fury was ditched off Choda Island after engine failure. Pilot S. W. E. Ford was killed on the 7th when he failed to get clear of his Firefly when ground fire forced him to ditch ahead of the ship. Lt R. E. Wilson in Firefly WB363 was also hit by ground fire and ditched near Kirin Do, but he and his observer

Typical winter conditions aboard HMAS *Sydney* during the winter of 1951/52. It is perhaps interesting to note that the aircraft have 'Royal Navy' on the rear fuselage although in Royal Australian Navy service. *(Australian War Memorial)*

were rescued unhurt. Another Firefly was damaged landing on, as were two Sea Furies. The ship had to return to harbour after this when the aviation fuel was found to be contaminated. Although rumours were rife about sabotage it was found that the supply ship, RFA *Wave Premier,* had contaminated pipes. This meant an enormous task for the maintenance ratings aboard *Glory* as all the contaminated fuel in the ship and aircraft had to be purged and replaced with fresh. So it was 2 July before she was back on station, and then the Task Group commander, Admiral Scott-Moncrieff joined them for a couple of days to watch the flying. It was while he was aboard that the ship had its 1000th operational sortie flown. The weather for once was good and the Air Group were clocking up over fifty sorties per day. This may not seem much on paper but it meant a lot of the enemy had a rough time. This constant launching, patrols, strikes and landings took their toll on ship, aircraft and aircrews, one result being the loss of the catapult after an accident and aircraft reverted to RATOG for launching. Lt J. H. Sharp and Aircrewman I. G. B. Wells were killed when their Firefly was shot down in flames seconds after releasing their bombs. Another Firefly, WB380, was lost when it crashed north of Sariwon on 16 July killing its crew, Lt R. Williams and his observer, Lt I. R. Shepley. Three Sea Furies were lost over the next three days, two of the pilots being saved.

HMS *Glory* was then sent to the Han River estuary to join the USS *Sicily* where they carried out 101 sorties around the neutral area of Kaesong while peace talks were going on. During this period the aircraft expended more than 1000 rockets, over 100 500lb bombs and nearly 49,000 rounds of 20 mm ammunition. Despite poor weather conditions and the number of sorties flown, no aircraft were lost to any cause. Operations between 16 and 24 August were curtailed by the arrival of Typhoon Marge, but were back on line by 1 September. With a spell of good weather the ship went back to achieving fifty-odd sorties a day, a record being set on 9 September when eighty-four were flown. Although the main concentration of effort was along the Han, strikes were also made at Chongchon and Chinnampo and many river craft were destroyed or damaged. The only casualty was a Firefly flown by Lt Morris. He was hit by flak and had to put down in some mud flats south east of Haeju in enemy territory. After the helicopter had rescued them the Firefly was set on fire. This brought to a close the patrols of *Glory,* for having completed 2892 operational sorties, she was now relieved by HMAS *Sydney* at the beginning of October 1951.

HMAS *Sydney* was an Australian light fleet carrier which had been launched as HMS *Terrible* on 30 September 1944 and sold to the Australian Navy in 1948. She was commanded by Captain D.

H. Harries RAN and her Air Group commander was Lt/Cdr M. F. Fell RN. The Air Group consisted of 817 Squadron with Firefly FR5s and commanded by Lt/Cdr R. N. Lunberg RN, two Sea Fury squadrons, 805 and 808 commanded by Lt/Cdr W. G. Bowles and J. L. Appleby respectively, and a rescue helicopter loaned by the US Navy. This was to be the first occasion that an aircraft carrier of a Dominion Navy had gone into action.

Sydney began her first patrol on 4 October 1951 off the west coast. The targets for the first day of operations on 5 October were a bridge at Chinnampo, another bridge at Songhwa and a reconnaissance along the Chodo/Changyou road. Lt/Cdr Lunberg led the first section of Fireflies away at 07.00 hours, all armed with two 500 lb bombs. Fireflies usually flew as a section of four aircraft and when the bombs had gone they would go down and strafe targets using the 20 mm cannon. However, the weather that day was not very good consisting of overcast and low lying mist. The following day it was another bridge at Allyong, and on the 7th buildings at Souchin. After three days operations *Sydney* moved to the east coast for a two-day attack on enemy installations and troop concentrations in the Kojo

area. The weather on the 10th was again poor with an 1800 ft cloud base. Nevertheless, Lt/Cdr Lunberg led off a section of Fireflies at 07.30 hours making bomb attacks on gun sites and spotting for HMS *Belfast*. Later that morning he led another strike and attacked a supply dump. At the end of the day sixty-nine sorties had been flown by the Air Group. On the 11th two of the Firefly sorties attacked troop concentrations in the Kojo area and at the end of the day a record ninety-three sorties had been flown, twenty-seven of them by the Fireflies. *Sydney* then withdrew to Sasebo to replenish, but on the 14th she put to sea to avoid an approaching typhoon. Unfortunately the warning arrived too late and at sea that night she was the subject of 90 mph winds. One Sea Fury was washed overboard and four other aircraft damaged beyond repair.

On 18 October *Sydney* returned to the attack, the Fireflies going for railway tunnels and bridges with some success, while others attacked buildings at Sinchon. Trafalgar Day was celebrated by a highly successful series of strikes against enemy junks in the Yalu estuary which, it was believed, were concentrating for an invasion of Taehwa Do Island. On 23 October one of the Firefly targets was a railway bridge east of Changyou. Lt/Cdr

Two railway bridges go down after bomb attacks by Fireflies from HMS *Glory*. *(Lt/Cdr J. Hone)*

A replacement Firefly being hoisted aboard HMS *Glory* at Iwakuni in Southern Japan. *(Imperial War Museum)*

Lunberg leading the early strike said, 'This was the first attack where we used 25 to 30 second delay fuses on the 500 lb bombs. I was most disappointed as leader to get a hit and see the bombs bounce off the bridge before exploding.' Later in the day *Sydney* provided an air search for ditched American airmen in the north east of Korea Bay. A Sea Fury pilot detected a survivor and towards dusk a Firefly dropped a dinghy and supplies. The airman was later rescued by a boat from the Australian frigate *Murchison*. The 25th also turned out to be a memorable day. One of the early Firefly strikes was a rail bridge north of Wonto and Lunberg was frustrated again as his bombs bounced off the bridge to explode harmlessly alongside. He strafed targets in Anak to vent his feelings. One of the Sea Furies was hit by flak and had to ditch, Lt Wheatley being rescued by the helicopter. Lt/Cdr Appleby was also hit by flak and just managed to limp into Kimpo airfield. Then in the afternoon five Fireflies went after the rail tunnels south of Sariwon but ran into intense flak and Sub-Lt N. D. MacWilliam after being hit carried out a skilful forced landing in enemy territory. *Sydney*'s helicopter was despatched with

Sea Furies, and an odd RAAF Meteor 8, as top cover. The Firefly crew on the ground meanwhile had been keeping the enemy at bay with their sub-machine guns and as the helicopter arrived USN Aviation Mechanicians Mate, C. G. Goulding leapt out and immediately shot two of the enemy who had crept to within fifteen yards of the Firefly. The rescue was effected without loss and an hour later the helicopter, and its escorts, landed with the last light of the day at Kimpo. On the 26th Lunberg led an early morning strike against some rail tunnels at Hyuam-Dong but failed to close them. The railway line from Chaeryong to Changyou was cut by bombs and box cars and a power house strafed. That day *Sydney* returned to Sasebo for replenishment.

The next patrol ran from 5 to 13 November 1951 with a sad start when Lt K. E. Clarkson was killed when he failed to pull out of a dive while attacking enemy transport. Lunberg said: 'Our targets this time were again mainly railway ones, the Sea Furies concentrating on marine targets. On the 5th we went back to the bridge north of Wonto and on the 6th a bridge at Soktong-Ni. The latter was difficult due to low cloud and poor visibility and we were led initially to the wrong target. It was a bridge at Sach'ang on the 7th and on the 8th back to Wonto, which I mercifully hit. On 10th and 11th, we attacked a bridge at Soktan-Ni, eventually breaking it on the 11th and experiencing heavy flak at Chaeryong. The 1000th operational sortie was flown on the 12th and the next day, the last of this particular patrol, I led the section against some troop and store targets at Kumsong-Ni after which there was a large smoke cloud to 4000 ft.'

On 18 November *Sydney* sailed from Sasebo forming part of Task Group 95.8 under the command of Rear-Admiral A. K. Scott-Moncrieff DSO RN flying his flag in HMS *Belfast,* for a co-ordinated strike against the industrial centre of Hungnam on the east coast. The guns of the Task Force opened fire shortly after dawn on 20 November as a preliminary to ten attacks by *Sydney*'s aircraft. Over two days more than 100 sorties were flown before *Sydney* departed for the west coast. Here snow and high winds prevented resumption of flying operations until the 24th but adverse weather still limited operational flying. Sub-zero temperatures were experienced but

flying resumed on 27th with another Firefly strike on the Wonto rail bridge. Both this one and one at Upchon-Dong were broken and the last bombs were dropped on another at Ongjin. On the last day of the patrol a railway bridge at Soktan-Ni was bombed successfully being finally broken by pilot Oakley.

A spell of fine weather set in for the next patrol, 7 to 17 December 1951, which allowed the ship a high rate of continuous sorties. Targets were rail bridges, troop concentrations in the Changyou/Hanchon areas, the Chinnampo waterfront, small coastal ships and communication transport. The Fireflies attacked a rail bridge north of Sinch'ang-Ni on the 13th with Sub-Lt Roland breaking the span. On the 17th the Fireflies were loaded with two 1000 lb bombs to suppress some enemy 76 mm gun positions at Am'gak. The patrol ended on 18 December with a tally of 383 sorties, of which 817 had done 123. Twenty-five aircraft suffered flak damage and five had been lost, the majority of the hits being sustained in the heavily defended Am'gak Peninsula area.

A brief respite for *Sydney* ended on 27 December when she left to relieve USS

Firefly VX420 237/R of 810 Squadron, ashore in South Korea. Note the absence of UN stripes, which seemed to disappear as the war went on and aircraft were repaired and returned to service with whichever unit was on station at the time. *(J. M. G. Gradidge)*

Arming a Firefly with standard 3 inch R/Ps with 60 lb warheads. The pigtail drooping at the rear has to be plugged in to make the rocket 'live'. *(Lt/Cdr J. F. K. McGrail)*

Badoeng Strait on the west coast. The weather was bad over the next couple of days but some operations were flown and Sub-Lt Simpson brought his Firefly back damaged by light flak. Lt/Cdr Lunberg picks up the story:

'We had more success on the 31st when we broke the rail bridge north of Sinchang-Ni and damaged the diversionary bridge at Singang-Ni as well. On New Year's Day we gave air support to UN troops invading the island of Yongho-Do and I was hit by light machine gun fire and made an emergency landing back on the carrier. The next day was another sad one for the ship, Sub-Lt Coleman flying a Sea Fury disappeared in cloud and was never seen again, despite searches over the sea for wreckage, and in the afternoon Sub-Lt Dunlop, also in a Sea Fury iced up and was hit by flak on his way to Seoul. I was leading four Fireflies on 3 January 1952 when we went after some more bridges along the Chonsan-Chaeryong-Changyen line. Myself and Genge fixed the diversionary bridge while

Bailey and Lee hit one to the north. The 5th saw one of the few successes at blocking rail tunnels. This one was north east of Ongjin and Lee put his bomb right in the entrance. Large puffs of smoke came out of the other end with suspected steam from the bombed end. We sailed for Sasebo the next day after flying 105 sorties.'

Sydney now sailed for her last patrol of the series, this running from 17 to 24 January and Lunberg continues:

'This patrol started with my fortieth operational patrol against rail bridges at Samchon and Sinwon where we left them both broken. The next day we made a bombing attack on the village of Hanun-Dong and Sub-Lt Rowland went so low he was hit by his own bomb casing in the tailplane! It was back to village attacks on the 19th when we went to Kachyou and Tangcha on the Yonan Peninsula, leaving large fires everywhere. On the 20th we went to the Wonto bridges and one just west of Haeju. In a model attack we cut both Wonto bridges and removed the span of the other. My last operational sortie over Korea was 23 January when we bombed the village of Taetan.'

During her period in the war zone *Sydney*'s aircraft flew 2366 sorties of which 743 were by the Fireflies of 817. During 564 of those sorties the Fireflies expended ten 1000 lb bombs and 1118 500 lb bombs. Three DSCs, one Bar to a DSC and one DSM were awarded to *Sydney*'s personnel for Korean service, only three pilots were killed and one wounded.

HMS *Glory* replaced *Sydney* for a short spell running from February to April 1952 during which some 689 sorties were flown, 104 in one day. The Fireflies of 812 were now commanded by Lt/Cdr J. M. Culbertson. The final patrol for *Glory* started on 18 April.

HMS *Ocean* arrived in May to take over from *Glory*. Aboard was the 17 CAG comprising 825 Squadron with Fireflies and commanded by Lt/Cdr C. K. Roberts, and 802 with Sea Furies commanded by Lt/Cdr S. F. F. Shotton. The first patrol did not get off to a very good start with a Firefly and Sea Fury both ditching to unknown causes. All the crews were rescued but Lt K. Macdonald was killed when his Sea Fury crashed on the Am'gak Peninsula after being hit by flak. Losses came thick and fast, a Firefly ditched on

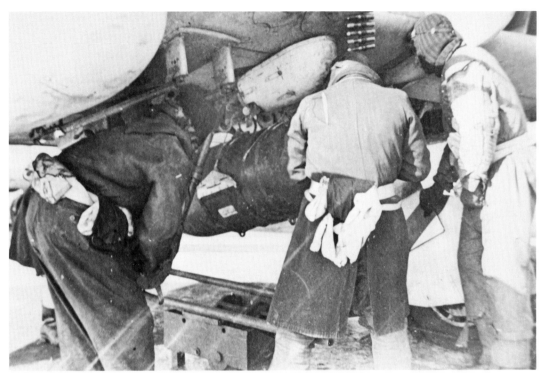

Smartly dressed deck crews winch up a bomb to its underwing carrier on a Firefly. The links of 20 mm ammunition hanging over the leading edge are part of the aircraft being re-armed. *(Lt/Cdr J. F. K. McGrail)*

16 May, a Sea Fury was lost on 18 May when the pilot baled out after being set on fire by flak. Another Firefly was shot down the following day, crashing about seven miles north of Kaesong unfortunately with Lt/Cdr T. J. C. Williamson-Napier and Aircrewman I. L. M. Edwards losing their lives. Although the weather for *Ocean*'s second patrol, which started 29 May, was kind, the stocks of rockets and bombs were limited and the Air Group was restricted to sixty-eight sorties a day. There was some flexibility with this because if the weather wasn't good enough for a day or two then the sorties could be increased when the weather improved. Despite these restrictions some 544 operational sorties were flown during the patrol. Engine reliability became a problem around this time with 825 having three Fireflies with connecting rod failures. To round the patrol off

Lt McGrail of 821 Squadron about to climb into a Firefly before a strike against Korean targets. Lt McGrail carried out 118 operational sorties while in the war zone. Note the scantily clad lady on the engine cowling. *(Lt/Cdr J. F. K. McGrail)*

two Sea Furies were lost on 4 June to enemy action but the pilots were rescued.

For the next patrol there had been a change in target selection policy whereby attacks could now be made on electrical installations where previously it was not allowed. A series of co-ordinated attacks was made by elements of the US 5th Air Force and Task Force 77 on 24 June when they went for the main industrial areas around Fusen, Kyosen, Chosin and Suiho. Low lying mist restricted operations for a few days but then a series of strikes was made in the Taedong estuary and to suppress the flak a naval bombardment was laid on. The crew of a Firefly were rescued when they ditched west of Choda on 24 July, but the new CO of 802, Lt/Cdr R. A. Dick, was killed when his Sea Fury was shot down over the River Taedong. Bad weather settled in again and the skipper of *Ocean* steamed north and found the conditions much better. Although this allowed the ship's aircraft to operate again, displaying the advantages of a moving base to a fixed ground one, they were seventy miles further north and found themselves meeting the enemy in the air. On 24 July four Fireflies returning from a strike, one of them badly damaged, were attacked by four Mig 15s with some others giving cover. Three of the Fireflies were damaged and one, VT478, had to ditch in the sea west of Choda but was picked up later. A similar attack was made on a formation of Sea Furies but they held their own and damaged one MiG. A return to Sasebo was a welcome respite, but not for long.

The ship returned to the west coast on 8 August in what was now a hotly contested air space battle between the US 5th Air Force and the communist air forces of China and North Korea. The requirement for supportive strikes for UN forces by the FAA, which was usually at least two a day, meant it would not be long before there would be other encounters with the MiGs. The next day four Sea Furies were attacked by eight MiGs north of Chinnampo and although no Sea Furies were lost, one MiG was shot down, the credit going to the flight leader, Lt P. Carmichael. Four more Sea Furies were attacked later in the day and Lt Clark's aircraft was hit, setting the drop tanks on fire. Lt H. M. McEnery managed to get a long burst in and damaged one MiG as they withdrew. Lt Clark now got rid of his drop tanks and with some skilful flying landed back on deck. It was his first operational flight. The day was rounded off with two other Sea Furies being attacked over Chinnampo, one having to make a wheels-up landing on Choda.

MiGs attacked the Sea Furies again and on

11 August two Fireflies were attacked over Haeju but after taking avoiding action the enemy flew off. The US 5th Air Force was asked if it could provide Sabres for top cover but said it was too heavily committed elsewhere. On 27 August a Firefly was hit in the radiator and had to ditch off Choda, the crew were rescued and were back flying the next day. By the time the patrol ended on 4 September the squadrons had flown 583 sorties, but they bettered this figure during the next patrol from 13 to 23 September when they achieved 749. During this patrol it was announced that all the rail bridges between Pyongyang and Chinnampo were at last down. It wasn't expected to last however, the enemy seemed to be able to put them up again virtually overnight. Other activities on this patrol were Sea Furies attacking and breaching sluice gates and some road transport that was destroyed. On the last patrol Lt D. G. Mather was hit by flak and force landed well into enemy territory. The ship's helicopter flew all the way to rescue him, with ten aircraft from *Ocean* for cover. The helicopter was required again three days later when Lt C. M. Jenne had to ditch his Sea Fury. *Ocean* now returned to Sasebo where HMS *Glory,* back for a third session, had arrived to relieve her.

The Air Group now comprised 821 Squadron equipped with Firefly FR5s commanded by Lt/Cdr J. R. N. Gardner, and 801 Squadron with Sea Furies commanded by Lt/Cdr P. B. Stuart. No 821 Squadron had been an anti-submarine squadron with the Firefly AS6 but for the Korean detachment they exchanged them for the FR5. Training was carried out at Malta, especially weapons training, after which they sailed for the Far East. They did however fire their guns before getting to Korea. Sean McGrail who had joined the squadron at Malta recalls the event: 'This was during the Malayan Emergency. We bombed and strafed bandit positions in the jungle in Selangar State. The aim was to drive the bandits to surrender themselves to soldiers. We all did two strikes, so that would be about 30 for the Fireflies of 821 Squadron.' Between 1 and 8 November the ship carried out exercises off Hong Kong and then sailed for her first patrol 12 to 19 November 1952. Fortunately the weather was kind and there was flying every day. The Fireflies were airborne at 07.20 hours on the first day providing a TARCAP (Target Combat Air Patrol) and then attacking a bridge near Changyou. In the afternoon they supported UN ground forces by attacking enemy troop positions. This went on for the best part of the patrol with the 18th being particularly busy. First strike of the day was a rocket attack on a store depot near Changyou followed by another rocket attack on a gun emplacement up the west coast. One or two aircraft were hit by light flak and Lt R. N. Jones was killed when his Sea Fury was shot down attacking a railway bridge. In the afternoon the Fireflies attacked and destroyed a transformer station near Changyou, but Lt Robbins was shot down and a CAP was set up over him until rescued. But the day was not over! Nine Sea Furies and six Fireflies were all damaged by enemy gunfire and another Firefly, WB242, went down when it lost its coolant and the engine failed, but the pilot was OK. The following day the Fireflies attacked enemy gun installations on the coast and brought the whole cliffside down with 1000 lb bombs. After a most eventful introductory patrol *Glory* sailed for Sasebo and replenishment.

The second patrol was from 29 November to 7 December 1952. The majority of days were spent attacking enemy troop positions and command posts with rockets and cannon, although there was an interesting strike on 5 December when some camouflaged invasion barges were found near Changyou-San. The following day a Firefly ditched about sixteen miles from the ship but the crew were rescued by the helicopter. During this patrol the weather, while still allowing flying, turned very cold and at one stage the coolant pipes on the Fireflies contracted to the point where they were causing leaks. It was after the end of this patrol that a tragedy occurred. The rescue Dragonfly helicopter was caught in a cross-wind over the flight deck and despite an attempt to recover the situation it was blown into the sea with the loss of its pilot, Lt A. P. Daniels and his winch operator, ACI E. R. Ripley.

The final patrol period for 1952 was 17 to 26 December when better weather allowed good reconnaissance for selecting targets for the rocket carrying Fireflies, the Sea Furies concentrating on bridges and rail targets. On the 20th Lt P. G. Fogden flying Firefly VT422 was attacking a junk when there was an explosion in one wing and he went in with no chance. Two days later another Firefly ditched after being hit by flak but the pilot was picked up by an amphibian from a shore base. Operations continued and on Christmas Day the Fireflies changed their rockets for 1000 lb bombs to go for bridges north of Haeju, Lt R. E. Barratt in Firefly VT471 being shot down and killed. The squadron went back next day and destroyed the bridge. The ship now withdrew to replenish and presumably, let in the New Year.

The first day of the new patrol, 5 to 11 January 1953, started badly with the loss of three Sea Fury

pilots. The target for the Fireflies was a tunnel north-east of Ongjin dam and Lt McGrail in WB410 on seeing a Sea Fury pilot bale out, jettisoned his bombs and became an R/T link co-ordinator for the ensuing search. The following day Firefly VT412 ditched north of Kirin after being hit by flak, the pilot being rescued later. Persistent hammering of enemy positions was still the priority: 6 January, vehicle shelter in Ongjin destroyed in the morning, an enemy HQ in the afternoon; 7 January, cutting railway lines south of Sinwon; 8 January, destroying rail trucks around Sinwon, another enemy HQ west of Ongjin; 10 January, enemy command post and gun positions destroyed, troop positions in the afternoon; 11 January, rocketing and destroying tank shelters east of Changyou. The ship withdrew and the aircraft flew ashore to Iwakuni for a few days.

The enemy appeared to be assembling concentrations of troops along the Ongjin Peninsula and in villages south-west of Chinnampo for what seemed to be hit and run raids on friendly islands using rubber boats. When *Glory* returned to the fray for her sixth patrol, 6 to 15 February it was these positions that the Fireflies and Sea Furies attacked. Four Sea Furies were attacked by MiGs on the 6th but sustained no losses. Not all losses were due to enemy action, Firefly WB366 returning from a mission went over the side when landing on but the crew were picked up, and another Firefly ditched after action the next day, the crew also being picked up. Some Sea Furies were also lost, two with the pilots being killed.

Patrol 7 began on 26 February and continued until 6 March, many of the targets still being the troop concentrations on the Ongjin Peninsula. There was however, a new type of raid, on 4 March the Fireflies started to drop leaflet bombs in the Ullyul area and again on the 6th, but this did not in any way interfere with the normal business of hitting the troop positions. The last four patrols ran from 16 March to 14 May and followed the same pattern – relentlessly they struck at enemy positions, showing the value time and time again of an off-shore strike force. During the period of this series of patrols *Glory* had achieved 1666 operational sorties expending 8768 rockets, 232 1000 lb bombs, 841 500lb bombs, forty leaflet bombs, twenty depth charges and more than 230,000 rounds of 20 mm ammunition. There had been 1869 deck landings with no accidents except the one that went over the side, and one that went into the barrier, and that was only because he picked up the 10th wire. On Sunday 5 April 1953 a day's flying programme was set up which resulted in 120 sorties being flown by 821 and 801 Squadrons, an all-time record. On 17 May HMS *Ocean* arrived at Sasebo to take over.

Ocean's Air Group consisted of 810 Squadron with Firefly FR5s commanded by Lt/Cdr A. W. Bloomer, and 807 Squadron with Sea Furies commanded by Lt/Cdr T. L. M. Brander. The first patrol began on 22 May 1953 with attacks on enemy buildings, communications, gun positions and troops. The weather, while allowing flying, gave poor visibility but some 560 sorties were flown, many in support of the Commonwealth Division. Some bombardment spotting was done for HMS *Newcastle* and USS *New Jersey*.

The second patrol began on 8 June and targets were much the same as the previous one with 539 sorties flown. On 29 June a Firefly WB264 was hit by small arms-fire and had to ditch but the crew was picked up by a helicopter from Pengyong-Do. The following day a Sea Fury had engine failure and ditched in the sea, the same rescue service come to his aid. By now the peace talks, which had been going on for some time reached an all-time high. On 8 June the President of South Korea had rejected the cease-fire terms and two days later the communist forces launched a new attack against South Korean positions. On 23 June the South Korean Government again rejected cease-fire terms. Two days later HMS *Ocean* returned to the combat zone and continued striking targets in support of the land forces, before returning to Sasebo on 6 July.

The fourth and last patrol began on 15 July and ran to the 23rd. It wasn't a good patrol to finish on. The catapult became unserviceable on the first day and using RATOG a Firefly VT482 crashed into the sea with the loss of both crew members, also a Sea Fury fired his RATOG too soon and hit the sea. The weather was poor and 434 sorties were flown, which was a disappointing figure to finish on. The ship returned to Sasebo arriving on the 25th.

On 8 July the UN Command and Communist forces agreed to negotiate an armistice without the South Koreans participating. On 13 July the Chinese launched yet another offensive against South Korean positions and it was *Ocean*'s Air Group that continued to support any UN strike requirements. While the Armistice talks were going on some North Korean PO-2 biplanes would come over at night and drop small bombs on targets of opportunity.

The Polikarpov PO-2s were sent over to harass American bases at night using fragmentation bombs. These 'Bedcheck Charlie' missions were reported in the press as nuisance raids, designed to hamper the American forces. They achieved little until 17 June 1951 when two PO-2s made a night attack on Suwon airfield, destroyed a North American F-86 Sabre, damaged eight others and wounded several Americans. Early attempts at stopping these intermittent raids using F3D-2 Skyknights and F4U Corsairs met with little success. The Skyknights, being jet aircraft, were too fast anyway and at least one flew into a PO-2 from astern. One or two were shot down, probably more by luck than judgement, as both a Douglas B-26 Invader and a Grumman F7F-3N Tigercat downed one each. As the war progressed other Soviet types made nocturnal raids such as the Yakovlev Yak-18 and the Lavochkin La-11, although again with little success. One US Marine Corp pilot shot down five of the night intruders flying a Corsair during June/July 1953 but this was an exceptional case. What was also embarrassing to the UN forces was that the PO-2s continued to make such raids when peace talks were taking place.

What was needed was a relatively slow aircraft, preferably fitted with air intercept radar and quickly available. The authorities did not have to look far. In June 1953 the US 5th Air Force Headquarters requested HMS *Ocean* to form a Firefly Night Fighter Detachment to be based ashore in Korea to combat the 'Bedcheck Charlies'. The Firefly FR5 seemed to fit the bill perfectly. On 7 July 1953 the first Firefly from 810 Squadron, WB395, fitted with APX-6, which was an Identification Friend/Foe (IFF) Mk 10 set, was flown ashore to Pyongtaek-ni by the CO, Lt/Cdr A. W. Bloomer DSC with Sub/Lt R. K. Simmonds as observer/AI operator. Initial trials were a success and two other Fireflies flew ashore on 18 July with full operations beginning on 22 July. The USAF Ground Control Interception (GCI) station was at Kimpo, just west of Seoul and about forty miles north of Pyongtaek-ni, the airfield the Fireflies were to operate from. The GCI controllers kept the Fireflies on a racetrack patrol between Inchon and Seoul and would vector the aircraft on a long curve of pursuit to intercept any contact not showing IFF. Three two-hour Combat Air Patrols (CAP) were flown every night while the detachment was deployed. Although the Night Fighter Detachment consisted of three Fireflies, these could be drawn from any available squadron aircraft as at least five different ones have been identified. No special markings were carried.

Actual interceptions were few, Captain David

HMS *Glory*'s flight deck during the winter of 1952/53. Only the very worst conditions would stop the carrier operating.
(Lt/Cdr J. F. K. McGrail)

Ashby, then a Sub Lieutenant Observer in 810 Squadron, and who served in the Night Fighter Detachment, recalls that the only aircraft he was able to visually identify was a darkened DC-3 trying to get into Kimpo without squawking IFF. On another occasion, his pilot, Lt Pete Spelling opened fire in the general direction of a lost close range ASH radar contact, but with no obvious results. Initial contact ranges were rarely more than three miles and the problem was not helped by the fact that none of 810's aircrew had at that time been trained in night fighter techniques.

Bombed-up Fireflies of 821 Squadron taxi forward ready for another strike against Korean Targets. *(Lt/Cdr J. F. K. McGrail)*

HMAS *Sydney* returned for a further spell of duty after the armistice was signed, and here three Fireflies from her Air Group patrol off the Korean coast. *(Australian War Memorial)*

The Armistice (which is still in force, a peace settlement never having been agreed) between the United Nation forces and the communist forces came into effect on the night of 27 July 1953. In the preceding ten days the Fireflies had flown thirty-one sorties maintaining six hours of CAP each night. As both sides kept a wary and distrustful eye on each other the Firefly operation continued. By 9 August, when US Marine Corp Douglas A3-D Skyraiders (also equally unsuited to the night intercept role) took over the job, the Fireflies had completed over 200 sorties. Although these operations were of little military significance, this virtually unrecorded episode in the history of the Fleet Air Arm night fighter story was considered a success due to the fact that from the time that the CAP's were initiated until 9 August no further bomb attacks were made by enemy night intruders. The Fireflies returned to HMS *Ocean* on 10 August 1953.

As in all adversity there is always the irrepressible spirit and good humour of some characters who have the ability to raise the spirits of others. The last 'land on' of the day in Korean waters was frequently at a time when the Wardroom bar was opening . . . imagine then that you are returning to the ship around dusk, you have been out on two strikes that day, friends have been lost or injured, the last target was a swine with lots of flak, you're weary and have the deck landing to face. As you curve in on the approach you cannot suppress a smile as you see *Glory*'s batsman, that splendid bearded 6ft 4in figure batting the last few aircraft on, already changed into mess undress to avoid a waste of good drinking time!

There can be little doubt about the contribution the Firefly made, and indeed, there can be no finer trial of an aircraft's capabilities than that of actual combat conditions, exemplified by the Firefly's performance in two wars.

Chapter 12
Fireflies for Ethiopia

To FULLY understand the background to Ethiopia acquiring Fireflies, and other military equipment, one must delve into its geo-political background. What follows is a brief summary which might help the reader. Ethiopia was one of the few African states not subjected to colonial rule. This was very important later in its history and gave it a lot of clout with other African nations. The horn of Africa, where the continental bulge projects itself into the Indian Ocean, contains the hostile pair of Ethiopia and Somalia as well as Africa's largest territory, the Sudan, and one of the smallest, the Republic of Djibouti. Ethiopia, the most densely populated of the four countries was an imperial state that incorporated two highly contested regions, the Province of Eritrea, always looking for independence, and the Ogaden, which has always been claimed by Somalia. Fierce disputes in this strategic region abutting the Red Sea and the Indian Ocean made the Horn of Africa the site of explosive tensions. Basic things like water and grazing rights, with complex feudal systems along its borders, were the

main causes of friction. Military intervention was one of the ways Ethiopia wanted to control these situations.

In 1935 Italy had invaded Ethiopia forcing the Emperor, Haile Selassie into exile in England. Deliverance came in May 1941 when Britain's Eighth Army continued its sweep through North Africa to remove Italian and German domination. The restored Emperor was able to strengthen his earlier position along the border by getting the victorious powers to agree to Ethiopia retaining the Ogaden (hitherto an Italian colony) as a federated state.

In October 1948 at a dinner party at Addis Ababa for the Sudan Goodwill Mission, the British Legation was rebuffed by Haile Selassie about the failure to provide military equipment he sought. A British Military Mission was visiting the capital at that time but were experiencing problems with the Foreign Office on what could, or could not, be released for use by foreign powers. The Emperor also said he was in need of military aircraft, 'some fighters and bombers'. He

Two Imperial Ethiopian Air Force Fireflies from the first UK batch are serviced in the midday heat. *(Via Ole G. Nordbo)*

stated that he would prefer to buy from Britain than from Sweden, who were also offering military equipment. Later that evening he sent a message to the Legation saying he wanted six of each type.

In November 1948 the Ethiopians asked through official channels for six fighters and six bombers, types to be agreed. The authorities in the UK looked at the types of aircraft available, usually ex-service after reconditioning, i.e. Spitfire IX, Oxford, Anson 18, Wellington X and Mosquito FBVI. New types discussed included the Brigand, Sea Fury and Firefly. Other problems such as operation of aircraft in hot and high conditions, radio, ammunition and aircraft spares were also raised. Some fourteen Saab B17s had already been acquired from Sweden as light bombers and the 'real bombers' were expected to be larger than those. Only the Halifax was available with the performance required, but it was considered unsuitable due to the fact that there were no trained aircrews and the subject of starting to train Ethiopian nationals to fly multi-engined aircraft from scratch didn't bear thinking about. When a British attaché queried the use of such aeroplanes, he was told they were required for 'self defence'. In a report put out by the chargé-d'affaires at Addis Ababa it was pointed out to the Foreign Office that the Imperial Ethiopian Air Force was not a properly constituted air force. It was in fact, the Emperor's personal air force administered from the palace, usually via his personal and private secretary, Ato Tafara Worq. It had no proper HQ (the Commander operated from his hotel room!) or staff and was commanded by retired Swedish Air Force Brigadier General Hard. His Commander-in-Chief was another Swede, Count von Rosen.

There then followed a protracted period when Ethiopia and the UK were constantly agreeing to disagree. The Ethiopians wanted aeroplanes quickly; the British Government frequently stalled as they discussed types available, their suitability and whether it was even a good idea to sell such types to Ethiopia. A large order for thirty-five Spitfires was mentioned but in the immediate post-war period the whole world seemed to want Spitfires and who was to get what was a problem. During 1949 the Ethiopians, after some sort of response, asked for six Spitfire Mk 9s as a start, with a follow up order for Mk 14s later. Nothing happened for a while and the Ethiopians, fed up with constant stalling, lost interest, the Spitfires reserved for them being released to Eire. Sweden were offering Mustangs but von Rosen was

adamant, he preferred the Firefly. It would fill both roles as fighter/fighter-bomber, was robust and had good strike capability.

Fairey informed the Foreign Office in January 1950 that the Ethiopian Vice Minister of Finance had contacted them about the purchase of up to twelve Firefly trainers and target tugs, reconditioned machines being acceptable. This was obviously a back door ploy to get the Fireflies and convert them for active use themselves later. They exploited the situation by stating that they had few trained national pilots or navigators/ observers and needed the aircraft so that training could commence ready for the delivery of other Firefly types later. Fairey, obviously interested in the sale, requested the Foreign Office to clear the sale of Firefly FR1 and Trainer aircraft.

Maurice Wright, a director of Faireys, visited the Foreign Office on 30 May 1950 and informed them that Count von Rosen had been in touch and was very keen to buy thirty-five Fireflies. Fairey were somewhat concerned. Here was good business for British industry and the government seemed only capable of dragging its feet. Von Rosen wasn't only looking for the aeroplanes, he also wanted 20 mm ammunition, rocket projectiles and 1000 lb bombs. Money was not a problem, the whole contract would be financed by the sale of UK bonds via the Sabean Utility Corporation in Cairo. Wright pointed out that the value of the order, including spares support over a number of years, was over half a million pounds. The Foreign Office told him they were keen for the deal to go through, but it would depend on how many Fireflies the Admiralty would release. When approached, the Admiralty declared that they were short of Fireflies and were certainly not prepared to release thirty-five.

From reports filtering back from Ethiopia it was becoming apparent that the aircraft were intended for use along the Eritrean border where the situation was deteriorating rapidly.

Count von Rosen had arranged to visit Fairey during May where he informed them of his intention to buy the Fireflies, confirmed on 1 August 1950 when he ordered thirty-five and asked for deliveries to start in January 1951. He said he wanted to form a complete strike wing in one go.

During July 1950 the Admiralty said that in view of the world situation there was no way they could release any Fireflies for resale. This was obviously tongue-in-cheek as they were under pressure to release Fireflies for other countries, including Siam who wanted twelve. The Korean

A military parade marches past a line-up of Fireflies, most of them from the Canadian batch. The first machine is camouflaged, but the others have a two-colour scheme. *(Via Ole G. Nordbo)*

war compounded the problem, some Firefly FR1s had been used operationally and reserves were needed for attrition purposes. When these were replaced by the Firefly 5 nobody could foresee how long the war would go on, or how many Fireflies would be needed, both for action and training. This situation was explained to the Ethiopians who were plainly disappointed, but said that they would still like to buy as many as possible when they became available. The Emperor was now prepared to buy twelve new Firefly 5s straight off the production line, but the Korean problem only made it more difficult – the Admiralty were adamant they wanted all production Firefly 5s. In October 1950 von Rosen said he wanted the thirty-five Fireflies as one order – not in dribs and drabs. During late October/early November the Admiralty, under increasing pressure, declared that they would be prepared to release twenty-one Firefly FR1s as they were about to be downgraded. The Firefly Mk 6, shortly to enter Service, would release some Mk 5s to reserve status or for training. They could release nine Firefly FR1s early in 1951 for Ethiopia with a possibility of more later – but there was no chance of any Mk 5s. On

14 November Fairey announced the Ethiopian order for thirty-five Fireflies. This was a crafty move by Fairey because with the large order being public knowledge something would have to be done. At a meeting on 7 December between Fairey, the Foreign Office, Ministry of Supply and Admiralty staff, the topic of discussion was the Ethiopian Firefly problem, which had been going on for over two years. The Admiralty dug its heels in and said there was no immediate prospect of releasing further Firefly aircraft until it was clear what their own needs would be. Commander Ben Hurren from the Fairey Sales Department said that he was under considerable pressure to sell Fireflies and was being approached by more and more countries. He cited Denmark, Sweden, Saudi Arabia and Lebanon, all looking for various marks of Firefly to suit their needs. He said that given the go-ahead Fairey could start a new production line at Stockport for the Mk 6, so releasing useful factory space at Hayes for conversions and re-conditioning. Although the Admiralty would not shift on the subject of more Fireflies they agreed to release the ones for Ethiopia. Consequently, when they and Fairey signed the final agreement on 22 December it was

for thirty-five aircraft in batches nine, nine and seventeen.

The first nine, eight FR1s and one T2, were released from Admiralty stocks at Abbotsinch during February/March 1951. These were delivered to Fairey's Stockport/Ringway factories for overhaul and/or re-conditioning before being painted up. The Fireflies were:

IEAF No	Ex-FAA serial
601	MB434
602	MB476
603 (T2)	MB382
604	MB497
605	MB737
606	Z2026
607	Z2100
608	Z1955
609	Z1982

with the first being handed over to Lt Col Asefa at Ringway. The follow-on orders were never processed but in March 1954 a memo from Addis Ababa to Fairey informed them that they had purchased fourteen Fireflies from Canada and nine from the Netherlands. The aircraft from Canada were to start being shipped on 10 March, with some of these and/or the Dutch machines being used for spares. The Canadian Fireflies delivered to Ethiopia were nine FR1s (DK535, 537, 545, 560, 561, 565, PP402, 462, 467); three T1s (DK445, DT975, MB443) and two T2s (MB694, PP408). So far, any tie-ups between the IEAF and FAA serials has not come to light. There has been no trace of the nine Fireflies ever being delivered from the Dutch to Ethiopia. In fact, the African Department of the Foreign Office was informed by Ben Hurren that the nine Fireflies were supposedly coming from Caracas but were in such a poor state that they were not worth the cost of transporting them.

The Fireflies delivered to Ethiopia were used for the purpose they were bought – attacking dissidents along the borders. In 1969 most of the Fireflies were still in a hangar at Asmara in flyable condition – although the engines had been inhibited. They had not flown for four years, since the Swedish advisors had moved out and American aid moved in. The Americans quickly sorted out the situation, bringing in their own country's products and relegating older material to the scrap heap. The Fireflies were pushed out and left in the sun and heat – the results being seen in the photographs. The majority of the airframes and engines had less than 500 hours on them. These same machines were offered for sale in the seventies but the general condition was poor and there is no known record of any sales.

Fireflies pushed out to die at Asmara in the mid-1970s. 616 is an ex-Canadian machine, while in the background are two trainers and another FR1. *(Author's collection)*

Chapter 13
Target Towing

A N ADMIRAL once said he would rather have one Fleet Requirements Unit (FRU) than a couple of squadrons of fighter aircraft. He also highlighted some of the essential functions of an FRU, firing practice for shore batteries, ships' guns and aircraft in flight. Each of these categories allowed practice under simulated combat conditions, using the weapons that would be used against an enemy. For this reason, an aircraft towed a wide variety of targets, ranging from the more conventional sleeves, not unlike a windsock, through towed flares, streamers sensitive to radar pick-up and special gliders which could have wing spans approaching full size aircraft. One of the latter incorporated a twin-fuselage layout which was considered the best general purpose target and became the most widely used.

Apparently the maximum satisfactory speed for target towing in the post-war era was no more than 240 knots, beyond this speed a new set of factors had to be considered. At the other end of the scale, a biplane, would not be representative of a modern combat aircraft. There was of course, the chance that the towing aircraft might get shot down instead of the target! This led to the well known anecdote of a pilot one day calling up the controlling firing office and saying: 'I'm pulling this bloody thing, not pushing it.' Or another one passed to the author: 'I am in the front one, but if you carry on at this rate I shall be safer in the one at the back.'

The idea of using the Firefly for target towing first came out at an Admiralty meeting in 1945, and although discussed, it was not taken further. However, a different Admiralty document relating to post-war FAA needs, estimated that there would be a requirement for ninety-two target towing aircraft for the FRUs. Again, nothing further was done and it fell to a foreign civilian company to get something moving. Svensk Flygtjanst AB was a Swedish civil company providing, among other things, a target towing facility for the Swedish forces. After the war they acquired some Miles Martinets but by 1947 it was becoming apparent that they needed replacing. Svensk thought the

A cutaway showing the positions of the crew and equipment of the Mk 1 target-tower. *(Author's collection)*

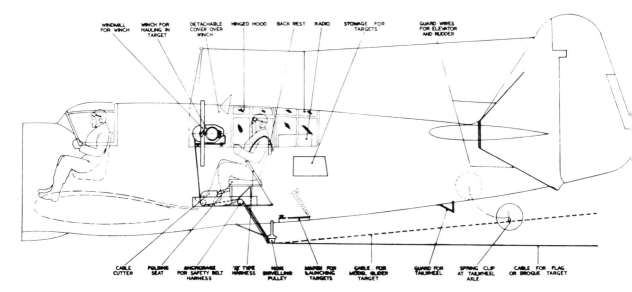

Close-up detail of a Firefly TT Mk 1 windlass. When not in use, it was rotated to a horizontal position to reduce drag.

(Author's collection)

Firefly an ideal candidate because (a) even in its Mk 1 obsolescent version it had sufficient life and speed for a 7000 ft tow, (b) under civil operating conditions, the work which a comparatively small number of Fireflies could achieve, would take the place of four squadrons of target towing personnel who, in the service, had many other duties to perform, and (c), the Firefly fell into the speed operating requirement perfectly.

Fairey looked at the technical problems and agreed that it would be suitable for conversion. The target towing installation comprised a standard Type B Mark 2B cable winch, driven by a windmill for target retraction, a sleeve target stowage compartment and launching hatch. To facilitate changing sleeve targets and finally releasing a target, a foot-operated cable cutter was fitted to the floor to the operator's cockpit. Cable guards were fitted under the fuselage and on the tail unit to prevent the cable fouling the tail wheel or control surfaces. A spring clip was attached to the tail wheel axle to support the cable when paid out for take-off with a glider target. The roomy rear cockpit gave the target operator full freedom of movement. A seat was attached to the starboard side of the cockpit, which folded up when not in use. There

was also a back rest complete with safety harness at the edge of the rear decking. An additional anchorage point was provided for a harness used when the operator was standing. A small windshield, mounted just forward of the decking, provided a clear view and protection of the operator if he wished to check the target astern. The target stowage compartment was aft of the cockpit, with the hinged door of the loading hatch just below. Normal radio and radar equipment was removed from the forward decking to make room for the winch. The actual towing cable ran from the winch under the decking, through rollers at the forward end of the cutter, and out through the bottom of the cockpit. When the operator was ready to cut the target cable, he removed the lever supplied from its stowage clips, inserted it into the socket at the aft end of the cutter and depressed it by foot, and in so doing, cut the cable. The only other modification was the mounting of the windmill operating arm just forward of the operator's cockpit on the port side. Maximum cruising speed with the target streamed, or a towed glider target, was 185 knots at sea level. It might be an idea at this stage to look at the operating procedures for target towing.

The glider type targets had negative incidence on their wings so that when they were released from a tug aircraft they plunged straight to the ground. Two types were mainly used, one had a 16 ft wingspan and conventional layout, the other had a wingspan of up to 32 ft, twin fuselages and tail units. The method of operation was to handle the target to a position into wind for take-off, and lay out a thin gauge wire attached to the target, extending about seventy-five yards ahead of it. The towing aircraft then manoeuvred to head into wind ahead of the target and pick up the wire. This wire was tied by a straightforward knot to another wire leading to a drum inside the rear cockpit of the tug aircraft. The drum was mechanically rotated by a windmill which was driven externally by the slipstream, and had enough cable to stream a target up to 7000 ft behind the aircraft. Although the target had no lift as such, it was remarkably light, and, it was possible, if somewhat tedious, to haul in the 16 ft target by hand. The pilot of the tug opened the throttle and once airborne kept the aircraft low over the ground, retracting the undercarriage soon after lift off (around 15/20 ft) with the target skidding along the ground behind. When the aircraft had reached a speed of 130 knots the pilot pulled sharply up into a steep climb, lifting the target clear of the ground in one clean go. The target was then directly behind the aircraft, but about 200 ft below. When the desired altitude was reached, the aircraft levelled out and the operator streamed the target out to the required distance. For landing, if the gunners had not shot the target down or the towing cable away, the aircraft was positioned about one mile to the lee of the aerodrome at about 500 ft, throttled back and fully flapped. The approach was of the deck landing type with plenty of power but losing height progressively until the target contacted the ground. At the critical moment, the cable was cut, the target skidded to a halt and the aircraft opened up to go round again and make a normal landing.

A mobile radio ground unit was used to communicate with the pilot during these operations. It could be set up or removed to another point in just over a minute. Changes of wind could be coped with and the radio unit itself could give correct line of approach for a shoot.

One of the reasons the Firefly was chosen was that it was a quick manoeuvring aircraft, especially in turns. The fact that the winged target had to trail astern and below meant that the target flew faster than the aircraft in a turn. The radius of the target turn was greater, and its path further for the same period of time. The pilot needed to have his wits about him some days. Despite the recommended maximum speed at sea level being 185 knots, it was found that the best speed for a tow was between 215 and 235 knots. This was because troubles were experienced with the larger targets which rolled on their back at around 175 knots and flew inverted! It resumed its normal position on reducing speed, but occasionally a savage jerk was felt down the cable. This instability problem was overcome by extending the target twin tail fins below the fuselage datum point. In practice, Service requirements for ground to air firing dictated a speed of around 170 knots – though the Firefly maximum towing speed was found to be around 260 knots.

Sweden went on to operate nineteen Firefly TT Mk 1s, Denmark bought a couple and India five. The Admiralty, while not interested in the Mk 1 became more enthusiastic over another idea. Fairey suggested that later marks of the Firefly would also be suitable for target towing and came up with a modification design change. This resulted in the Firefly TT Mk 4, where Modification 850 allowed a standard Mk 4 to be changed into a target towing aircraft. The actual changes to the aircraft were small as the winch was a Type G Mk 3 with target towing exchange unit Type B Mk 2. The winch and associated equipment were carried in a nacelle beneath the aircraft and this had a fully-feathering windmill propeller. The four 20 mm cannon in the wings, engine mounting ballast and ASH radar were removed, although the nacelle was retained for aerodynamic reasons. For severing the winch cable in an emergency a trigger shaped handle, painted yellow, was positioned on the starboard side of the pilot's cockpit and on the control panel above the launching chute in the operator's cockpit. In the event of having to jettison the winch nacelle itself, there was a hand lever in the pilot's cockpit. The Admiralty liked this idea more than the Mk 1 and ordered 28TT Mk 4s, and India ordered five to supplement their Mk 1s. As there was little difference between the Firefly 4, 5 and 6, it meant the target towing modification could be fitted to any of those marks. The Royal Australian Navy took advantage of this to modify some of their Firefly Mk 5 and Mk 6 aircraft using kits sent out from Fairey. The Dutch also converted some of their Fireflies to the target towing role using these kits. The idea of conversion kits had been dreamed up by Fairey when the Royal Danish Air Force bought some surplus Firefly Mk 1s from Canada and wanted them for target towing.

In February 1950 the Ministry cleared the Firefly Mk 4 and Mk 5 for operation with preliminary practice target towing gear. Although the FAA was

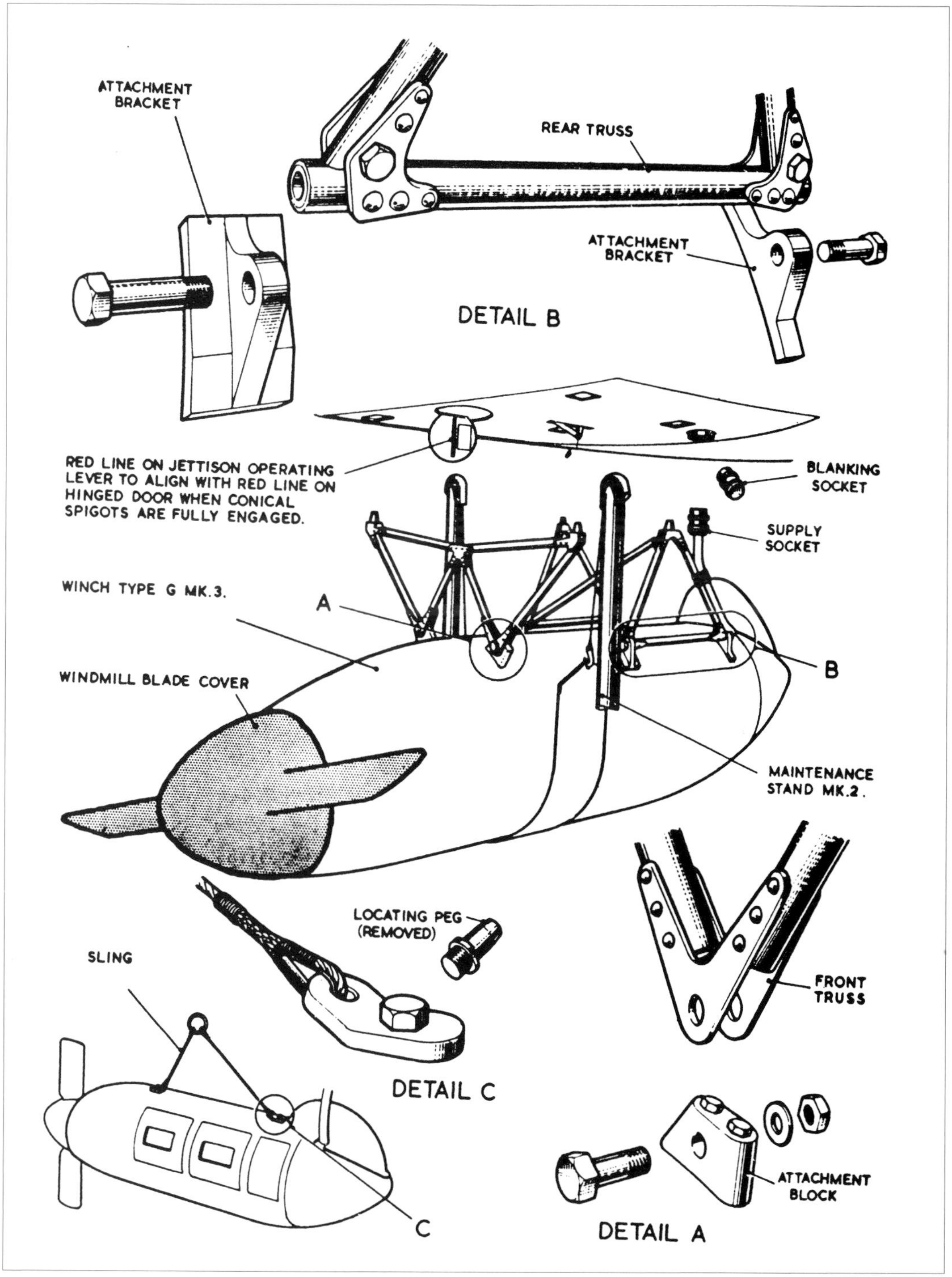

ATTACHMENT BRACKET

REAR TRUSS

ATTACHMENT BRACKET

DETAIL B

RED LINE ON JETTISON OPERATING LEVER TO ALIGN WITH RED LINE ON HINGED DOOR WHEN CONICAL SPIGOTS ARE FULLY ENGAGED.

BLANKING SOCKET

SUPPLY SOCKET

WINCH TYPE G MK.3.

A

WINDMILL BLADE COVER

B

MAINTENANCE STAND MK.2.

LOCATING PEG (REMOVED)

FRONT TRUSS

SLING

DETAIL C

C

ATTACHMENT BLOCK

DETAIL A

Diagram showing all the detail associated with the Type G Mk 3 winch, as used on the Firefly TT Mk 4 and the Mks 5/6 in service with other countries. *(Author's collection)* cleared to operate these types, the A&AEE at Boscombe was asked to conduct trials with a Firefly Mk 5 to establish its suitability for towing targets under ICAN temperate summer and tropical conditions. Trials were to include the use of a 2 ft Type M4 and 4ft Type M3 low drag sleeve, and a 32 ft Mk 2 winged target. The Firefly, WB406, undertook these trials between November 1950 and May 1951 at Boscombe. It was fitted with a G Type Mk 2 fully feathering windmill winch mounted under the fuselage at the centre section, with the winch drum carrying 6300 ft of steel cable. The cable was painted between 40 ft and 5 ft from the end in yellow, from the five-foot mark a red band, one inch wide, was marked at one foot intervals to the end of the cable. The trials, although successful as expected, did show up that the 32 ft winged target suffered damage at speeds in excess of 150 knots and disintegrated on one occasion. It was pointed out that they would probably be unsuitable for high speed work.

At the end of May 1951 the Firefly T Mk 1 and T Mk 2 were considered suitable for target towing work subject to the application of Fairey Modification 12 which was the target towing gear fitment, and some slight alterations such as repositioning of a control lever, Bowden control lever run etc. It is doubtful whether any Trainers ever acted in the target towing role.

Of the Admiralty's twenty-eight Firefly TT Mk 4s, some of these were already at Fairey's Ringway factory for Cat 4 repairs or reconditioning, and all it needed was an order to convert these while still at the factory. The twenty-eight converted were VG957, 958, 961, 962, 965, 966, 967, 968, 974, 977, 979, 982, 988 and 993, VH126, 127, 132 and 143, TW722, 723, 733, 734, 737, 739, 744, 750, 751 and 753. Most of these went on to serve with the FRU squadrons, No 700 and 771 Squadrons. The latter had reformed in July 1948 and the Fireflies arrived in 1950. The unit became the Southern Fleet Requirements Unit on 1 September 1952, moving its HQ to Ford in the process. The unit amalgamated with 703 Squadron on 17 August 1955 to form 700 Squadron. The new squadron formed up as a Trials and Requirements Unit, absorbing the tasks of 703 and 771 Squadrons. Although it operated a variety of aircraft it boasted nine Firefly TT Mk 4s. The following year 787 Squadron's tasks were absorbed when it too disbanded. In February 1957 the civil company, Airwork, who had their own FRU at Hurn, took over the role of fleet requirements and the Firefly target towing facility disappeared.

Australian conversions amounted to two Mk 5s, VX388 and WB271, and four Mk 6, WB518, WD828, 840 and 901.

Superb air-to-air portrait of Firefly TT Mk 4 VH132 of 771 Squadron, out from Ford. The clarity of the picture allows a close study of detail, note for instance that the winch propeller is feathered. *(B. J. Lowe)*

Chapter 14
Dutch Fireflies

URING 1945, in what was the first private sale of military aircraft by a British aviation company since before the war, Fairey sold thirty Firefly Mk 1 aircraft to the Royal Netherlands Naval Air Service (MLD). Deliveries were agreed with the Admiralty so that production was drawn from previous orders and manufactured alongside the FAA aircraft. The first deliveries were to begin in January 1946. The Fireflies were to be numbered F1 to F30 inclusive and camouflaged as per FAA Fireflies but with an inverted orange triangle on the front fuselage just forward of the pilot's cockpit. It was also

Six of the fifteen Fireflies of 860 Squadron aboard HNMS *Karel Doorman* en route to the Netherlands East Indies in 1946. The second machine, F22, was to be shot down by terrorists. *(Royal Netherlands Navy via David Oliver)*

agreed that Firefly airframe components would be made under licence by Aviolanda Maatschappij voor Vliegtuigbouw NV. This was to assist the Dutch aircraft industry get back on its feet after the war.

The first six were handed over at Heston on Friday 18 January 1946 at a small ceremony when the first machine, F1, was christened *Pioneer* by the wife of Lt/Cdr Beets, Royal Netherlands Navy. Others at the event included Lt/Cdr Bastiaan Sjerp RNN, Rear Admiral Feteris RNN and Rear Admiral Slattery, who was Vice-Controller (Air) at that time.

The first six Fireflies allowed their new owners, No 860 Squadron, RNNAS, to work up at St Merryn in the UK prior to their embarkation in HNMS *Karel Doorman*, the ex-British carrier, HMS *Nairana*. More aircraft joined the six and after working up fifteen of the Fireflies embarked on the carrier to steam to the Dutch East Indies, where there was a rebellion. Flying ashore on 12 October 1946 Firefly F13 crashed on landing at Kemajoran airfield, Java. It was only eighteen months since the Fireflies of 1770 had wreaked havoc in Sumatra and now they were back in action in the same area. No 860 was to operate mostly from Morokrembangan airfield and the seaplane base at Soerabaja. The Fireflies had been bought because they were considered a good strike aircraft and this is what they did, usually as single seaters, but occasionally with another crew member, either official or otherwise! They were soon in action and Gerrit Zwanenburg, although in the Dutch Marines, has cause to remember them.

'Yes indeed, the Firefly flew actions against the rebels in the former Netherlands East Indies. They flew ground support missions for us as fighters with rockets and cannon. I know from experience as I was slogging along on the ground as a Marine and often the spent 20 mm shells rained down on us! Some of the Fireflies were lost in action. I well remember F22 crashing halfway between Soerabaja and Malang after being shot down on 21 July 1947. We got to the aircraft just too late to rescue the pilot, the rebels took him away and

A rare picture of a Dutch Mk 1 Firefly, F12, flying above Java in 1946. At this time they were still in British markings with Dutch triangles. F12 returned to Holland in 1951 and was converted into a trainer. *(Royal Netherlands Navy)*

later executed him. F24, I recall, flew into a mountain north west of Malang on 14 May 1947 killing the pilot and a corporal of the Marines who was just along for the ride. F27 was shot down on 4 August 1947 but I cannot remember the details. Our Marine Brigade operated mainly south of Soerabaja and initially only took part in patrol actions. After mid-July 1947 we were involved in major actions during which we took the whole eastern part of Java from Soerabaja to Malang. During these actions the Fireflies gave us air cover, shooting up enemy positions with their cannon and rockets. The earlier mention of spent shells raining down on us was again evident when we had to take a bridge over the river Kali Mas at Porrong. One Firefly came so low firing his guns the casings were bouncing off our heads – whose side was he on anyway? They were mainly used as ground support fighters with only a pilot aboard. Sometimes a navigator or wireless operator went along but this wasn't the norm. On another occasion in January 1947 my friend managed to go along on a raid and they had to shoot up targets near Modjokerto with rockets. The pilot flew so low that debris

or parts of his rockets hit and damaged the aircraft. The pilot nursed it home to Soerabaja and made a wheels-up landing on a rifle range – appropriate don't you think?'

The Fireflies continued their work but the people wanted their independence and eventually the Dutch East Indies became Indonesia ruled by Sukarno All told the Fireflies flew in the region of 4000 operational sorties and only lost two to enemy ground fire and two in accidents. At the end of hostilities in 1951, 860 returned to Holland taking with them eleven of the fifteen Fireflies they set out with.

The first batch of Firefly Mk 1s were operated by Nos 860 and 861 Squadrons, with a few later serving with No 1 Squadron in the Netherlands Antilles. These saw their time out there and were scrapped but seven were converted into Trainers. A number of the Mk 1s were lost in accidents, F2 going down near Margate on 14 October 1946, F9 was lost in the North Sea during its delivery flight en route to the Netherlands on 13 February 1946, F14 crashed on Valkenburg airfield on 20 January 1950 and F15 came down on a school at Apeldoorn on 2 December 1946.

During 1949, F1, F4, F5, F8, F12, F23 and F29 were converted into Trainers. This was done by the Aviolanda company of Papendrecht, previously a member of the United Dutch Aircraft Factories Group. The conversion was the same as that done by the Fairey company, i.e. cutting away the rear fuselage top fairing and replacing it with a new structure which allowed a standard front cockpit hood assembly to be fitted at the rear. The rear instructor's cockpit was raised twelve inches and all controls were duplicated.

During late 1946 the Dutch ordered forty new Firefly FR4 aircraft to supplement the Mk 1s then in use. These were numbered F31 to F70 inclusive, with deliveries starting in April 1947 and werecompleted by December that year. The FR4s served with No 1 Squadron, usually based in the Netherlands Antilles, Nos 2, 4 and 5 Squadrons in the Netherlands and No 7 Squadron at Biak, Netherlands New Guinea. Of these FR4s, nine were lost in accidents – F35, F50 and F56 aboard HMS *Illustrious* and F69 aboard HMS *Theseus*. F70 crashed at sea, as did F68 out in Netherlands New Guinea. Eight, (F31, F37, F41, F42, F44, F47, F48 and F49) were converted to target

towers. Many of the others survived into the late fifties, and seven even soldiered on until 1961.

At the beginning of 1949 the Dutch Navy took delivery of fourteen Firefly NF Mk 5 aircraft, and these were interspersed with the FR4 units. K76 crashed in the sea near Kijkduin, K78 caught fire while being refuelled at Valkenburg and burnt out, K80 was in an air collision with K84 on 1 June 1950 and K81 crashed near Haarlem on 12 May 1950. Seven survived until 1961 when all Fireflies were scrapped. Prior to this, in 1952, the Dutch heard that the Canadians were disposing of their Fireflies and in February 1953 managed to acquire four AS Mk 5s (VH139, VH141, VX414 and VX415) under the Mutual Air Plan. These were numbered P86 to P89 inclusive but the tie-ups are not necessarily in that order. The last two were never used, being broken up for spares in June 1956. P86 served with No 2 Squadron before joining No 1 Squadron in the Netherlands Antilles and survived until 1958. P87 served with No 1 Squadron until broken up in September 1957.

The Fireflies went through a complicated four changes of serial number identity. The thirty Mk 1 and forty Mk 4 all received F numbers, but by

An extremely rare and exciting shot of three Dutch Fireflies in close formation making a rocket strike at terrorist positions. Note that full Dutch markings have been applied. *(Royal Netherlands Navy)*

Magnificent line-up of ten of the eleven Firefly FR4s at Heston, prior to them all being delivered on 22 April 1947.

(Westland Aircraft Ltd)

1949 these had given way to a K prefix, although all the aircraft did not use this code if they had been written off or converted to Trainers. The Trainers were coded differently, just to confuse the issue. For example, F1, when converted to a Trainer did not get a K code, but became L11, whereas F4 became K4 when it was converted to a Trainer. The Mk 5s started with the K code, i.e. K71 to K84 inclusive. Then they were changed again to a P code, so that F3/K3 became P3, but those converted to Trainers used a U code so that F12/K12 became U12, not P12. In fact some Fireflies had five changes of code, for by 1960 any surviving machines received a three digit code, i.e. F33/P33/005. Trainer F12 became K12, L12, U12 and eventually 003, before being struck off charge on 29 March 1960.

Camouflage and markings present no problem. The Mk 1 Fireflies were sprayed up in British FAA colours with roundels. The Dutch inverted orange triangle with black surround, was positioned on both sides of the rudder, and on each side of the fuselage just forward of the pilot's cockpit. No fuselage codes were carried but the serial was put beneath the starboard wing. Later, the number appeared on the fuselage. Although letters were allocated to the aircraft number, they were in fact, never used. The FR4 and NF5s were also delivered in British FAA colours, but used the Dutch roundel in place of the British one. The aircraft number was usually put on both sides of the engine cowling and under the nose just aft of the spinner. In some instances the aircraft number would be added, much smaller, to the undercarriage doors. 'Kon Marine' was stencilled on the rear fuselage under the tailplane. The last few Fireflies in service had 'Kon Marine' put on the fuselage in much larger letters and the three-digit code that had been introduced was placed on the upper starboard wing in very large numbers. This was repeated on the engine cowling but smaller. For the last airworthy Fireflies out in Biak, a large 'B' was added to the fin, the national flag disappearing, as did the last Dutch Fireflies shortly afterwards.

Chapter 15
Firefly Fiasco

IT WAS FOUND, amongst other problems relating to the Admiralty's anti-submarine programme, that the new two-seat anti-submarine aircraft to Specification GR17/45 (Gannet) was going to be too heavy for operation from the light fleet carriers. They would have to be modified before Gannets could operate from them, also, the Admiralty could not make its mind up whether the Gannet should be a two, or three-seater, and there were development problems with the engine, the Armstrong-Siddeley Double Mamba. Under the circumstances their Lordships realised that they needed to maintain an anti-submarine presence during the modernisation programme and decided an interim aircraft, capable of carrying British sonobuoy equipment and ASH, should be made available. This was in addition to the Firefly AS6 programme which was already under way. Their requirements were passed to Fairey for comment.

But all was not well at Hayes. The addition of a third seat and equipment in the rear cockpit, with difference performance demands, dictated once again a major redesign of the Firefly structure. To compensate for the extra weight in the rear the engine had to be moved forward slightly and a Griffon 57 was chosen as the power plant with an annular chin radiator. This meant that the leading edge radiators were removed and the wing plan reverted to the elliptical shape of the Firefly 1 but with extension of the leading edge near the fuselage and larger ailerons. It was decided to make the tailwheel non-retractable.

A meeting was convened on 7 February 1949 between the various departments of the Admiralty, Fairey, Rolls-Royce and the Air Ministry. The Admiralty's tentative requirements were outlined much as above, but stating that the aircraft landing weight was not to exceed 13,000 lb and, it must be

A clean-looking Mk 7 MB757 with the mocked-up observer's canopy. This aircraft with the Barracuda-type powerplant, cockpit hood and elliptical wings of the Mk 1, and the tailplane of the Mk 4, is not unpleasant to the eye. *(Westland Aircraft Co)*

ready for entry into Service by mid-1950! On hearing about the original proposal Fairey had suggested the Firefly Mk 5 powered by a Shackleton-type power unit with contra-props. It was confirmed that sonobuoys and the receiver installation would be available for Service trials by May 1949, with first production aircraft available by September that year. This was based on agreement of production line priorities.

In the light of the new requirements Fairey came up with another plan for the meeting. Hollis-Williams of Fairey stated that the proposed aircraft, referred to as a three-seat Firefly 6, would use a Firefly Mk 5 structure with a Barracuda Mk 5 pattern power plant, with chin-type radiator – not unlike the FIII – in lieu of the existing leading-edge type. It was to have an enlarged rear cockpit with full installation of British sonobuoy equipment and enough room for two operators. Guns were deleted and the contra-prop idea was dropped. It was proposed to install a Griffon 57 with a single propeller and water-methanol injection to give 25 lb boost at take-off instead of the normal 18 lb. Firefly Mk 1 type wing tips would be fitted to improve take-off and endurance. The proposed large bubble canopy for the rear cockpit would provide a good view, and most of the other changes, based on Firefly operational experience, were of a relatively small nature. The only one of note being the two extra inches of the increased stroke oleo under-carriage leg then being developed. This would cater for the 12 ft/min rate of descent on to a deck at 14,000 lb AUW, instead of the normal 12,300 lb. There was a proposal that a Griffon 37 might be fitted initially until the modified Griffon 57 came along. This was rejected at the meeting on the grounds that the Griffon 37 was on the obsolete list.

Fairey said that given the go-ahead and subject to the engine being available, they could have twenty-five aircraft available for the required time of mid-1950. Mr Hollis-Williams then outlined the programme proposals for the prototypes. This would commence with a mock-up flight test aircraft, the rear canopy being an airflow approval layout before proper testing of a perspex one. The first complete prototype could be ready at the end of eight months, with other prototypes, if required, following at six weekly intervals. Only two prototypes were proposed as it wasn't envisaged that there would be many problems, and based on the assurance that the Admiralty would provide the necessary Barracuda Mk 5 power plants. Rolls-Royce stated that design work would be needed for a modified engine gear casing, revised engine

feet, coolant pump and provision of cartridge starting. In view of the time scale, the Admiralty gave the go-ahead. Thus, the seeds of disaster were sown. No one had raised the doubts experienced in the past over the Firefly FIII or of the directional stability problems associated with under-the-nose radiator installations. It appears nothing had been learned. The changes required to the Griffon 57 would result in a new model number, the Griffon 59.

A Naval Staff Requirement, No NR/A28, was issued on 18 June 1949 for an interim anti-submarine aircraft with a first draft of the specification on 7 January 1950. The requirements included a three-seat version of the Firefly AS5 (still referred to as the Mk 6 in the text) capable of operating from the smaller fleet carriers around the world on anti-submarine duties. A top speed of not less than 230 knots at 5000 ft was asked for, but a high cruising speed was not considered important. An approach to the deck would be made at eighty knots, without using more than two-thirds engine power. The rest of the specification followed pretty well what had originally been agreed.

By September 1949 the revised anti-submarine Mk 6 was being referred to as the Firefly Mk 7 to avoid confusion with the production Mk 6. When the Design Branch Specification No M101P was issued, it was for a Firefly Mk 7.

In the meantime, Fairey had allotted Firefly Mk 1 MB757 as the flight trials mock-up aircraft. An Engineering Department memo dated 12 January 1950 was titled: 'Conversion of Firefly FR Mk 1 to three-seater anti-submarine'. The project engineer outlined the requirements, and implications involved in converting a standard Firefly FR Mk 1 into a three-seater anti-submarine aircraft. Because of the nature and after effects these changes represented it is worth noting what was said. The pilot's cockpit was to remain unchanged, except for the introduction of the GM4B compass which was essential for sonobuoy operations. The main fuel and oil tank bays were unaltered. Rear cockpit modifications allowed a two-seat arrangement with just enough room. The two twenty-three-gallon fuel tanks in the leading edge of the centre section were removed, and radio equipment and main battery installed. To compensate for the loss of fuel, the wing tank and the ASH nacelle would be located on the outer portion of the wing. This would necessitate the re-introduction of the Mk 4 series wing which offered other advantages, including power folding as already introduced on the Firefly Mk 5. A non-retractable tail wheel would be standard, and the

If they had stuck any more on MB757 at this point she would have sunk into the ground! Still in mock-up form and undergoing trials at Boscombe Down, she carries the wing nacelles, bombs and sonobuoys. There is also a metal plate above the exhaust to reduce glare. *(Crown Copyright)*

The transformation begins. The first 'true' Mk 7 WJ215 with a definite and more angular look. A single piece pilot's hood has been fitted, and a dorsal fin to the tail in an effort to help directional stability. An uglier metal exhaust baffle plate is fitted, and the streamlined containers beneath the wings are sonobuoy containers. *(Crown Copyright)*

increased stroke oleo leg modification on the main undercarriage would be incorporated. Guns, ammunition boxes and armour plating would be deleted saving some 900 lb in weight. To meet C of G considerations it was assessed that 470 lb of ballast weight would be required on the engine mounting. It was possible to avoid this if they decided to install the Griffon 12 in a Mk 4 engine mounting, to which would have been added fittings to accept existing radiator and air intakes. This would move the engine five inches forward and bring the propeller disc into the same position as on the Firefly FR4, but with a reduced ballast of 100 lb. This section finished with the words: 'It should be noted that this may have a slight adverse effect on fore and aft stability'. An understatement indeed, in the light of what eventually happened.

In March it was stated that the Admiralty had an initial requirement for fifty Firefly Mk 7 aircraft for 1951/52, but when the order came it was for fifty-two.

At an Advisory Design Conference on 6 April it was envisaged that most of the requirements would be met, but Fairey revealed that due to continually changing equipment requirements the maximum AUW was approaching 16,000 lb and

with drop tanks and other external stores they could not meet the request for continuous level speeds of 230 knots. After some discussion it was agreed that this figure could be dropped and replaced by 210/220 knots. The conference agreed that the design was suitable for economic production of 120 aircraft at a maximum rate of five aircraft per month. On 30 August 1950 Fairey received an amendment to the last Mk 6 order to cancel the last two machines and use them, 'as economically as possible in the construction of the first two Firefly Mk 7 aircraft'. These were WD924 which became WJ215, and WD925 which became WJ216. The Director of Contracts informed Fairey on 17 November that twenty-six Firefly AS Mk 7 would be added to the other orders, serials to be WK348 to WK373 inclusive.

Back in August, Fairey had proposed a new rear cockpit hooding to the MOS. This consisted of a two-piece hood, the forward section sliding aft, and the aft section sliding forward inside the front portion. Both halves hinged upwards on a single structure and could be jettisoned together. This was agreed for the production aircraft.

When MB757 was mocked-up, various Fairey test pilots flew it for evaluation. The first thing

A really fine air-to-air picture of WJ216 in full naval colours. Gone is the dorsal fin and in its place is a taller, more angular fin and rudder. *(Author's collection)*

they found was that the pilot's vision during a deck approach was limited. After some deliberation the Design Office said that all the pilot's controls and associated equipment was to be raised by twelve inches to overcome this problem. After more flights the test pilots were of the opinion that the apparent increase in view did not represent a great deal of improvement. It was said: 'Whilst in direct view over the propeller boss the angle of vision is increased from five to eleven degrees, giving an increase of deck vision of from 49 ft to 87 ft forward, the chief test pilot assures me that the critical point of view for deck landing is some fifteen degrees off the bow. This would infer that improvement at this point can only be achieved by keeping the increase in height of the forward fairing within the existing shoulder. This would lead to a steep shouldered top fairing with consequent restrictions on the size of the dashboard.' It was a *Catch 22* situation – started by the changing of the basic design.

Fairey had by now realised that there might be stability problems as well, and in January 1951 came up with an improvement by increasing the span of the tailplane, from 16 ft to 18 ft. Flight trials with increased span tailplane fitted to Firefly VT393 were to be carried out and if approved would be incorporated on the two prototype Firefly Mk 7s.

On 11 January 1951 Fairey was informed the Admiralty was buying another 101 Firefly AS Mk 7 aircraft, serials to be WM761 to WM779, WM796 to WM832 and WM835 to WM899 inclusive. Deliveries were to start 1 April 1952 and continue to 31 March 1953. By now the Admiralty had all flags flying and ordered another 105 on 23 February with a follow up order of fifty-one on 8 June – a total of 337 including the two prototypes, and all AS Mk 7. Any reference to these orders in other publications being for the Firefly T Mk 7 are not correct.

First flight of the prototype WJ215 was made on 22 May 1951. All three aircraft, the two prototypes, WJ215 and WJ216, and the development airframe MB757, flew initially with the standard Mk 6 fin and rudder. From flight test experience it was realised that more directional control was required and a taller, more angular fin and rudder was tried on WJ216, and after a further change was incorporated on production aircraft. WJ216 was chosen because WJ215 had been converted from a Mk 6 on the production line and was a pre-production standard incorporating the following design changes:

Mod 940	Increased travel oleo
Mod 1000	Three-seat conversion
Mod 1238	Eighteen-foot tailplane incorporated
Mod 1244	The further improvements to the oleos.

Starting on 2 June 1951 WJ215 was involved in trials of general handling characteristics at aft C of G positions at different weights, and with the elevator horn balance beaks removed; directional control in untrimmed dives; vibration records; fuel consumptions with the Griffon 59 fitted and nacelles removed from the wings. On 11 June it was handling characteristics at forward C of Gs including stalls, ADDLs, stick forces and longitudinal control. During July more trials were conducted, this time at Boscombe Down. It was reported:

'On take-off trials the mean distance using 2750 rpm plus 25 lb/sq in boost (with water/methanol) at 14,500 lb AUW was 1047 ft in zero wind and 575 ft in a 21 knot wind. Without the water/methanol these figures became 1117 ft and 610 ft respectively. There was little change in stability when sonobuoy containers were fitted, up to about 250 knots, but above this speed the containers prevented the tendency to instability due, I think, to the change in tailplane and elevator loadings caused by the container aerodynamics and their centre of pressure.'

An assessment was made of the general worry – longitudinal handling characteristics – by both Fairey and Boscombe test pilots, the former saying that handling was within the defined limits. Boscombe disagreed. In a report of September 1951 where the performance of WJ215 was compared against a standard Mk 6, they stated that the directional and longitudinal handling behaviour, especially at low speeds, i.e. deck landing approaches, was worse than those of the Mk 6. Further comparative trials were made with a Mk 7 against Mk 6 WD886 and WH629 in January 1952, but the results were the same, the forward view was poorer. Take-off performance was inferior to Fairey's declared measurements and the undercarriage was 'not good'. Among the comments in the summary was '. . . a very considerable improvement beyond the present standard must be made'. However, in a MOS letter to the RTO at Fairey on 18 September it was pointed out, in all fairness, that on the take-off tests the Mk 7 had more drag than the mock-up, and the directional stability problem compared to MB757 was thought to be due to repositioning the engine further forward. Throughout 1951 MB757 was involved in numerous comparative trials against WJ215, which at times included exchanging items, such as the rear cockpit hood or wing nacelles. The only real difference was that MB757 was still powered by a Griffon 37 but the Design Office could correct figures to allow for this. WJ216 joined the programme in November 1951 carrying out comparative trials with a Barracuda-type radiator nose and Mk 7 four-blade propeller. Level speeds were assessed at different heights between 5000 ft and 15,000 ft, while fairings were added behind the observer's cockpit hood, presumably in an effort to clean up the airflow.

On 3 October 1951 a Firefly AS Mk 7 meeting was called to action alterations (about twenty-three) required for production aircraft. The most important of these included a complete redesign of the pilot's cockpit, inclusion of the increased span tailplane, hydraulic damper for the deck hook, redesigned fin and rudder contours and to incorporate ASV 19A radar instead of ASH. The other improvements were of a minor, but necessary nature, although very relevant at the time. Of these, the pilot's cockpit changes entailed a great deal of redesign and was a major setback. This was because it now had to meet new requirements for an SBAC approved cockpit layout. The tailplane had to be completely redesigned as just extending its span didn't help longitudinal stability at all, although it was retained at 18 ft. It was found that the ASV 19A nacelle on the wing was of considerably larger diameter than the ASH one, thus adding more drag. The whole situation was rapidly getting out of hand, not helped by the fact that the Americans were offering the use of Grumman Avenger AS Mk 4s through the Mutual Defence Aid Program (MDAP) and looked more suitable. Constant requests for changes and modifications, compounded by the poor flight results, meant that the programme had slipped back from mid-1950 to mid-October 1951 when the first production Firefly AS Mk 7 left the line. Events to change things were precipitated in February 1952 when a memo was circulated within the Admiralty stating that the A & AEE considered the Mk 7 inferior in view and control to other marks of Firefly and that deck landing by night under normal conditions would not be possible without a high accident rate. They also said

that only when Fairey had raised the directional characteristics to an acceptable standard would it be possible to condone an CS(A) release for day operations, including deck landing in moderately calm conditions. The general view at the Ministry was that the view and control deficiencies had been known for some time. Nothing had been done about the view and precious little had been achieved on control characteristics in the last six months. If the situation was allowed to continue, another six months would pass with nothing achieved. Someone, from somewhere, had to get a grip of the situation and sort it out.

It fell to the Assistant Director of Naval Development and Production to make the following statement:

'I am firmly of the opinion that the Firefly Mk 7 is basically unsuitable for its role under operating conditions. It is unsuitable for day or night deck operations whilst its flight characteristics are inferior to previous marks of Firefly and it is considered by A & AEE that it will prove very unpopular in Service. I have based opinion on the following main facts:

'(a) The view has deteriorated and no improvement can be affected without considerable redesign.
(b) The undercarriage is relatively weak and falls short of present day requirements. It has this week (5 February 1952) collapsed during ADDLs. Its capacity is only sixty per cent of the present standard.
(c) Little improvement in the control features has been achieved. Directional characteristics are still bad and aileron effectiveness at low speeds has worsened. Rudder lock-over happens in the climb.

'To improve any of the deficiencies and to bring each up to acceptable standards must involve considerable redesign which will require time and labour. We can go on hopefully expecting improvements from short-term work, but I consider that it would be wrong to continue this policy. Only long-term studies will provide the remedies. In such a case the impact on the Gannet programme would have to be carefully considered. It is certain that any diversion of design effort from the Gannet would have

Firefly T Mk 7s in full song as 719 Squadron keep closed-up for the Coronation Fly Past. Nearest is WK368 337/GN, middle is WJ188 322/GN, far left is WJ165 329/GN and in front is WM770 330/GN. *(Flight International)*

very serious effects on its programme. This position is further aggravated by the failure of the laminar flow propeller to meet 'G' plus yaw case, and production of blades has stopped pending a redesign of root portion.

'The Admiralty should be informed immediately of the unsatisfactory technical state of the Firefly 7, and I strongly recommend that they are advised that the Firefly 7 will be unsatisfactory in the operational conditions associated with its role. Night operations from carrier decks will not be possible.'

It should perhaps be pointed out at this stage that during the research for this book the author was informed that there was a lot of lobbying and pressure put on certain people to get the Firefly 7 programme cancelled in favour of accepting larger numbers of the Avenger from the USA.

In an effort to try and save something and redress the situation, Fairey met with Ministry representatives on 14 February with some ideas on

how to improve the directional problems. This was to:

1 Offset the fin slight.
2 Increase the fin height and area.
3 Introduce a narrower chord rudder with the tab higher up.

They offered to have the modified aircraft flying that weekend but could offer no short-term solutions. They still had not overcome the rudder overbalance or aileron problems at slow speeds, which they reckoned were bound up with the directional behaviour. While Fairey were doing their best to try and come up with an answer, the men from the Ministry met again on 21 February to see what could be saved from the programme. They thought under the circumstances that the most desirable course would be for it to be used for observer and aircrewmen training, and its value would be greatly enhanced if night operations from airfields could be granted. This would reduce the demand for Mk 6 Fireflies engaged in training, so that more would be available for front-line anti-submarine squadrons until the Gannet entered Service, or sufficient Avengers were received from America. A line of action was proposed for the training Firefly Mk 7:

1 Meet with Boscombe Down to discuss trials necessary for CS(A) release in the training role.
2 Cancel trials aboard HMS *Illustrious* as its use as a trainer did not require deck landing clearance.
3 Fairey to be informed and to stop all action on the AS Mk 7 except for the development of the revised fin and rudder.
4 Contracts department informed of changed requirements.
5 Place the Firefly Mk 7 on the 'Restricted' modification list as soon as the deletion of the various items of equipment had been covered.

Fairey modified the controls as requested and WJ215 went back to Boscombe. The results were not long in forthcoming, by the end of March they reported: '. . . sufficient flying has now been done for it to be concluded that while the new fin and rudder and modified ailerons have made detailed improvements to the control characteristics, the overall assessment of the

aircraft remains very much as before, i.e. that night deck operations would inevitably involve a high accident rate, that day deck landings will need a high degree of judgement, even under good conditions, and that instrument and night flying in particular will be very tiring. It has been confirmed that the view is definitely worse than that of the Mk 6 and very much worse than that of the Mk 1.' The Ministry said that they were unable therefore to give consideration to a CS(A) Release for any deck operation and Fairey were to be informed of the change in role. (Fairey were led to believe the Boscombe trials were still part of the modification programme to the AS Mk 7.) Clearance for Service use was expected by August with only minor changes, the actual specification for the Firefly T Mk 7 being very similar except for the deletion of any reference to anti-submarine duties.

On 23 April 1952 Air Marshal Sir John N. Boothman (at the Air Ministry) wrote to Sir Richard Fairey:

> 'I regret to inform you that despite the considerable improvements in the control characteristics of the Firefly AS7 that have been effected by your efforts, we cannot recommend this aircraft to the Admiralty for use in the anti-submarine role.

Firefly T Mk 7s WJ188 T and WM764 P in the hangar at Llanbedr, 23 July 1959. Used for shepherding or as chase aircraft, they needed the extra fuel carried in the drop tanks. *(A. Pearcy)*

WM770 761/CU and Mk 4 VH127 at Lossiemouth in April 1962. Both were going to be preserved but only the latter made it, WM770 was sold as scrap and ended its days in the infamous Quarrywood scrapyard in Scotland not long after this photograph was taken. *(S. L. Waring via G. J. R. Skillen)*

'In our opinion, day deck landing would require a high degree of judgement even in good conditions and night deck operation might well involve a high accident rate. While instrument and night flying would be very tiring, the pilot's view is considered to be worse than the Mark 6 and very much worse than the Mark 1.

'The aircraft is, however, considered to be suitable for observer training duties from airfield bases by day and night with the gyro gunsight removed. Its use in that role has been recommended to the Admiralty.

'Discussions are in progress with the Admiralty on what should be done to adapt the aircraft to the training role, and these intended modifications will be communicated to you shortly. You are already aware of the probable reduction in the numbers required but it is expected, subject to Treasury approval, that some 160 aircraft will be required in the training role. I understand also that some seventy may be required for the purposes of the Controller of Guided Weapons and Electronics.'

The details of the Firefly's use by the Guided Weapon division is told in the chapter about target drones.

The first production machine, WJ146 made its maiden flight on 16 October 1951, and after acceptance flying by Fairey it was returned to Fairey at White Waltham on 9 March 1953, where it made a perfect wheels-up landing. It then went to Fairey's Hamble factory for repair and was delivered to Anthorn on 29 April 1954. Here it was placed in Long Term Storage (LTS) until 1958 when it was scrapped. This was the first of 151 Firefly T Mk 7s built, 110 at Hayes and the last forty-one at Stockport to make way for Gannet production at Hayes. The problems associated with the production of the Firefly Mk 7 were never truly resolved and this resulted in about half of the aircraft being placed in LTS and never used. The last T Mk 7 Firefly was delivered to the FAA in December 1953.

Those that did enter service were used by various training squadrons, by 719 between February 1953 and June 1956 at Eglinton; by 750 between March 1953 and June 1955; by 765, a piston engined pilot's school at Culdrose during February 1955 to September 1956; by 796 for a short time between March and November 1956 and two RNVR squadrons, 1840 and 1841 of the Channel Air Division at Ford. Observer training has always been an important part of naval aviation and the duties could be very diversified, hence the unofficial motto, 'Find, Fix and Strike'. Following the end of the Second World War observer recruitment came to a standstill, but not for long. With the wide range of aircraft entering service and new tasks and equipment it was soon recognised that observers still had an important role to play in the FAA. Recruitment came from four sources, fleet entry, which was a general service lieutenant specialising in the Air Branch; aviation cadet, who entered on a short-service commission for either four or eight years; National Service entry and finally regular naval ratings who volunteered for aircrew duties. Taking a new entry in 1956 as an example, their course with the Observer's School at Culdrose lasted thirty-nine weeks and was broken down into three parts. Part 1 comprised radar, basic navigation, wireless telegraphy etc. with thirty-four hours flying; Part II concentrated on applied navigation with forty hours day flying and eight at night; Part III included fifty hours day and eight hours night flying on advanced navigation, tactical work, photo reconnaissance and wider aspects of maritime warfare. All the flying was done in the Firefly T Mk 7. After receiving their 'wings' a two-month series of exercises followed before being posted to an operational squadron. This was one of the last tasks the Firefly performed for the FAA as by 1955 the Gannet was being introduced into service.

Chapter 16
Svensk Fireflies

AS A FIREFLY operator, the Swedish company, Svensk Flygjanst AB, was unique in that it was a civil company which operated target-towing services for the Swedish military forces.

Svensk Flygtjanst AB – Swedish Air Services Ltd – was a private company formed in 1935 by Tor Eliasson, who, at that time was just twenty-one. His first aircraft was an Avro Avian, which Eliasson bought in England and flew to Sweden. The first few years were spent on banner-towing, passenger flights and flying lessons. The private flying school he formed before the war, became the largest in the country. To do this he added other Avians, de Havilland Moths, Bucker Bestmans, a Bristol Fighter and a Sikorsky amphibian.

At the beginning of the war a contract was signed with the defence forces to provide target-towing, target flying and certain types of special missions. During the war a great number of different types were acquired and used: Moths, Miles Falcon, Caudron, Arado, Fokker CVE and Fiat CR42 to name some. After the war the contract was continued and other aircraft acquired – Miles Martinets, Saab B17s and the Fairey Firefly. In 1955 two Gloster Meteor T Mk 7 were added, followed by four Meteor TT MK 20 which were used for Danish defence work. Douglas AD4W Skyraiders arrived in 1963. Other activities of the company after the war were crop spraying, air taxi work, passenger flights and charter work. The latter developed into a semi-regular airline to Prague with Fokker Trimotors, Junkers W34 and de Havilland Rapide.

In 1948 Svensk Flygtjanst considered their Miles Martinets too slow for the target-towing work they were getting and looked for a suitable replacement. The choice of the Firefly was obvious, because of its cruising speed, its rear cockpit was large enough to take the equipment and operator, both its airframe and engine were well proven and, its low initial cost as a surplus military machine. Once an agreement had been reached between the two companies Fairey sought the release of some Firefly 1s from the Admiralty. For once they agreed and released some, the first

being DK568 which, after being converted into a target-tower became TT Mk 1 SE.BRA. All the aircraft were painted yellow overall with the text, 'SVENSK FLYGTJANST AB STOCKHOLM' on the fuselage under the front cockpit. Registration letters and anti-dazzle panel forward of the pilot's cockpit was in black. On some of the fleet, but not all, a red arrowhead was painted on the rudder, and on the occasional aircraft, on the drop tank. General instructions, usually stencilled on a military aircraft, were in black and Swedish, examples being:

Handtag = Hand hold
Fotsteg = Foot step
Lyfrslinga = Hoist sling

Group Captain Gordon Slade, at that time Chief Test Pilot to Fairey, delivered the first aircraft, SE.BRA, on 6 December 1948. The delivery flight from Ringway was to Valkenburg in Holland, then to Kastrup, Denmark and on to Bromma in Sweden where the aircraft was handed over. This was the first of nineteen Firefly TT Mk 1s acquired by Svensk and was to serve them well. Over the period of the contract all the Fireflies bought from the Fairey company were delivered by Fairey test pilots. Some of them had interesting trips, although Sam Moseley's was, thank goodness, not typical:

'SE.BRF was the one I most remember. I had an adverse weather forecast for the Valkenburg/Kastrup leg for the morning of Friday 13 January 1949! However, the weather in the afternoon was expected to clear; Valkenburg and Kastrup required a most elaborate flight plan for the trip, together with details of all navigation aids in the Firefly. These were confined to about four VHF channels! Anyway, I elected to go and took off. At 10,000 ft the weather was clear, no cloud etc. all the way via Kiel to the mainland and islands of Sjadland, Falster, Mon etc. Every one of the islands was covered with low cloud (lifted fog). I descended and endeavoured to fly under this cloud, but it was too low, nearly extending to the coastline. Neither was it possible to fly low round the coast. I remember coming to a bridge joining two of the islands, and deciding it would be foolhardy to fly under it, I climbed slightly to go over it and found myself in cloud again! So climbing for safety I went up to 10,000 ft again and proceeded to Kastrup. I called them constantly on the approach frequency, to no effect. When I had overflown Kastrup on ETA (Estimated Time of Arrival), Malmo came on in answer to my Kastrup calls. Malmo then alerted Kastrup, who then answered me stating that they had thick fog, with visibility less than forty yards! They asked me what navigational aids I had and I told them, nothing other than VHF radio. The top of this thick fog was 700/800 ft and I asked if they had GCA (Ground Control Approach radar). I knew they hadn't officially, but it was the only way to get down that I knew of. I also asked for any alternative suggestions – but they had none to offer. The cause of the fog was a mild day (all of Denmark was under snow) and a thaw had followed with high humidity, but by 3 p.m. the temperature started to fall and fog formed.

I told them at Kastrup that Kiel had been open when I overflew it about an hour earlier and that I intended to return there. By the time I was fifty miles from Kiel I could see fog had formed there and the whole of Jutland was now under cloud. There were now only two courses open to me, bale out and lose the aeroplane, or force-land and hope for the best. I then remembered a small bit of Sjaelland (high ground off Denmark) showing through the fog as I flew over. I raced back. There was a small area still open about 1500 yards in diameter, and underneath, farmland, all covered in snow. I made about five or six dummy runs over telegraph wires into a small snow-covered field, and deciding I could make it, went in with wheels and flaps down. Unfortunately, under the snow the field was half turf, and half ploughed in long strips. Having landed OK I was just congratulating myself when, on crossing one of the ploughed sections, the Firefly started to bog down, and the tail started to come up. I debated, but decided against using some engine power to increase elevator effectiveness, due to the limited size of the field – and she slowly turned over. The hood was open and I wasted

SE.BRL at Farnborough in September 1950. To give them the extra endurance, the Swedish Fireflies always operated with drop tanks, but it was rare for them to be used in military service. *(Author's collection)*

SE.BRL in less happy times. She suffered an engine failure on 28 September 1963 while towing off the coast near Halland, and crashed in the surf. *(Author's collection)*

SE.BRG and SE.BYD at Bulltofta Airport, Malmo, in the early 1960s. Note the different coloured spinner on .BYD. Later on, BRG also had a three-colour spinner, red tip, white band and yellow rear. *(Lars E. Lundin)*

no time in scrambling out. Fortunately, not too much damage was done, mainly due to the soft ground and snow. Well, the Danish authorities required a comprehensive report of the sequence of events leading up to the accident. I submitted this saying I was equally interested to see their side of the story. Their report arrived after some weeks – it was almost word for word the same as mine!'

The rest of the Fireflies were delivered, including three acquired in 1957/58 as substitutes for aircraft lost in accidents, from the Royal Danish Air Force who had cancelled their operation. None of the three flew, being set aside for cannibalisation to keep the others flying. The identities of the Swedish aircraft were:

SE.BRG and CAW were handed over to Swedish aircraft museums, and SE.BRD was flown to Staverton, Gloucestershire, on 5 May 1964 to join Peter Thomas's Skyfame Museum. It is perhaps appropriate that this machine should be the one to return to the UK as it was previously Z2033, the original trainer mock-up trials aircraft. The reason the Fireflies were retired in 1964 was general wear, corrosion, fatigue and lack of essential spare parts. During their time with Svensk target-towing, the Fireflies flew some 14,962 flying hours. The total time on the airframes when withdrawn from service varied between 1500 and 3300 hours.

Reg	Ex-RN	Delivered	Cancelled	Remarks
SE.BRA	DK568	06.12.48	03.06.64	Scrapped
SE.BRB	DK459	12.01.49	03.06.64	Scrapped
SE.BRC	Z1908	14.01.49	21.03.63	Crashed
SE.BRD	Z2033	15.02.49	16.03.64	To Skyfame, UK
SE.BRF	DT986	13.01.50	24.11.54	Crashed
SE.BRG	DT989	28.06.50	03.06.64	Scrapped
SE.BRH	MB387	28.06.50	03.06.64	Scrapped
SE.BRI	DV121	24.07.50	03.11.54	Crashed
SE.BRK	MB503	24.07.50	11.02.53	Crashed
SE.BRL	DT939	23.09.50	03.06.64	Scrapped
SE.BRM	DK430	12.09.50	21.03.63	Scrapped
SE.BYB	MB624		21.03.63	Scrapped
SE.BYC	MB728		03.06.64	Scrapped
SE.BYD	MB702		03.06.64	Scrapped
SE.CAU	PP469		03.06.64	Scrapped
SE.CAW	PP392		03.06.64	Scrapped
SE.CHL	Z1842	Ex-RDAF 625		Spares
SE.CHM	Z1850	Ex-RDAF 626		Spares
SE.CHN	MB579	Ex-RDAF 630		Spares

Chapter 17
Firefly Drones

SOON AFTER World War II the development of missiles made it imperative that some form of remotely-controlled target aircraft was developed. During the war the de Havilland Queen Bee, a radio-controlled version of the famous Tiger Moth was used. What was needed however, was a high speed target; experiments with radio-controlled Spitfires and Martinets had come to nothing. It was also realised that the rapid development of advanced guided missiles would require something for the future along the lines of a jet powered machine capable of operating at speeds up to 500 knots and from ground level to 50,000 ft. The MOS specification for this would eventually be filled by the Australian produced Jindivik. In the interim, the staff at Aberporth in Wales had assessed a French version of the German V1 produced by the Nord Company, but it proved unsuitable. The department for guided weapons at the MOS then asked the RAE at Farnborough if they could provide some form of converted aircraft, with a reasonable performance, to use until the new aircraft came on line. Their first choice was ex-FAA Fireflies. There were plenty around, they were rugged and had a fairly good performance, and, they had room for any special equipment which might need fitting.

Development of the Firefly as a target drone began in 1952 by the RAE although Fairey was closely concerned at all stages, and was subsequently responsible for 'productionising' the system. This wasn't the first time Fairey aircraft had been involved with guided weapon research however. Work on Remotely-Piloted Vehicles (RPV) had been going on since 1917 but had gone quiet at the end of World War I. Interest was revived in 1922/23 when the earlier model of 1917 was flown powered by an Anzani motorcycle engine. Some twelve launches took place during 1923/24 with varying degrees of success, or total loss of control! During the period 1922/25 a series of trials took place with what was intended to be an aerial target. These machines were launched from HMS *Stronghold* and escorted by a Fairey

IIID (N9641) seaplane flown by F/Lt H. L. Macro from the School of Naval Co-Operation at Lee-on-Solent. Flying alongside these often out-of-control machines to record their behaviour was an unenviable job as they would make erratic manoeuvres with no warning. It really fell to the RAE and Fairey to develop the first real British drone.

In 1929 arguments raged back and forth over the controversial effectiveness of air attacks against warships. The Air Ministry, at that time, had been impressed by the success of bombing exercises against the undefended target ship HMS *Centurion*. Their Lordships at the Admiralty remained unconvinced that such attacks could be pressed home in the face of defensive gunfire. A radio-controlled target to simulate bombing and torpedo attacks promised to resolve the controversy. Accordingly, the RAE was asked to develop such a target. The Fairey IIIF was chosen as a suitable basis for the target, since it met the requirements of being launched from ship's catapults, simulating level and dive-bombing attacks and alighting on the sea; and it could be flown conventionally for check purposes. A completely new set of automatic equipment was developed for the 'Queen', as the IIIF target was to be called, based upon the principles of the RAE Pilot's Assister, the automatic pilot developed in 1925. Three Fairey IIIFs were converted to Queens and the first of these was flown – as a landplane and with a check crew on board – in the autumn of 1931. It was then taken to Lee-on-Solent for floats to be fitted and was allocated to HMS *Valiant* for the first pilotless test flight. This was made on 21 January 1932 and was a complete failure; the Queen struck the sea eighteen seconds after being launched and was destroyed. The trouble was traced to the method of achieving longitudinal control through the elevator, which was by means of an accelerometer-monitored gyroscope. Modifications were made and the second Queen was launched on 19 April 1932. The second Queen survived for twenty-five seconds before diving almost vertically into the sea. This second failure was attributed to the inability of the automatic control system to hold on rudder which would have counteracted the yaw which developed during the launch. A more powerful and aerodynamically balanced rudder was fitted to the third and last Queen. After some hesitation over the use of the surviving target – the possibility of its being flown to a safe height by a pilot who would then bale out was seriously considered – it was finally decided to risk all on another pilotless flight. This was successfully made on 14 September 1932, and lasted nine minutes, slight damage occurred in the landing in a rather rough sea. The culmination of the Queen's story came in January 1933, when the third aircraft was taken to Gibraltar for the Home Fleet's Spring Cruise. It was duly mounted aboard HMS *Valiant* for a shoot in Tetuan Bay. On the day in question, a fresh wind was blowing and the sea was so rough as to make a successful automatic landing doubtful. However, as the Commander-in-Chief thought it unlikely that the aircraft would be required to land, he ordered the exercise to proceed. The next two hours were to have far-reaching consequences in several directions, for the Queen remained airborne and unscathed by the whole weight of fire of the Home Fleet, which included the battleships HMS *Nelson* and *Rodney*. At the end of the shoot, the Queen alighted successfully and was retrieved by HMS *Valiant*. Among other things, the episode showed the need for the Fleet to improve its standard of ship-to-air gunnery and demonstrated the value of a pilotless aircraft for this purpose, although it appears a pilot aboard would have been quite safe on this occasion. For production purposes the IIIF was larger and more complex than necessary and, the Fairey Aviation Co., then being fully committed to other work, a new drone was developed from the Tiger Moth and put into production as the Queen Bee. The surviving IIIF Queen ended her days honourably, in May 1933, when she was shot down by HMS *Shropshire* during exercises with the Mediterranean Fleet after being airborne for about twenty minutes.

From the meetings held about the future of the Firefly Mk 7 it had been mentioned that its use as a target drone would be considered. The RAE was informed and contacted Fairey. A meeting was held at Hayes on 8 April 1952 between Fairey design staff led by H. E. Chaplin and four representatives from the RAE. They were to discuss the implications of fitting an auto pilot and associated equipment in the Mk 7. The aircraft had to be capable of being flown manually with an observer to calibrate the auto pilot, probably prior to each controlled flight. Briefly, the requirement involved stripping all existing equipment from the rear cockpit and installing radio control, auto-pilot, and trials instrumentation units. It was agreed that most of the radio control and auto-pilot units could be mounted in the compartment over the main fuel tank and at the forward end of the observer's cockpit. The trials instrumentation units, consisting of cameras requiring an all-round view, were to be mounted in special nacelles carried on the wing tips. The pilot's cockpit would remain substantially unaltered except to remove unnecessary equipment and have new controllers fitted. It was agreed that the standard internal fuel tankage of 176 gallons would be adequate for range requirements and the fifty-five-gallon nacelle tank deleted. It was also agreed to remove anything to save weight, such as wing folding mechanism, flame dampers, water/methanol system, heaters etc. which would be left to Fairey. A standard production Mk 7, WJ149, was required to be at the RAE by the end of April for trial purposes. This would be modified and followed by two further machines, WJ151 and WJ152, so that there would be three prototypes. Eventually six machines became test or chase aircraft, the additional ones being WJ147, 150 and 153, and they were known as T Mk 8s but were all upgraded eventually to U Mk 8 status. Total requirement, Fairey was informed, was for seventy aircraft, in addition to the prototypes, with deliveries of eleven aircraft in the first year, twenty-two in the second and 30/40 in 1954/55. Later, the number of development machines was increased to six. For the purposes of remote-controlled flight the controls for the throttle, propeller, flaps and arrester hook incorporated radio-controlled electric actuators. The 'fixed' commands available to the ground operators were: Take-off, climb, cruise, slow level, beep down/ beep up, left turn, right turn, descend-flaps up, descend-flaps down, roll left, roll right, camera operate, camera event, signal fail and engine cut.

During radio-controlled flight the throttle was operated electrically by an ULTRA throttle unit mounted on the port side of the cockpit. The propeller levers on the quadrant were locked in the 2600 rpm position. The automatic pilot installation was known as the Type H and developed from the standard Mk 9 auto-pilot system. In addition to the stabilisation of the aircraft in normal flight, i.e. detecting and correcting disturbances from normal, the auto-pilot was designed to initiate controlled movements to the aircraft in flight in response to remotely transmitted command signals. Each camera nacelle contained four weapon assessing cameras and a special purpose fifth one.

The changes incorporated into the aircraft were covered by Modification 1500 and consisted of thirteen parts:

Part 1 Installation of Type H auto-pilot
Part 2 Installation of throttle control unit
Part 3 Installation of radio equipment, VHF and intercom
Part 4 Installation of two-position jacks to operate undercarriage, flaps, propeller lever and arrester hook
Part 5 Installation of weapon assessing gear in wing tip nacelle
Part 6 Installation of oxygen equipment for crew
Part 7 Installation of emergency diving system
Part 8 Removal of –
    (a) Wing folding jacks
    (b) Wing tank and ASH nacelle
    (c) Flame dampers replaced by stub type
    (d) Cockpit heating
    (e) Water/methanol system
    (f) Gun sight
    (g) G45 camera
    (h) ADRIS
    (i) All existing radio equipment
Part 9 Special colour and identification scheme
Part 10 GM4B compass repositioning of detector in tail
Part 11 Installation of 6 cm oscillator
Part 12 Electrical supply (junction and terminal boxes etc.) to suit requirements
Part 13 Deck-hook gear re-installed.

Most of the early development flying, with pilot and observer aboard, was done from White Waltham in collaboration with the RAE. Before the end of 1952 one of the six Fireflies was sent to RAE Llanbedr where Short Bros. and Harland's Flying Services Division maintained a unit on behalf of the MOS. With a check pilot on board this aircraft was used to develop remote control techniques until, by the end of 1953, its behaviour and speed could be controlled from Aberporth. The first unmanned flight from Llanbedr was made in February 1954.

Meanwhile, a contract for the production of thirty-four drones was placed with Fairey, production to be at the Stockport/Ringway factories. These were designated Firefly U Mk 8, and used many of the components and parts originally laid down for Firefly T Mk 7 production, contracts of which had been curtailed.

The first Firefly U Mk 8 took to the air on 27 November 1953.

As mentioned, most of the early development flying was done by Fairey at White Waltham. The first two Mk 7s, WJ216 and 217 were used for trials in the Mk 7 programme but afterwards were completed as Mk 7Ds as drone pilot test beds. The assigned Fairey test pilot for this work was David Masters, an ex-RAF pilot, and he recalls those days:

'The project was certainly an interesting one. To begin with, one could hardly choose a more difficult or unsuitable aircraft for landing by remote radio-control than a single-engined, tail-wheeled propeller driven aircraft! Since the slightest throttle movement sharply affected longitudinal and directional trim, the response to elevator and rudder movements, and even the stalling characteristics just before touch down, you can understand that in those days any computer complex enough to handle all the changing information and behaviour patterns would have filled a couple of Beverleys! The result was that there had to be remote manual over-ride of the auto-pilot during the take-off and landing, by two strategically placed observers, sited in positions of some risk. As you no doubt realise, a pilot of a manually-controlled aircraft – particularly one like the Firefly – relies heavily on the feel of the controls for information about changing response rates etc. Since the observers could have no such information, and since the commands that could be transmitted to the aircraft were limited in number (and subtlety) the near-the-ground control of the Firefly was not so much incomplete, as bloody primitive! Furthermore, the Smith's auto-pilot made available for the aircraft was quite unsuitable. According to its manufacturer's handbook, it was not to be asked to carry out-of-trim loads for more than the passing moment; to fly a Firefly at speeds ranging from take-off to max cruise it had to carry heavy out-of-trim loads continuously!

'The throttle control was also a bit of a problem. The throttle motor was controlled by a Black Box designed and supplied by Ultra. The throttle behaviour induced dangerous instabilities in turns, for example, due to the effects of over-correction and false airspeeds fed in from the wing pitot head during yaw produced by throttle movement. The throttle

An excellent study of the third Firefly U Mk 8 WM856 showing the wing tip nacelle position and the layout of the wing. The red and yellow scheme made the drone very colourful and a modeller's delight. *(Crown Copyright)*

control amplifier was a mystery to everyone, apparently, except Ultra! It was heavily marked 'Secret', with no drawings available to us etc. Unfortunately, only one man at Ultra really understood the thing, so when he was killed in a car accident, we were a bit poorly placed. After a lot of unsatisfactory dealings with all concerned, we took the lid off the contraption and nosed around inside. We took the law into our own hands, as it were, and made a modification or two that improved things considerably!

'I flew a number of tests at Llanbedr, and one or two with 728B Squadron in Malta allowing the thing to be radio-controlled whilst I sat in the cockpit and prayed. The trouble was that one had to let things get to a pretty pass to see whether the remote-controllers were going to be able to retrieve the situation. This meant that one had to judge very accurately the point at which disaster was inevitable, and take suitable action about two seconds (or a few feet) before it. After, for example, an ill-judged encounter with the

runway during a landing attempt, one could arrive at a height of twenty or thirty feet, in an obscene and lunatic nose-up attitude with the airspeed rapidly disappearing and the engine more or less off duty. If, after a short period (about a thousand years) it seemed that the remote-controllers were undecided what to do, or dead maybe, one could (a) throw out the auto-pilot (if the electric clutches responded smartly enough), or (b) unlock the throttle from the throttle-motor by rotating the twist-grip (if it hadn't jammed under load) or (c) return the aircraft to the ether by coaxing the engine into renewed life and manufacturing some airspeed from somewhere. All very exhilarating!'

General development continued and on 29 September 1955 at Aberporth a Venom carried out the first air launch of a guided and controlled missile which destroyed a Firefly U Mk 8 WM886. There was a rumour at the time that the Firefly was more aimed at the missile than the missile at the Firefly! Things did not always go according to plan either. On one sortie with a pilot aboard the engine failed and the pilot made a forced-landing in a field near a village. Another time one had engine trouble on the approach with flaps and undercarriage down and just dropped out of the sky, splat onto rough ground. The fuel tanks burst and there was fuel all over the place, with a resulting fire. The pilot rescued his RAE observer and both suffered burns, but the pilot was later awarded the George Medal for his action. One of the test pilots, G. R. MacDonald recalls one of his trips:

'The incident to the Firefly U Mk 8 which finished up on its nose occurred on an occasion on which I was "shepherding". The pilotless aircraft were controlled by radio transmissions from ground stations, either Llanbedr or Aberporth. Take-off was accomplished by a man situated at the downwind end of the runway, equipped with a left-right switch, an engine out switch and the main transmitters from which other commands such as "take-off" were initiated. Landing was accomplished by a team consisting of an azimuth site operator, a pitch site operator and a master controller. The "shepherd" pilot gave instructions regarding attitudes and headings when the pilotless aircraft was climbing, descending and en

route to the range, but did not actually transmit command signals to the pilotless aircraft. On the occasion in question, everything went reasonably smoothly until the pilotless aircraft was on the approach. It was then found that it was not responding in pitch. At this time a new runway was being constructed at Llanbedr and it so happened that a contractor's bulldozer chose this morning to sever the cable leading from the pitch site to the main transmitter. Overshoot procedure was carried out and the Firefly was sent round again in the normal (very wide) circuit while emergency measures were taken on the ground. The transmitters were still serviceable and there was a device available which had been constructed by RAE to enable signals to be sent out automatically with visual tracking of the aircraft. The master controller opted to use this device but had no experience of using it! A quick decision was necessary at this stage as the aircraft had been on the range for over two hours and was low on fuel (as was I). The first attempt with the emergency set up resulted in a heavy landing, and the aircraft was sent round again from the bounce. Flying alongside I noticed that one landing gear leg was bent back at an angle. An interesting landing was therefore inevitable. On the second attempt an extremely smooth landing was made, but due

WM810 A and WJ149 E at RAE Lanbedr. *(A. Pearcy)*

to the previous damage to the undercarriage the aircraft slowly pitched onto its nose and slid a long way on two propeller blades. This was somewhat of an embarrassment to me as I had insufficient fuel to divert and the pilotless aircraft finished up on the intersection on the two runways. I eventually landed over the top of the other Firefly and landed in half the usual distance with heavy braking, but it was a near thing.'

The use of the target Fireflies was not restricted to UK operators either. In November 1959 six Banshee jet fighters of 870 Squadron of the Royal Canadian Navy were temporarily detached from their carrier, HMCS *Bonaventure,* while on NATO winter exercises. Armed with Sidewinder missiles the pilots demonstrated their skill by shooting down five out of six Firefly drones over the Aberporth ranges.

When a further batch of forty Firefly target drones was ordered by the MOS in 1955, the Firefly Mk 7/8 were out of production. No reason was given for not considering the Firefly Mk 7s languishing at the naval LTS depot. Instead, it was decided to convert standard Firefly Mk 5s which were surplus to FAA requirements. These new conversions were designated Firefly U Mk 9, for which Fairey was wholly responsible. Because of the different aerodynamic characteristics of the Firefly Mk 5, considerable changes to the automatic control system were required. WB416 became the prototype U Mk 9 and was used for testing any changes required on the production aircraft, it eventually became surplus to requirements and being non-standard was reduced to scrap in July 1961. The conversion of the aircraft was carried out at the Stockport/Ringway factory. Development trials were carried out at Ringway with the help of design teams from the Guided Weapons Division of Fairey at Heston. The first production Firefly U Mk 9 flew from Ringway on 13 December 1956, and subsequently Fairey conducted remote-control trials at Llanbedr before operations started in October 1957. During the years of Firefly drone operations, aircraft frequently had mishaps and accidents which required their presence back at Ringway for repair. Afterwards these would be placed in a pool storage at Ringway ready for when they were required again.

The actual conversion used most of the equipment fitted to the U Mk 8 except for:

Mod 1576 Strengthening of the wing spars and attachments for camera nacelles.

Mod 1584 Strengthening of camera nacelle attachment lugs.

Mod 1599 Fitment of flares under outer wings to assist tracking of aircraft under drone conditions.

For tracking of the aircraft six flares were provided three mounted line astern under each wing tip and were fired on command in pairs. Modellers might like to know that each flare holder was coloured to correspond with its respective supply socket and fired in the following order:

First pair	Aft	Light blue
Second pair	Central	Yellow
Third pair	Forward	White

Mod 1616 To introduce a command destruction system.

Mod 1617 To introduce 'signal failure' orbiting control.

Mod 1647 To provide for 'undercarriage' when command 'destroy' was operated.

The fuel system was the same as for the Mk 5 except that long range tanks were not carried and the suspension units removed. Auxiliary fuel tanks fitted to both port and starboard wings as standard equipment.

Interestingly it was decided to equip one FAA squadron with the Firefly U Mk 9 to meet the requirement for targets for HMS *Girdleness* equipped with Armstrong Whitworth Seaslug ship-to-air missiles. Lt/Cdr John G. Corbett RN was the CO and he recalls the early days:

'No 728B Squadron was formed at RNAS Stretton, near Warrington, on 13 January 1958. We had three aircraft initially, WB307, VT497 and VT487. These were joined by WB341, VX429, VT493, VX418, VT463, VT481 in February. Stretton was selected because it was convenient to Faireys at Ringway and Llanbedr in Wales. Our nomenclature by the way of 728B was selected rather than being given a separate squadron number for political motives. By this method the Navy maintained three separate squadrons labelled 728A, 728B and 728C while making it appear on paper that they had only one. It took two months at Stretton organising our supply lines and gathering information from Llanbedr before we moved to Hal Far on Malta. Hal Far was selected because it was already in use with two runways terminating at the cliffs and enjoying an excellent weather factor for

This rough-looking Firefly Mk 5 VT413 arrived at Ringway in October 1956 for conversion to a U Mk 9. It still has a FAA fuselage code, the crew's names and a fin code, all indecipherable in this view. *(via G. A. Jenks)*

Firefly U Mk 9 WB350 L on the ramp at RAE Llanbedr. It arrived at Ringway for conversion in May 1957 and was delivered to RAE Llanbedr in April 1958. It was repaired at Ringway in 1959 and listed as issued to 728B Squadron in June 1960, although there does not appear to be a record of it with that unit and it may have gone to Llanbedr. *(A Pearcy)*

A remarkable picture of U Mk 9 VT487 590 in pilotless flight on 8 July 1958 while serving with 728B Squadron at Hal Far, Malta. *(A. J. Standbridge)*

A most interesting study of VT485 595 shepherding pilotless VT487 590 over the Mediterranean. The two machines belong to 728B Squadron, which at that time was based at Hal Far, Malta. *(A. J. Standbridge)*

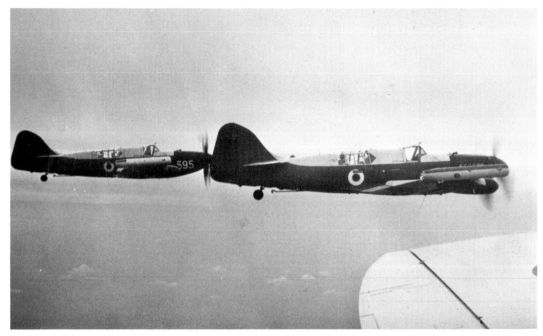

photographing the flight of the missiles.'

Before this pilots and ratings from the squadron had spent some time at Llanbedr studying MOS operations with the Firefly Mk 8, and in particular to study the ground-control equipment. They also had a chance to study the first few U Mk 9s that Llanbedr had received, WB410 having arrived on 9 July 1957 and VX421 which made the first U Mk 9 sortie on 8 October 1957. The squadron moved out to Hal Far at the end of February 1958 and started an intensive period of training. John Corbett continues:

'After arrival at Malta I was mainly pre-occupied in coaxing Maltese labourers into installing equipment and controlling things from the ground. I found I could not fly and resolve the overall problems at the same time, although I got more flying in later when things had settled down. We had the Firefly 9s which were much more difficult than Firefly 8s because it had the old type undercarriage with the high rebound factor and Mk 4 fin and rudder which, directionally, was much less stable. A complication we had not foreseen was that an aircraft running off the runway at Llanbedr sank into the peat and stopped before it could get into trouble, whereas at Hal Far it ran until it hit an obstruction, or ground-looped with resultant undercarriage failure. We found the unmanned accident rate and reliability factor quite unacceptable. The unreliability was greatly improved by looking at every single component and submitting it to the question – ''It this bit 100 per cent essential to the continuation of the flight?'' If the answer was ''no'', the component was consigned to the dustbin, whatever its theoretical advantages and regardless of the reputation of its sponsor. The accident rate was improved by lengthening the hook. To do this we used a Seahawk deck hook and connected it to the Firefly Mk 5 frame by a locally produced adapter, in fact I think the first hook to be fitted came from a ditched Seahawk. The Fairey Stress Office blew up when they heard because the Modification was unapproved and might bend slightly in use, but I preferred to change the bent adapter every fifth flight at the expense of four man hours work than write an aircraft off every flight. A modification we proposed in the light of experience with the Mk 8, was a command which put the aircraft into continuous orbit in the event of radio failure. If the fault in the control transmitters could not be rectified, or if the aircraft could not obey transmitted commands for any other reason, the ''emergency dive'' system could be brought into operation by completely separate transmitters and receivers.'

In addition to providing support to HMS *Girdleness,* 728B also supplied Fireflies for the guns of the Fleet, and Firestreaks of No 893 Squadron, who were operating the Sea Venom at that time. No 728B operated thirty-three Firefly U Mk 9s of which at least seventeen were shot down in their role as targets. One of these, WB331 only made two flights with the squadron, being shot down on the second sortie by guns of the Fleet on 2 September 1961. By now the roles of target drones was being increasingly taken over by the Meteor and Canberra. The last Firefly U Mk 9 drone in RN service, WB391, was shot down by the guns of HMS *Duchess* on 27 November 1961, and ended an era.

Chapter 18
Thai Tales

DURING 1949/50 the Royal Thai Navy expressed an interest in acquiring a number of Firefly aircraft. They were impressed with its operational history and strike capability.

A contract was signed for ten Firefly FR1s and two T2 operational trainers. The selection of the Firefly was made for a number of reasons, the principal one being that they wanted their own air arm, to be independent of the air force, and they wanted them quickly.

Fairey acquired the twelve Fireflies from the Admiralty. At that time, surplus Fireflies were parked at Abbotsinch and those selected were moved to the Stockport/ Ringway factory during January/February 1951. The Royal Thai Navy seconded an engineering officer to Ringway to oversee the reconditioning and test flying of the aircraft. These were carried out between June and December 1951 at Ringway.

In the meantime, test pilot Sam Moseley, who was going to do the test flights after the Fireflies were re-erected in Thailand, went out to see what facilities were available:

'In October 1950 I went out to Siam (later called Thailand) to assess the facilities at the Royal Thai naval airfield at Sataheep. I found virtually nothing at Sataheep, no hangar, no electric power or engineering facilities of any sort, and a rather rough runway cut in the jungle and barely 400 yards long! I told Admiral Sin, Commander-in-Chief of the Royal Thai Navy what we would require and that the existing facilities were quite inadequate. He assured me that by the time they (the aircraft) were required (October 1951) they would be available. I had grave doubts about this, but could not do other than accept his assurances . . .'

A Firefly in the original Royal Thai Navy markings, outside the Fairey hangar at Ringway. *(R. Pugh via G. A. Jenks)*

Back at Ringway, the first Firefly, SF1 (ex-MB469) was test flown between 2 and 4 June, and by the end of July the first five aircraft were ready. These were in the colours of the Royal Thai Navy with dark sea grey on the upper surfaces, light blue on the fuselage below the decking and extending up the fin. The spinner was red. The Thai roundels were on the wings but the fuselage insignia was an anchor. After clearance test flights the Fireflies were disassembled and crated for shipment to Thailand. However, when Sam Moseley returned there he found a few changes . . .

'In November 1951 the first three aircraft arrived by sea at Klong Toi (Bangkok

Royal Thai Air Force officers and porters, standing on a Fairey packing crate containing one of their Fireflies.
(Author's collection)

seaport). I, in charge of a party of six fitters arrived in Bangkok on 25 November 1951. The Fireflies were still in their packing cases on the quay! On going to the Royal Thai Naval Headquarters to find out if Sataheep was ready, and to get the shipping documents so that the cases could be customs cleared, I found only one junior lieutenant. A month or two earlier, the Royal Thai Navy had endeavoured to effect a coup d'état, and had abducted the premier! This attempt had proved a dismal failure and the Commander-in-Chief, Admiral Sin, and practically all the naval officers, were in the cooler! Although we at Fairey had suspicions of this affair, I can't help feeling our agents in Thailand had been singularly remiss in keeping us informed of events.

'After much frustration and inertia, it was finally decided that the Fireflies should go to the Royal Thai Air Force. This did not go down very well. They did not want the "cast offs" of the Thai Navy, who were in disgrace, and with whom the air force were not even on speaking terms. However, this did mean that the aircraft were assembled, flight tested and handed over to the air force at Don Muang, where facilities were much more adequate. The Fireflies were also painted in air force markings.'

On paper at least, the Fireflies were transferred from the Royal Thai Navy to the Royal Thai Air Force on 22 December 1951. They were then assigned to No 1 Squadron of the IV Wing and declared operational on 5 March 1952. The air force was not happy with their new mounts, they lacked the glamour of a single seat fighter and were slow. They had no need of a fighter that required two crew. Sam Moseley found other problems . . .

'It was also my responsibility to get the Thais to order some spares, of which they had none for the Fireflies. I had three types of provisioning schedules, (1) Good for about five years, (2) twelve months' supplies and (3) the very barest minimum to keep things going – but the Thais were not disposed to order anything at all. The net result was that when they started to fly the aircraft (which they did not do much) and had the odd incident, we were asked to rob the later aircraft, which, although having arrived, was as yet unassembled. Things like propellers

Fitters putting the finishing touches to two of the Fireflies at Don Muang air base. Note the markings have been changed to the RTAF insignia. *(Author's collection)*

One of the two Firefly trainers, SF6 (Z2037). Colours followed the traditional pattern of yellow overall, but with a red spinner. This machine has had a small accident, as the tail wheel is missing. *(Author's collection)*

and main wheel tyres being examples. And so, although we eventually built all the aircraft, I did not fly the last three or four because they were incomplete and missing minor, but vital, parts. I tried to get them to buy a few tyres at least, but they said ''no'', and pointing to the grounded aircraft, said ''There are our spares'', meaning the last few Fireflies. Our position at that time was not helped by the fact that we had to work alongside MAAG – the American Military Aid Advisory Group. The Americans had just GIVEN the Royal Thai Air Force about forty brand new Grumman F8F Bearcats with oodles of spares.'

Sam Moseley had flight tested the first assembled Firefly SF2 (ex-MB445) on 10 January 1952, and the others followed until 4 March when the last of the airworthy ones, SF4 (ex-MB407) was test flown. He returned to the UK on 6 April 1952.

No 1 Squadron operated the Fireflies infrequently until 1 March 1954 when they were withdrawn from use. For some strange reason, considering the Royal Thai Air Force did not like the aircraft, one Firefly SF11 (ex-MB410) was preserved and this can still be seen in the RTAF Museum at Bangkok.

Chapter 19
India – and Other Tales

IN THE immediate post-war period the purchase of military aircraft, either new or reconditioned, from the UK, was a very involved process. Contact would be made either through the manufacturer in question, or the British Government representative for that particular country, i.e. a military attaché. These in turn would contact the Foreign Office for details of whether arms could be sold to that country, the political climate between the two, what the aircraft were going to be used for and whether there would be any repercussions from countries affected but friendly to Britain etc. The Foreign Office would assess the situation, contact the Ministry of Supply for details of aircraft available and whether they would be released for sale. The manufacturer would be drawn in and informed of the interest in their product(s) and what the situation was like regarding new aircraft or reconditioned ones. More often than not, at that time, the Arms Working Party of the Joint War Production Staff would be involved as they usually knew what the situation was with regard to surplus military aircraft. Everyone, in those days, was after Spitfires!

INDIA

In 1953 the Indian Navy found that they had a requirement for an aircraft capable of providing target towing duties. The market and supply in this field was a relatively small one, the most successful one, they found, being the converted Fairey Firefly Mk 1. After contact with Fairey an order for five Firefly TT Mk 1 aircraft was placed.

Fairey bought the five Fireflies back from the Admiralty and these were transferred from the holding station, RNAS Anthorn, to Fairey's Hamble factory for conversion. The five machines were delivered during June/July 1954, and became:

INS111	DK566
INS112	DK477
INS113	PP488
INS114	DK479
INS115	DK552

The conversions were completed early in 1955 and delivered in two batches, the first two, INS111

and 113, being delivered on 5 February and the other three on 12 April 1955.

The five aircraft were used by No 550 Squadron based at Cochin for target towing and other fleet requirement duties.

By 1956 spares were becoming a problem and the aircraft were being fully utilised, so it was decided to acquire some more. Although Firefly Mk 1s were still around it was decided that the later mark of Firefly would be more suitable and Fairey sold them five Firefly TT Mk 4 aircraft. The five Mk 4s were all received at Ringway during May 1957 for conversion. These became:

INS116	VG964
INS117	VG985
INS118	TW749
INS119	VH128
INS120	VG980

The first two Firefly TT4s for the Indian Navy were handed over to Lt/Cdr M. G. Shriklande at Ringway on 2 September 1958. The following day two Airwork ferry crews took off for India flying through Bahrain on the 9th. The other three left on 17 December, passing through Bahrain on the 20th. All five joined the TT1s at Cochin and were used until general wear and lack of spares gradually grounded them. Nine were sold for scrap and one set aside for the Indian Naval Museum at Cochin. This was still apparent in the late 1960s but nothing further has been heard.

ARGENTINE

On 1 April 1946, the Chief of the Argentine Naval Commission in London, Captain Teodoro E. Hartung, wrote to Fairey and asked for a quote for six Firefly Mk IV aircraft, saying that if there was a problem they would pay cash! He and other members of the Commission were in the UK buying aircraft; during 1946 they were to order 150 Miles Magister trainers, twenty Vickers Viking airliners, fifteen Bristol Wayfarer freighters, three Avro York military transports and three Avro Tudor airliners, plus other equipment.

Fairey immediately got in touch with the Foreign Office to enquire whether there was any objection

Three Firefly TT Mk 4s, INS118/119 and 120, at Sharjah in the Arabian Peninsula. This was an overnight stop on 21 December 1958 while on their delivery flight. *(Author's collection)*

to submitting a quote for the Fireflies, including associated radio and armament equipment. The problem was that the FAA were about to get their Firefly IVs and it would never do to let another country, especially in South America, be on par with the Royal Navy. The reply to Fairey, later in the month, was that the British Government could not give a green light to this order and asked the people involved to 'stall' the Argentinians. It was inferred that the economic climate was due to change which would prevent the sale of arms to Argentine. It was suggested a delaying message be sent talking about production problems, Admiralty priority and European friendly countries having preference (the Dutch had just placed their first order). The message was obvious, no orders for Fireflies.

AFGHANISTAN

The Afghan Government put in a request to Britain for modern combat aircraft which resulted in an Air Staff recommendation to supply twenty Firefly FR Mk IV aircraft – but this was later rescinded and nothing came of it.

FRANCE

The French Navy at one stage looked to be like the Dutch, a strong customer. Post war, the French aviation authorities were buying military aircraft purely as a stop gap until their own industry could get back on its feet. A request by the Aeronavale for demonstrations of the Firefly was met enthusiastically by Fairey. Peter Twiss took Firefly IV TW729 to Buc, near Toussus le Noble, south of Paris and then to Les Mureaux for demonstrations. Duncan Menzies took the Firefly Trainer F1 also to those places, but the interest was only lukewarm. Fairey Director, Maurice Wright wanted to land a Firefly IV along the Champs Elysées to demonstrate its performance characteristics, but the idea was considered a little too 'up-market' and dropped. Fairey kept up a presence while there was an interest including having a complete Firefly IV on their stand at the 1946 Paris Salon, but the French were just not interested.

FINLAND

In April 1950 Fairey approached the Foreign Office asking if they might negotiate with the Finnish Government who might be interested in the possible sale of Firefly 1s or Vs, Trainers or target tugs. Nothing, however came of these negotiations.

IRAQ

Iraq expressed an interest in modern combat types of aircraft, particularly with good strike capability. The Firefly was suggested and Group Captain Gordon Slade flew a Mk IV out to Iraq for them to assess it. The Iraqis were looking for a sliding rear canopy that would allow the use of a flexible operated 0.5 in calibre machine gun. Robert Carter, an apprentice remembers being involved: 'Early in 1948 there was some scheme to install a flexibly mounted gun in the rear cockpit, I believe it was for

Iraq. When any scheme of this nature was being considered it was usually tried in any available aircraft, by the largest and smallest men or boys in the shop. Even then at the age of eighteen I was fairly hefty, and I found myself wrestling with a large gun (unmounted) in the rear cockpit of Z2118. It didn't come to anything, there just wasn't room for the pair of us.' The negotiations dried up.

EGYPT
This was another case of contacting Britain with an interest in acquiring modern combat aircraft. The time was right to include Egypt with a demonstration by the Firefly IV Group Captain Slade was taking out to Iraq. Nothing came of this however.

LEBANON
Continuing the interest shown in the Firefly by other Middle East countries, Lebanon were actually in negotiation with Fairey for the supply of twenty-four Firefly Vs. Unfortunately the deal fell through.

SAUDI ARABIA
During May/June 1950 the Royal Saudi Air Force asked the UK if they could purchase the Firefly, initially six Firefly Vs plus one other to be converted into a Firefly V trainer. Although the Admiralty agreed in principal to release this small number from the production line, they did not like the idea of follow up orders and word was passed to the Saudis that the Firefly would possibly be unsuitable for use in Arabia.

SYRIA
Syria was another country requesting modern combat aircraft and again the suitability of the Firefly came up. In February 1951 the Foreign Office supported the Fairey sales office by asking the Admiralty to release, at least some Firefly Mk 1s, if not later marks, for reconditioning for sale to the Syrian Air Force. The Admiralty replied that they had no surplus Fireflies and they were not prepared to release any production line machines. Also, did the Foreign Office not realise that the Firefly was still not on the 'open list'? No sale.

There has been evidence of interest by other countries, including detailed negotiations, but the paperwork does not seem to have survived.

This smart-looking Firefly IV TW692, seen at Heston, is being readied for the demonstration trip to Iraq by Group Captain Gordon Slade. *(Westland Aircraft Ltd)*

Chapter 20
What Was it Like to Fly?

THE FIREFLY was an interesting aeroplane, it was well liked by the crews that flew it and despite the early directional problems it subsequently went on to show that the basic design, even if two-crew as directed by the Admiralty, gave a sound performance and had tremendous versatility demonstrated in two major wars and some minor ones. The author found no pilot who did not like flying it, indeed, one ATA pilot, Alec Matthews, said he preferred ferrying them to any other type. The Pilots' Notes for the Firefly Mk 1 states that for general flying: 'At all normal loading the aircraft is easy and pleasant to fly and stability about all axes is reasonably satisfactory'. While the 'Notes for the Trainer Mk T1/T2' says much the same, it notes that there was some slight lateral instability under climbing conditions.

Sean McGrail says: 'The Firefly Mk 1s and Trainers were quite different from the later marks in handling qualities. The early series were much more lively and responsive with aerobatics a pleasure. They were all pleasant to fly and deck land and after the hook damping modification there were fewer barrier landings.' R. B. Lunberg said: 'I thought the Firefly an excellent aeroplane and weapon platform, but, as usual, we tried to cram too much (equipment) into it. I don't think it was a very good aeroplane for the observer though, it had what I thought was an exceedingly cramped rear cockpit, not half as good as the Barracuda.' John Hone thought: 'The Mk 1s were light and pleasant to fly – for a strike-trained pilot the nearest we could get to a single-seat fighter, and for the observer, of course, the only way he could know what flying a fighter was like. In all the Fireflies the pilot was most ideally seated for the feeling of being almost part of the aircraft – you felt astride it, in the centre of things, and you could really fly it from there. You also felt strangely secure, there being miles of it in front of you – a fellow crew member behind and two large platform wings stretching out and supporting you on either side.' John Corbett's recollections are more reserved:

'I preferred the Mk 1 Firefly if only because its fuel consumption could be reduced to forty-five gallons per hour, and it had extra fuel

tanks in the stub plane (centre section). Fuel and endurance to a naval aviator are supremely important. Mks 1 to 6 were all very prone to vibration due to the rough running characteristics of the Griffon engine. This led to an enormous amount of servicing, often quite unnecessarily. I found it was the smooth runners which seemed more likely to have con rod failure. Its chief handling fault was the rudder. Full left rudder was required during a deck landing approach which left nothing in hand should one have to hurriedly apply full power at the last moment, and full right rudder was needed to keep the aircraft flying accurately in a terminal velocity dive. This continual changing rudder as speed increased made it jolly difficult to keep a bead on the target. At the same time, the aircraft became monstrously tail heavy and unless nose down trim was applied continually, the aircraft would take charge during recovery resulting in blacking out and occasionally, tailplane failure. It was very bouncy with the short-stroke oleos and unless a good three-pointer was made, it bounced badly pecking the propeller on the flight deck if hooked to a wire, or entering the barrier if not. Because the tail wheel was fully castering it was highly directionally unstable and many highly thought of pilots made fools of themselves by ground looping during the landing run and invariably wiping off the undercarriage. Its most vicious characteristic was a tendency to torque stall if full throttle was applied too quickly when trying to go around again. This characteristic was at first denied, but undoubtedly caused many deaths, particularly those who flew into the mast funnel and island of aircraft carriers attempting a late wave-off.'

One who does remember the effects of torque stall was Alan Braithwaite who said:

'I was on the approach to the deck and everything seemed fine, but there was a slight crosswind and I found I was needing more and more left rudder, until I realised it was all starting to go wrong and as I came in over the stern and felt the downdraught I slammed on full power to go round – the Firefly just half-rolled and went straight in the drink. Fortunately I got out, but my favourite Firefly now lies at the bottom of Lyme Bay. I always remember that day as it falls on my wedding anniversary, and each year when we go out to celebrate I make a toast to the fact that I am not at the bottom of Lyme Bay with my other love.'

The problem in general, says John Corbett:

'. . . is that it really was a most unsuitable aircraft for deck landing, but this was largely because of the tail wheel configuration, and applied to all aircraft of that geometry. I am inclined to think that my own modest success in deck landing was due to coming in slightly faster and steeper than the book recommended so that I could see more ahead over the resultant lower nose position. Prangs were usually caused by chaps coming in too low with too much power on so they had an exaggerated nose up attitude and little rate of sink. When they got in the downdraught over the ship's stern they had to apply an enormous burst of power which built up their speed ten knots or more so they crossed the round down very nose up, straight and level with no sink at all, and due to the excess speed at the wrong time, could not re-establish the sink before they were in the barrier. By arriving at a decent steady descent there was room for considerable error in the planned glide path with the collision point (flight deck) still within the wires. Furthermore, by avoiding an enormous burst of throttle to cross the round down, the speed did not suddenly build up at the wrong moment and the slight excess speed throughout the glide was available to lower the tail to cushion the arrival without creating a bounce.'

This approach applied to all marks of Firefly, not just the Mk 1s. And, if you missed the wires it was into the dreaded barrier. John Hone recalls his first such excursion:

'I remember the incident, all deck landings had to be just right or led to disaster, the Firefly being no exception. With the Firefly, attitude was the most vital consideration, particularly in the early days of unmodified oleo legs and pre-American style deck landing technique. If

landed only slightly main wheels first it tended to bounce, and with any excess speed this meant a float into the barrier. When it happened to me it was still a frequent thing, so much so in fact that you felt it was only a matter of time before one's own own fun came. On the day in question, 17 November 1949 in Firefly WB295, as soon as I chopped the throttle and felt the nose drop I realised the inevitable – I can still remember the seemingly endless suspended feeling of the float and the desperate feeling of a need to brake to avoid the trap. When it happened it was quite gentle, rather quiet and really quite an anti-climax – but what a long walk it seemed up to the Commander (Air) on the bridge!'

On the later marks Sean McGrail says: 'The Mk 4, 5 and 6 were all similar to fly. They all had a non-standard blind flying panel which made scanning instruments under instrument flying conditions more difficult than normal, however, I found them a stable aircraft. The Mk 5 which I flew in Korea was not a bad weapon platform, although nothing as good as the Fury. I think we became very accurate at rocket firing because of this and

The cockpit of the early marks of Firefly. This may not be entirely to Service standard, as it is a factory shot.

(Westland Aircraft Co)

A near perfect approach for this pilot of a Firefly FR1 of 827 Squadron from HMS *Triumph,* about to touch down on the American carrier USS *Boxer* off the Philippines. *(Lt/Cdr B. C. Lyons)*

bombing in a 45-degree dive wasn't too bad either.' John Corbett remembers: 'The Mk 4 with its improved fin and rudder and lockable tail wheel cut down the accident rate but it is doubtful if the increased petrol consumption and loss of petrol storage to make room for the wing root radiators was worth the slight increase in performance.' John Hone says more enthusiastically: 'The Mk 4, 5 and 6, were, to me, the very stuff of which flying is made. It was an easy aircraft to fly with no vices, unless mishandled. It was a real beauty to look at which made you feel grand just to fly it – plenty of performance for someone who doesn't want a hot-rod – and you could get all the thrills of flying it with an exceptionally reliable engine for comfort. It was good on the flight deck, but if not done properly could get you into trouble. Once you got into the swing of things a deck landing became a rather exhilarating routine. It was a real machine for letting off steam amongst nice big cumulus in the sunshine with a spate of aerobatics thrown in.'

Eric Brown was also an enthusiast:

'For me, the deep throated growl of the superlative Rolls-Royce Griffon had epitomised sheer power from the moment, a few weeks earlier, that I had first experienced its exhilarating surge – and awesome thirst – pulling the Spitfire XII off the ground at Arbroath, and it was with pleasurable anticipation that I first hoisted myself over the cockpit sill of the Firefly. Offering maximum ratings of 1735 hp at 1000 ft and 1495 hp at 14,500 ft the Griffon IIB was provided with 145.5 imperial gallons of fuel in the main tank immediately aft of the cockpit and twenty-three gallons in each of the wing centre section leading edge tanks. With the wing tanks empty, main tank fuel was limited to 116 gallons to keep the C of G within the permissible limits, and with max internal fuel, at least thirty gallons had to be drawn off the main tank before switching to the wing tanks. After priming the engine and depressing the starter button, the Griffon fired immediately and was opened up slowly to 1200 rpm for warm-up.

With oil at fifteen degrees centigrade and coolant at forty, the throttle was opened fully to 2750 rpm plus 12 lb boost for a brief check, the engine giving vent to a very impressive roar which died down as I eased back the throttle and commenced taxying. The Firefly was very stable on the ground, thanks to its wide-track undercarriage, and the brakes proved smooth and positive.

'A quick check that all three trim tabs were zeroed, the propeller was fined, the fuel cock set on 'MAIN' and the flaps selected one notch down for take-off. The Firefly accelerated with commendable rapidity but demanded strong rudder movement to control a marked tendency to swing to starboard. The initial climb out was at 120 knots IAS, the flaps being raised at about 300 ft, climbing speed rapidly built up to 135 knots which was recommended for max climb rate up to 16,000 ft, the retraction of undercarriage and flaps having produced a measure of nose-up trim. I soon discovered that all changes of power and speed demanded attention to the trim tabs as they were accompanied by marked changes in lateral and directional trim, and the Firefly was not overly stable either in the climb or in level flight, being just about possible to fly 'hands-off' by dint of very careful trimming.

'Nevertheless, the Firefly was a pilot's aeroplane and its handling characteristics were good, although the controls tended to heavy up with speed, this being particularly noticeable on the ailerons, but it could be thrown about with reasonable élan, although spinning was not recommended. In fact, the Firefly responded to standard spin recovery action extremely well, recovery normally being affected in half a turn, but an IAS of at least 160 knots was necessary before pulling out of the ensuing dive. In diving the aircraft became very tail heavy as speed built up, also tending to yaw to port, and in order to avoid high g in recovery, it was advisable to trim the Firefly into a dive. Stall warning came in the form of a modicum of elevator buffet three or four knots before the onset of the stall, the nose and port wing tending to drop quite sharply, stalling speed in clean condition being about ninety knots IAS. In a steep turn a sudden reduction in elevator feel gave warning of an approaching stall and if the pull force was not immediately relaxed the Firefly would flick out of the turn. Recommended speeds for aerobatics were 180–220 knots for a roll,

260–280 knots for a loop and 280–300 knots for a half-roll off the top.'

One of the procedures to get aircraft off the deck/ground under certain conditions was to use Rocket Assisted Take-Off (RATO) and some pilot's had vivid memories of using them. But first, the procedure – the pilot's controls consisted of a master switch mounted on a panel against the pilot's right elbow, with the jettison switch just above. The firing button was mounted on the throttle. This button also operated the 'press-to-speak' operation unless Modification 501 had been incorporated when the latter was repositioned on the control column. To use RATO you measured the wind speed over the deck or runway and plotted that against the aircraft take-off weight and distance available, determined the correct firing point from the chart and noted the actual position on the take-off run at which the rockets would be fired. The cockpit check list was as for normal take-off but added RATO master switch ON. The run was started as for a normal take-off, extra care being taken to keep the aircraft straight. A better take-off would result if the tail was kept down throughout the run, when opposite the firing point depress the firing button. The rockets, either singly or in pairs would normally fire simultaneously within half a second of each other – if they didn't you abandoned the take-off. Once airborne, switch the master OFF and lock, when clear of the ship, and having reached a safe height of not less than 300 ft, raise the flaps and jettison the rocket carrier at a speed not above 150 knots IAS. If an observer was carried he could then check that the jettison was successful.

John Hone recalls using RATO for an unusual task!

'The question was asked, could a carrier leaving harbour provide its own anti-submarine patrol outside? i.e., patrolling outside the harbour waiting for the carrier. Only, it appears, under certain conditions of wind direction and strength – and not usually available in harbour due to restricted flight paths, no wind etc. But by using RATO these conditions could be extended. On 14 February 1950 HMS *Glory* was leaving Grand Harbour, Malta, at about four knots, minimum speed to have steaming way and had about 20 knots of wind from almost dead astern, hmmm. We ranged four Fireflies right up on the bow, mine being VT420, facing aft. This was totally alien to our normal take-off procedure.

One of the deck-landing faults was to not get it quite right on touch down and let the nose drop, with the resultant 'pecking' of the deck with the propeller blades, as shown here. *(Author's collection)*

The other was to miss or jump the wires and go into the barrier, as demonstrated here. Note that all the propeller blades have gone and the radiator has been pushed back. *(Author's collection)*

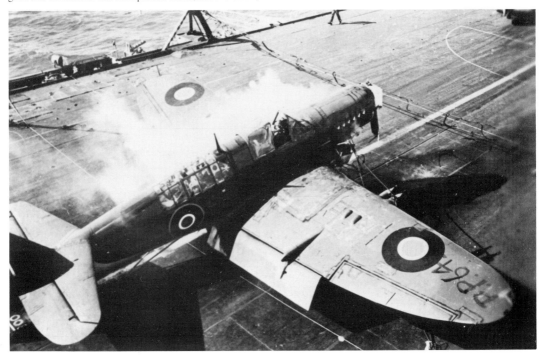

The first set off, fired his RATO and disappeared alarmingly over the stern only to re-emerge a few seconds later still flying and having to make a steep turn to avoid a cruiser moored further down the harbour. We were then waved off one by one and all launched successfully – bow to stern – and by the time *Glory* passed the breakwater we were patrolling outside.'

Sean McGrail recalls his experience which was a bit more memorable:

'I was on No 23 Pilot's Course with 737 Squadron at Eglinton, Northern Ireland at the time and on 22 July 1952 was practising RATO take-offs in a Firefly Mk 4, I had done one successfully, landing and got set up for another. I started the take-off run and at the selected point fired the RATO. The port motor broke away, and shot forward, shearing off all four prop blades at the root, while running at full power this was spectacular in the extreme. As I was taking off with the canopy open the flame from the rocket going past burned half my beard off before I abandoned the aircraft on the runway. I was flying again the next day – but minus a beard!'

Being a naval aeroplane there was always the problem of engine failure over the sea or battle damage which would necessitate a ditching. In the Firefly both members of the crew carried a K-type dinghy. The ditching characteristics were good provided all the external stores had been jettisoned, otherwise it was safer to bale out. Jock Fraser recalls his experience of ditching: 'On 14 March 1953 the London *Evening Standard* printed a series of adventures of the Goldfish Club, including my own. I read that we had broken cloud under leaden skies and the angry waves were leaping at us. Much to my annoyance as the navigator, we did not know where we were. The facts are completely opposite. There wasn't a cloud in the sky, the sea was flat calm and even in our dinghies we could see Blackpool Tower.' The details leading up to this ditching are recorded in the night fighter chapter, and in particular the section about 1790 Squadron:

'On the afternoon of 12 May 1945 we had gone out to HMCS *Puncher* for deck landing training and had our (survival) gear with us.

John Hone of 812 Squadron being RATO-launched from the flight-deck of HMS *Glory* in Valletta Harbour, Malta – but bow to stern instead of the reverse. *(Neville Franklin)*

The foam-covered Firefly in which Sean McGrain burnt off half his traditional naval beard when the RATO motor broke away and shot forward, shearing all the propeller blades. *(Lt/Cdr J. F. K. McGrail)*

Mine was in a grip stuffed down by the radio and Pat's (Lt P. A. Toynbee RNR) in a parachute pack which I had on my lap. As we glided down I said "cruising flap" to Pat and got a curt, "I know" in reply. I opened my cockpit canopy and just before we ditched I decided I didn't want a parachute bag in the way and chucked it over the side. You sat on your dinghy which was attached to the parachute by press-studs and your Mae West by a quick release grip. Before and after hitting the water I tried to release the dinghy from the parachute but could not. As I watched the tail go up I reckoned it was time to get out so I pulled the quick release grip and found myself clear of the aircraft (MB498). My parachute and dinghy floated up beside me. I started to inflate the dinghy using the CO_2 bottle and looked round for Pat who was swimming towards me shouting: "Jock, how do these bloody things work?" The very same thing had happened to his parachute and dinghy. I replied: "You wait until I am in my dinghy when I'll deal with you." We got in our dinghies and lashed them together. We had two of the squadron Fireflies overhead and while

one radioed Burscough the other attracted the attention of a frigate entering harbour off the Barrow. My bag had gone down with the aircraft but Pat saw his floating some distance away. Despite my reply of "Bugger your bag" to his suggestion that we paddle across to get it, we did so, and he must be one of the few who have ditched and boarded the rescue vessel carrying his bag!'

The Pilot's Notes for the Firefly Mk 7 says: 'The aircraft is easy to fly in still air conditions over most of the speed range, although some concentration is required to trim the aircraft accurately.' Aircrew had their own comments. Sean McGrail said: 'The Mk 7 was like a cow – nothing viscious but like an omnibus.' John Corbett felt that: 'The Mk 7 with an even bigger fin and rudder was a very good aircraft and I was astonished when Boscombe declared it unsafe to deck land. It was undoubtedly a lot safer in that respect than any of the earlier marks. Mind you, Boscombe test pilots did not always see things as do experienced deck landing pilots.' Lover of the Firefly John Hone said: 'The Mk 7 was certainly more staid, and in fact, felt strange. It was a different aircraft, yet it was still a Firefly with the same in-bred qualities of comfort and reliability.'

Summing up on the Fireflies in general, John Hone – 'A delightful aircraft to fly, giving the pilot the best combination of all worlds. You felt part of it, knew you were master of it in all respects – yet it would look after you and give you all the excitement and pleasure possible in flight.'

During the research for this book the author came across many stories concerning the Firefly and it is perhaps appropriate to round this chapter off with just a few . . . In 1957 a Firefly of 705 Squadron, operating at sea from Culdrose experienced engine trouble. The pilot told his observer to tighten his straps in case they had to bale out. On landing back at Culdrose the pilot found he was minus an observer. Misunderstanding his pilot's instructions he had immediately baled out – and was found later out at sea in his dinghy! David Carter recalls a hair raising incident: 'There is only one incident which really sticks in my mind. In HMS *Vengeance* during 1949/50 we were doing the first post war night exercises out in the Atlantic. A pilot from 814, Lt J. M. Ogden, found himself on finals with a complete failure of instrument lighting, and crawled over the round-down with his observer using a flashlight on the ASI and calling out the airspeed over the intercom. I saw the landing, which in the circumstances was very good!' Let us not forget also the sterling work done by the ATA during the time that they were in operation – making 1384 Firefly movements. Alec Matthews contributes two stories from his days as a delivery pilot:

'Unfortunately the war didn't close down at weekends, but I had a splendid weekend Saturday/Sunday, 12/13 August 1944. On Saturday I flew four Ansons and two Hellcats. I had never seen a Hellcat before and was therefore proud to deliver two to the Orkneys from Lossiemouth. Sunday also proved to be a very busy day, I flew two Fairchild Argus, a Martinet, an Anson and then a Firefly. This was DT931 and had been flown to Lossiemouth by a Prestwick pilot. It had a P1 (Priority 1) rating which meant it was to be delivered with the utmost urgency. Like the Hellcat I had not seen a Firefly before, and it was necessary to read the Pilot's Notes. I read the starting procedure, take-off and climb, a quick glance at cruising speed and I was away, intending to read landing details en route over the Pentland Firth to the Orkneys. Climbing away from Lossiemouth with hood open as per regulations, my Pilot's Notes were sucked out of my harness where they had been tucked, and disappeared into the Moray Firth! The Firefly behaved like a perfect lady as I practised landing on a cloud to ascertain landing and stalling speeds. It is now some forty-seven years ago but I remember approaching in the region of 100 knots, and realising I was too fast opened up and went round again, this time about ninety knots and she landed impeccably. November 1944 was a good month with twelve different types in my logbook. On Thursday 30 November I was flying Firefly DV127 from Prestwick to Lossiemouth when the weather began to close in. Arriving in the circuit I encountered a gaggle of Wellingtons coming in to land, so, being of a gentlemanly disposition I stooged round Elgin at low altitude to await my turn. There is a long straight road from Elgin to Lossiemouth, and in a fit of gay abandon I beat up a large black motor car. On my second run it suddenly dawned on me that, yes, you guessed it, it belonged to our American commanding officer. Next morning, before delivering my Firefly to the Orkneys, I was called to the CO's office and had a severe ticking off that I shall never forget. Eventually my CO and I became good friends and I see him every year. His name is Ed Heering, he still flies and has accumulated an incredible 35,000 hours, mostly as chief pilot to World Airways.'

I would however, like to complete this chapter with a superb story from Richard Griffiths:

'As you can imagine, the immediate post-war period, while those of us in the RNVR were continuing to do odd flying jobs while awaiting demobilisation, was a rather unreal and, above all, tedious one. You may also remember that Sub Lieutenants (A) RNVR were not renowned for their amenability to naval discipline, and some of the younger and more foolhardy of us used to relieve the tedium of flogging Ansons and Fireflies around the sky, while RN types practised air signals or radar in the back seat, by a spot of low flying amongst the glens and peaks of the Scottish Highlands. Thus, on a sunny morning on 15 August 1946 I took off in Firefly MB758 with Lt G. A. Carter RCN in the back seat, ostensibly to practise some ASH homings. We flew roughly north from Arbroath and before long there below us was the lovely Dee Valley, looking very fresh and beautiful in the morning sunlight. And further up the valley lay Balmoral Castle, where at that time, the King and Queen were in residence, as were the two young Princesses, Elizabeth and Margaret. I felt that the least I could do was give my Canadian passenger an opportunity to see the Castle at close quarters, and perhaps even to pay personal homage to the Royal Family. I dived down from about 5000 ft and shot across the roof-tops of Balmoral Castle going west to east. However, I then made a fatal error of judgement, and decided to take another and closer look on the off-chance of seeing one of the Princesses. I made a tight 180-degree turn and flew back east to west just a few feet above the large lawn which stretches out in front of the main porchway and entrance to the Castle. Alas, by then His Majesty King George VI had come out to see what all the noise was about, and arrived on the front porch just in time to see me flash across the lawn at nought feet – and also in time for him to get my number! Later that day a signal arrived at Arbroath addressed from FOFT to all Scottish Naval Air Stations, worded as follows: ''A Spitfire or Seafire was reported flying very low over Balmoral at 100 ft today Thursday. Number appears to be Mike Baker 758. Report forthwith if this can be traced to any aircraft from your station. Nil reports are required''. It subsequently transpired that it was the King himself who had made the ''sighting'' and it was clear that his eyesight was excellent in getting the number exactly right, but that his aircraft recognition was a little less reliable in that he made the not uncommon error of confusing the Firefly with the Spitfire/Seafire family.'

One can imagine the aftermath of this escapade, but S/Lt Griffiths was not court martialled, even though he was grounded until demobilisation a few months later. All was forgiven however, as Richard Griffiths flew again for the FAA – between 1947 and 1956 with 1832 Squadron RNVR at Culham, and later at RAF Benson, as a member of the Southern Air Division RNVR – but not in Fireflies!

The last of the three Firefly genre, the T Mk 7, was never allowed to demonstrate the role for which it was designed, that of anti-submarine detection. If it had, there appears to be little doubt that it would have done so with the same panache as its earlier breed. Despite the reports, pilots found it pleasant enough to fly. *(Flight International)*

Chapter 21
Production and Specification Data

Firefly F Mk 1

All metal two-seat low-wing monoplane designed for fighter and reconnaissance duties with Royal Navy. Powered by Rolls-Royce supercharged Griffon IIB or, after the 470th aircraft, the Griffon 12, driving a Rotol three-blade variable-pitch constant-speed propeller. Power plant was a complete unit, detachable from the firewall (Frame 1). Starting was by Coffman cartridge starter which was mounted on starboard side of engine. Engine controls consisted of push-pull rods operated from a conventional type of throttle box.

The fuselage was a light-alloy monocoque structure consisting of twenty-one U-frames and bulkheads to which the centre section was bolted, the whole being covered with flush-riveted light alloy sheets. The centre section was a light alloy structure comprising front and rear spars, diagonal bracing diaphragms, oil tank bearers, tension members, leading edge portions and providing housing for the retractable undercarriage wheels, the retracting mechanism and air bottles. The rear wedge and engine mountings were of steel tubing. Catapult launching spools and deck arrester gear were fitted to the fuselage. The wings were of stressed skin construction and consisted of two I-section spars of fabricated light-alloy plate, and plate ribs which supported the metal skin. The outer wing was hinged to the rear spar of the centre section and folded back parallel to the fuselage. Wing locking gear was mounted on Rib 6a and consisted of a telescopic lever which slid into a housing hinged on brackets attached to the front spar; the housing was coupled by a connecting link to a front extractor lever, the ball ends of which engaged in slots in the top and bottom latchpins. These extractor levers pivoted on ball bearings and were encased in forged housings. The restraining latchpins could be withdrawn after opening the hinged fairing on the leading edge, extracting the locking pin from the tubular housing by means of the ring provided, pulling out the tubular lever and pressing it down. The wings contained the fixed armament which consisted of two 20 mm cannon in each wing and fired electro-pneumatically by a push button on the pilot's control column, sighting being via a GM Mk 2 reflector gunsight. Also carried under the wings were the mounting units to carry bombs, rocket projectiles and long range fuel tanks. The cantilever tailplane consisted of I-section spars with plate ribs supporting a flush riveted metal skin. A conventional fin and rudder were attached to the rear wedge. The main fuel tank was housed between the two crew cockpits and located over the centre section with two other fuel tanks stowed in the leading edge of the centre section. Both cockpits were constructed in the traditional sense covered by transparent hooding to allow entry and exit both being jettisonable in an emergency. The main retractable undercarriage embodied two oleo-pneumatic shock-absorber struts while the tail wheel unit comprised a friction-damped, fully-castering, retractable oleo-pneumatic shock absorber strut and wheel. The hydraulic system, which obtained its power from an engine-driven pump, operated the flaps and undercarriage retraction mechanism. Electrical services were provided by two twelve-volt batteries connected in series.

Production of the Firefly F Mk 1 amounted to 297 aircraft with other marks such as the FR1, NF1 and NFII interspersed within those numbers. As the breakdown of such a list would take up far more space than allowed only the production serials are listed.

Z1826 – Z1845	
Z1865 – Z1914	
Z1942 – Z1986	
Z2011 – Z2058	
Z2059 – Z2095	All cancelled except Z2059/Z2060/Z2092 which were transferred to Mk 4 contract as TW677, TW678 and TW679 respectively.
Z2096 – Z2120	
Z2121 – Z2126	Cancelled, last two transferred to Mk 4 contract as TW687 and TW688.
DT926 – DT930	Cancelled, transferred to Mk 4 order as TW689 to TW693 respectively.
DT931 – DT949	

DT950 – DT961	Cancelled, transferred to Mk 4 contract as TW694 to TW699 and TW715 to TW720.
DT974 – DT991	
DV117 – DV134	
DV147 – DV150	
PP391 – PP437	The thirty Mk 1s for the Dutch were drawn from these serial batches.
PP456 – PP497	
PP523 – PP567	
PP580 – PP623	
PP639 – PP660	
MB378 – MB419	
MB433 – MB449	
MB460 – MB479	
MB492 – MB536	
MB549 – MB593	
MB613 – MB649	
MB662 – MB758	
DK414 – DK462	Built by General Aircraft Co.
DK476 – DK513	
DK526 – DK570	
DK588 – DK619	Last sixty-eight cancelled and not built.
DK633 – DK667	

Firefly F Mk 1A

Essentially an F Mk 1 converted by Service maintenance units to FR Mk 1 standard by using Fairey supplied installation drawings. Known as the 'ASHCAT' the actual number converted appears to be unknown.

Firefly FR Mk 1

Construction and armament as for the F Mk 1. ASH radar fitted in a nacelle mounted beneath the forward fuselage. ASH was AN/APS-4 radar, also known as ARI 5607. Radio equipment as for F Mk 1. Gyro gunsight fitted above instrument panel. Production amounted to 273 aircraft from the list of the F Mk 1.

Firefly NF Mk 1

Night fighter version of the F Mk 1 using ASH radar mounted in a nacelle and attached under the forward fuselage. All other equipment as for the FR Mk 1 except for a shroud fitted over the engine exhaust manifolds. Production was drawn from the F Mk 1 list and Fairey gave a figure of 140.

Firefly T Mk 1

Basically an F Mk 1/FR Mk 1 but devoid of operational equipment. The instructor's rear cockpit

was raised twelve inches to improve his view. Six aircraft fitted with one 20 mm cannon in each wing. Thirty-four listed conversions by Fairey.

Firefly TT Mk 1

Conversion of F Mk 1/FR Mk 1 by fitting a windlass arm on the port side of the fuselage just forward of the rear cockpit. Rear cockpit fitted with target-towing equipment and space for one operator. Guards mounted around tail area so that cables could not foul controls. Production conversions amounted to nineteen for Sweden, five for India and two for Denmark.

Firefly NF Mk II

Large production planned with orders for 328. Later reduced to thirty-seven, which were built with the majority later converted to NF Mk 1. Some remained as NF Mk IIs until scrapped.

Construction was the same as for the day fighter but there were twenty-two U frames instead of the usual twenty-one. Not fitted with a gunsight but had a projector unit suspended beneath the coaming. Other small changes to suit the role including a tandem generator system.

Firefly T Mk 2

As for T Mk 1 except all conversions had one 20 mm cannon per wing. Provision for carrying numerous weapon loads. Production conversions listed as fifty-four.

Firefly F Mk III

One aircraft only Z1835 powered by Griffon 61. Design unsuitable and project abandoned. This aircraft became the second prototype Mk IV with a Griffon 72.

Firefly T Mk 3

Conversion of FR Mk 1 for observer training purposes. Standard FR Mk 1 equipment retained and additional training aids, such as a drift recorder fitted. No actual figures released on number of conversions as they were done by Royal Navy units, but believed to be fifty.

Firefly FR/NF Mk 4

The Firefly Mk 4 changed its outline with the removal of the elliptical wing for a square shape and the oil and coolant radiators were moved from beneath the nose to the leading edge of the centre section. Otherwise construction followed the Firefly pattern and power came from a Griffon 74. An ASH transmitter/receiver contained within a pressurised bomb-shaped structure was mounted in a nacelle on the starboard wing, and to balance this a fuel tank was mounted in the same position on the port wing. These nacelles were designed to fit a modified bomb carrier, the shape of the nacelle tail cone was later changed. An aerial assembly was fitted to both sides of the fin and connected to RT-34/APS-13 unit in the observer's cockpit to give warning of approach from rear.

Production consisted of forty-three conversions from the F Mk 1 line, plus seventy-seven aircraft built as FR/NF Mk 4s with 133 being cancelled in favour of the Firefly FR/AS/NF Mk 5 series. Serials were:

VG957 – VG999
VH121 – VH144 77
VH145 – VH148 133 cancelled
VH163 – VH191
VH203 – VH245
VH270 – VH305
VH341 – VH361

plus forty new FR Mk 4 for the Royal Netherlands Navy.

Firefly TT Mk 4

Similar conversion to the Mk 1 except that the fully feathering Type G Mk 3 winch was mounted in a nacelle under the fuselage thus doing away with the need for a windlass arm.

Conversions by inclusion of Modification 850 amounted to twenty-eight. Royal Netherlands Navy converted eight to TT Mk 4 status.

Firefly FR/AS/NF Mk 5

Logical development of the Mk 4 but with later equipment and easy conversion for any of the three roles. Production amounted to 338 aircraft as follows:

VT362 – VT381
VT392 – VT441
VT458 – VT504
VX371 – VX396
VX413 – VX438
WB243 – WB272
WB281 – WB316
WB330 – WB382
WB391 – WB440

The last sixteen were converted to AS Mk 6.

The Royal Netherlands Navy received fourteen new NF Mk 5 Fireflies.

Firefly T Mk 5

Two conversions only of VT440 and VX373 for the Royal Australian Navy.

Firefly TT Mk 5

Two conversions only of WB271 and VX388 for Royal Australian Navy.

Firefly AS Mk 6

Construction followed the pattern of the Mk 4/5. Electrical equipment modified to accept wide range of anti-submarine detection gear including using British directional sonobuoys. Although cannon armament was deleted the wing attachment points allowed a wide range of weapons, anti-submarine equipment and long-range fuel tanks to be fitted.

Production, excluding Mk 5 conversions amounted to 133 production aircraft as follows:

WB505 – WB510
WB516 – WB523
WD824 – WD872
WD878 – WD923
WH627 – WH632
WJ104 – WJ121

Two Mk 6 WD924/WD925 were cancelled from the contract and transferred as the two prototype Firefly Mk 7s WJ215/WJ216.

Firefly TT Mk 6

Four conversions only of WB518, WD828, WD840 and WD901 for Royal Australian Navy.

Firefly AS Mk 7/T Mk 7

Construction followed Firefly structure pattern but fuselage had twenty-eight U frames and bulkheads. Wing shape returned to elliptical planform with the slightly projecting leading edge portions of the centre section housing flexible fuel tanks. Power plant changed to Griffon 59 driving four-blade Rotol variable-pitch constant-speed propeller. Tail wheel non-retractable. Design considered unsuitable for role and changed into a trainer.

Production, including the two pre-production machines transferred from the Mk 6 run, was for 337 aircraft. Of this total, 152 were cancelled, thirty-four moved to the drone programme and 151 were built, 110 at Hayes and forty-one at Stockport. Serial ranges were:

WJ146 – WJ174
WJ187 – WJ209

WJ215 – WJ216
WK348 – WK373
WM761 – WM779
WM796 – WM832
WM855 – WM899
WP351 – WP354   185
WP355 – WP400
WP421 – WP453
WP469 – WP490
WV967 – WV991
WW103 – WW128   152 cancelled

Firefly U Mk 7
One under this designation only, WJ194 before becoming a U Mk 8.

Firefly T Mk 8
Six aircraft only, WJ147, WJ149, WJ150, WJ151, WJ152 and WJ153, used as early development or chase aircraft. Afterwards made up to U Mk 8 standard.

Firefly U Mk 8
A Firefly Mk 7 converted into a pilotless target drone. Stripped of all unnecessary existing equipment from observer's cockpit and installation of radio-controlled Mk 8 Type H automatic pilot allowed control from the ground. Propeller locked at 2600 rpm for pilotless flight. Pilot's cockpit remained substantially unchanged except for removal again of unnecessary equipment and fitment of new controllers. Wing tip pods carried recording cameras. Production amounted to thirty-four aircraft drawn from the Mk 7 line:

WM810, WM823, WM856 to WM863 inclusive, WM880 to WM899 inclusive.
WP351 to WP354 inclusive.

Firefly U Mk 9
Final mark of Firefly range and was conversion of Mk 5. Changes mostly same as for U Mk 8.
   Production came to forty conversions of standard Mk 5 aircraft:
WB245, WB257, WB307, WB331, WB341, WB347, WB350, WB365, WB373, WB374, WB391, WB392, WB394, WB402, WB410, WB411, WB416, VH130, VH134, VX416, VX418, VX421, VX427, VX429, VT364, VT370, VT372, VT403, VT413, VT430, VT441, VT461, VT463, VT470, VT481, VT485, VT487, VT493, VR494 and VT497.

Total number of production Fireflies – 1702.

Rolls-Royce Griffon 74 engine. *(Author's collection)*

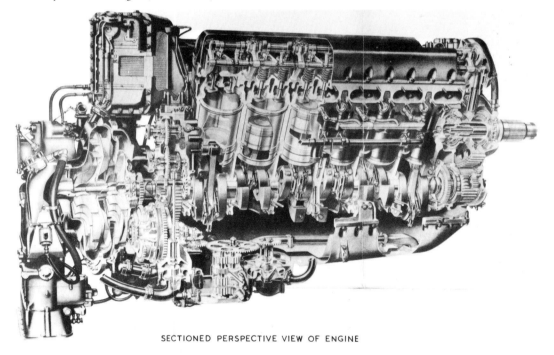

SECTIONED PERSPECTIVE VIEW OF ENGINE

FIREFLY SPECIFICATIONS

	Mk 1	Trainers	Mk 4/5/6	Mk 7	
Engine Type	Griffon IIB	Griffon 12	Griffon 74	Griffon 59	
Rating at sea level	1735 bhp	1735 bhp	2004 bhp	1960 bhp	at 2750 rpm
at 14,000 ft	1495 bhp	1495 bhp	2245 bhp	2435 bhp	at 2750 rpm
Weight – empty	8925 lb	9674 lb	9859 lb	11,016 lb	
– AUW	12,400 lb	12,655 lb	13,950 lb	13,970 lb	
– full load	14,900 lb	13,415 lb	15,615 lb	15,800 lb	13,792 lb for TT4
Fuel – internal	191 galls	191 galls	200 galls	229 galls	
– with drop tanks	371 galls	371 galls	381 galls	409 galls	
Max speed at sea level	247 knots	246 knots	277 knots	300 knots	
at 17,000 ft	277 knots	270 knots	335 knots	at 10,000 ft	
Take-off distance –					
into 10 knot wind	685 yards	120 yards in	675 yards		
20 knot wind	505 yards	27 knot wind	504 yards		
Time to 5000 ft	2.35 mins	2.05 mins	3.60 mins	4.20 mins	
Range – internal	774 miles	800 miles	582 miles	860 miles	
– with drop tanks	1364 miles	–	1300 miles		
Service ceiling	29,000 ft	28,400 ft	29,200 ft	25,500 ft	
Span	44 ft 6 in	44 ft 6 in	41 ft 2 in	44 ft 6 in	
Length	37 ft 7 in	37 ft 7 in	38 ft 9 in	38 ft 3 in	NFII was 38 ft 10 in
Height	15 ft 5$\frac{1}{2}$ in	15 ft 5$\frac{1}{2}$ in	14 ft 4 in	15 ft 11 in	
Width (wings folded)	13 ft 6 in	13 ft 6 in	13 ft 6 in	13 ft 6 in	
Armament – Fixed	4 x 20 mm	2 x 20 mm	4 x 20 mm	nil	AS5/AS6/T7
– Stores	8 x 60 lb R/P	in T Mk 2	in Mk 4/FR5		carried a wide
	2 x 500 lb	and various	8 x 60 lb R/P		range of sea
	or 2 x 1000 lb	weapon loads	2 x 500 lb or		markers,
	bombs	for training	2 x 1000 lb		sonobuoys,
			bombs		mines etc.

Griffons

In December 1939 Rolls-Royce took the decision to go ahead with the development of a new piston engine. It was designed to meet a new Admiralty requirement to provide high power at low altitude and possibly also be suitable for installation in existing aircraft already powered by the Merlin. The Griffon, as the new engine became known, not only utilised all the company experience gained on V-12 design such as the Kestrel and Merlin engines, but had the same cylinder arrangement and dimensions as the 'R' engine used in the Supermarine Schneider Trophy contest aircraft. For a relatively similar frontal area to the Merlin the Griffon had a 35.9 per cent greater swept volume, and taking the cylinder bore to six inches gave it twenty-three per cent more piston area than the Merlin. The engine was also the first Rolls-Royce aero engine to incorporate as standard practice the lubrication of the main bearings and big-ends from a hollow shaft. The Griffon incorporated a number of interesting design features which included the provision of a remote gearbox, shaft driven from the engine, on which were mounted the mechanically-driven accessories required to operate such features as a retractable undercarriage, wheel brakes, wing flaps, blind-flying instrument panel and the generator for the radio installation.

The Griffon was selected from the outset as the power plant for the new Fairey Firefly naval fighter; due to enter service in 1942 the Air Ministry and Admiralty put pressure on Rolls-Royce to get the engine cleared as soon as possible. The initial engine, a Griffon IIB fitted with a Firefly type cowling arrangement, was flight tested on Hawker Henley L3414 at the Rolls-Royce test facility at Hucknall, near Nottingham, starting in January 1940 and continuing into 1943, the year the Firefly went into FAA service. This first mark of Griffon was to power all Fireflies built until the 470th aircraft, after which the Griffon 12 was installed. The basic difference between IIB and 12 was that the latter had a strengthened reduction gear and increased boost. The engines had a maximum rating of 1735 hp at 1000 ft and 1495 hp at 14,500 ft, depending on boost.

The next mark of Griffon affecting the Firefly was the Griffon 61 which was earmarked for the Firefly FIII and was fitted with a two-speed two-stage supercharger and intercooler. The two-speed supercharger gave increased power at low altitudes combined with high power at high altitudes and improved fuel economy under cruising conditions. The pilot had a two-position control to select either the MS or FS gear ratio as required. The gear change could be made at any rpm and boost conditions without throttling back. The MS ratio always had to be used for take-off, and at altitudes below 8000 ft there was no flight condition under which an increased performance could be obtained in FS ratio. At altitudes above 8000 ft the optimum gear depended on the general flight condition and no general rule was laid down. Compared to the earlier Griffons the 61 had a considerably improved altitude performance. The rating was 2035 hp at 7000 ft and 1820 hp at 21,000 ft with 1540 hp available at take-off, depending on boost and supercharger gear ratios. The object of ratios of supercharging on an aero engine is to enable its power to be developed from the throttled sea level power in moderate supercharged gear (MS) to a height at which the throttle is fully open and the maximum power is being delivered. When the fully supercharged gear (FS) is engaged the engine is again throttled until the rated height is reached in this gear.

The Griffon 72/74 were developed specifically for the new mark of Firefly incorporating wing-root leading-edge radiators. The 72 was only fitted to the Firefly Mk 4 prototypes, the 74 being the production engine. The only difference between the 72 and 74 was that the former had a Bendix-Stromberg carburettor and the latter a Rolls-Royce injection pump. The 74 was to power the whole series of Mk 4/5 and 6 Fireflies. Power at 7500 ft was 1505 hp at 2600 rpm and 1450 hp at 20,000 ft. Using 150 octane aviation spirit gave 2245 hp at 9250 ft at 2750 rpm.

The final production Griffon engine for the Firefly was the Griffon 59 which powered the Firefly Mk 7. This engine, although similar to the Shackleton Griffon Mk 57/57A engine had a cartridge starter in place of the electrical system and a single propeller shaft driven through plain spur gearing instead of a contra-rotating reduction gear. The engine at sea level delivered 1960 hp at 2750 rpm in low gear with plus 18 lb/sq in boost, and 2435 hp at 2750 rpm in high gear with plus 25 lb/sq in boost.

Index